5.
S

**The most significant departure from Freud
in the last thirty years—**

TRANSACTIONAL ANALYSIS—fondly called T/A
by those familiar with it—is the revolutionary
technique developed by Dr. Eric Berne for understanding ourselves and the way we relate
to others—husbands and wives, those we work
with, children and parents, and friends.

TRANSACTIONAL ANALYSIS IN PSYCHOTHER-
APY was Dr. Berne's first book explaining the
principles of T/A. It had an incalculable impact
on all branches of psychology, psychiatry, and
mental health work. In it Dr. Berne explains how
our three ego states—Child, Parent, and Adult
—relate to each other and to the ego states of
others, in marriages, business associations, and
interpersonal relations of all kinds.

TRANSACTIONAL ANALYSIS IN PSYCHOTHER-
APY has been an established classic for nearly
15 years. After its publication Dr. Berne went
on to write the celebrated bestseller GAMES
PEOPLE PLAY in 1964, and PRINCIPLES OF
GROUP TREATMENT in 1966. His last book
written shortly before his death was WHAT DO
YOU SAY AFTER YOU SAY HELLO?

Transactional Analysis in Psychotherapy

A Systematic Individual and Social Psychiatry

Eric Berne, M.D.

BALLANTINE BOOKS • NEW YORK

Library of Congress Catalog Card Number: 60-13795

SBN 345-24637-3-195

This edition published by arrangement with
Grove Press, Inc.

First Printing: October, 1973
Third Printing: November, 1975

Printed in the United States of America

BALLANTINE BOOKS
A Division of Random House, Inc.
201 East 50th Street, New York, N.Y. 10022
Simultaneously published by
Ballantine Books, Ltd., Toronto, Canada

In Memoriam
Patris Mei David
Medicinae Doctor et Chirurgiae Magister
atque Pauperibus Medicus

Montreal, Canada, 1882–1921.

Contents

Contents

PART III

Psychotherapy

PART IV

Frontiers of Transactional Analysis

Table of Figures

Preface

THIS book outlines a unified system of individual and social psychiatry as it has been taught during the past five years at the Group Therapy Seminar of Mount Zion Hospital in San Francisco, at the Monterey Peninsula Clinical Conference in Psychiatry, at the San Francisco Social Psychiatry Seminars, and more recently at Atascadero State Hospital, and the Langley Porter Neuropsychiatric Institute. This approach is now being used by therapists and group workers in various institutional settings, as well as in private practice, to deal with almost every type of mental, emotional, and characterological disturbance. The growing interest in and wider dissemination of its principles have indicated a need for this book, since it has become increasingly difficult to fulfill all the requests for lectures, reprints, and correspondence.

The writer has had the privilege of visiting mental hospitals in about thirty different countries in Europe, Asia, Africa, and the islands of the Atlantic and Pacific, and has taken the opportunity of testing the principles of structural analysis in various racial and cultural settings. Their precision and predictive value have stood up rather well under particularly rigorous conditions requiring the services of interpreters to reach people of very exotic mentalities.

Since structural analysis is a more general theory

than orthodox psychoanalysis, the reader will be fairer to himself and to the writer if he resists, initially at least, the understandable temptation to try to fit the former into the latter. If the process is reversed, as it should be, it will be found that psychoanalysis easily finds its place methodologically as a highly specialized aspect of structural analysis. For example transactional analysis, the social aspect of structural analysis, reveals several different types of "crossed transactions." The multifarious phenomena of transference are almost all subsumed under just one of these types, here denoted "Crossed Transaction Type I." Other examples of the relationship between psychoanalysis and structural analysis are given in the text.

SEMANTICS

Later on, the term *transactional analysis* will be used to refer to the whole system, including structural analysis. In appropriate contexts, this term will be used in its stricter sense to mean the analysis of single transactions.

Social psychiatry is used here to denote the study of the psychiatric aspects of specific transactions or sets of transactions which take place between two or more particular individuals at a given time and place. Comparative psychiatric epidemiology, or the comparison of the psychiatric problems of various sociological, cultural, or national groups, which is also sometimes called "social psychiatry," can be adequately and perhaps better and more precisely denoted by the expression "comparative psychiatry." (This problem of nomenclature was discussed by the writer (1956), noting the early use of "comparative psychiatry" by Yap (1951).)

He often refers to human beings in general, of either sex. *Is* in a technical context means "is regularly, so far as the writer's experience goes." *Seems to be* means "appears to me to be, from repeated observations, but not enough to make me certain yet." Actual people are referred to by "adult," "parent," and "child." When these terms are capitalized as *Adult, Parent,* and *Child,* they refer to ego states, not people. The corresponding adjectives are "parental," "adult," and "child" or "child-like," sometimes capitalized and sometimes not, according to the context.

Psychoanalysis and its cognates as used in this book are meant to refer to what is known as "orthodox" psychoanalysis, that is, the resolution of infantile conflicts through the systematic use of free association, dealing with the phenomena of transference and resistance according to the principles of Freud. It may be borne in mind, however, that after fifteen years the psychoanalytic movement and the writer officially parted company (on the most friendly terms) a few years ago, and that the writer's concept of ego function is different from that of the majority of orthodox psychoanalysts, approaching more closely the viewpoints of Federn (1952) and his pupil Edoardo Weiss (1950).

Acknowledgments

THANKS are due first of all to those in San Francisco who encouraged me by their interest in transactional analysis in the early stages: Dr. R. J. Starrels, who has followed its development almost *ab initio;* Dr. Martin Steiner, who organized the first seminars at Mount Zion Hospital; and Mrs. Eugenia Prescott, of the San Francisco Department of Health, who organized the first evening seminar. I am particularly grateful to those who invited me or allowed me to lay my ideas before the critical judgment of their staffs and to demonstrate them in clinical practice: Dr. Norman Reider, of Mount Zion Hospital; Dr. Donald Shaskan, of the Veterans Adminstration Mental Hygiene Clinic; Dr. M. Robert Harris, of the Langley Porter Neuropsychiatric Institute; and Drs. Reginald Rood and Victor Arcadi, of Atascadero State Hospital.

The most dynamic developments have taken place at the San Francisco Social Psychiatry Seminars. It was most gratifying to have so many people attending there week after week for months and even years on end, often traveling long distances, and in most cases with considerable sacrifice of busy schedules. Those who regularly contributed their criticisms and addenda, and/or applied structural and transactional analysis in their own groups or individual cases and reported on the results, were most helpful in case-hardening the formulations. These include: Miss Viola Litt, secretary of the seminars; Miss Barbara Rosenfeld, who has devoted many hours each week to transactional analysis and has contributed many useful ideas; Mr. Harold E. Dent; Dr. Franklin Ernst; Miss Margaret Frings; Dr. Gordon Gritter; Dr. John Ryan; Mrs. Myra Schapps; and Mr. Claude Steiner. I am also grateful to those who have contributed or listened most regularly at the Monterey Peninsula Clinical Conference in Psychiatry (to dignify a pleasant, informal, and enlightening weekly experience with a formal title): Dr. Bruno Klopfer, Dr. David Kupfer, Dr. Herbert Wiesenfeld, and Miss Anita Wiggins, R.N. This list could be extended to include those who attended the seminars from time to time, and by their questions and observations stimulated further thinking. I have also appreciated the opportunities offered by all the program chairmen of all the meetings where I have been invited to lecture. And I am grateful to those who have offered to act as observers in therapy groups so I could determine whether my version of what happened was only my own fantasy or whether it had some consensus. Above all I am thankful to the patients who revealed to me the structures of their personalities and offered the opportunity to elaborate the principles of transactional analysis.

Finally I have to thank those who helped most with the writing of the book itself. The hundred or so clinicians who read it carefully and offered me their suggestions; my wife, for keeping my machinery running smoothly and for her patience during the many evenings I spent in my study; and Mrs. Allen Williams for her conscientious and intelligent secretarial service.

Carmel-by-the Sea, California
April 1960

Introduction

AN EGO state may be described phenomenologically as a coherent system of feelings related to a given subject, and operationally as a set of coherent behavior patterns; or pragmatically, as a system of feelings which motivates a related set of behavior patterns. Penfield[1] has demonstrated that in epileptic subjects memories are retained in their natural form as ego states. By direct electrical stimulation of the bared temporal cortex of either side, he was able to evoke these phenomena.

"The subject feels again the emotion which the situation originally produced in him, and he is aware of the same interpretations, true or false, which he himself gave to the experience in the first place. Thus, evoked recollection is not the exact photographic or phonographic reproduction of past scenes and events. It is reproduction of what the patient saw and heard and felt and understood." He noted further that such evocations were discrete, and "not fused with other, similar experiences."

He further demonstrated that two different ego states can occupy consciousness simultaneously as discrete psychological entities distinct from each other. In one case of such "forced" re-experiencing under electrical stimulation, the patient cried out that he heard people laughing. The patient himself, however, "did not feel inclined to laugh at the joke, whatever it may have been. He was, somehow, doubly conscious of two simultaneous situations. His exclamation showed his immediate appreciation of the incongruity of the two experiences—the one in the present, the other forced into his consciousness from the past." This refers to the fact that the patient was aware that he was in the operating room and addressed his exclamation to the doctor, while, at the same time, when such a memory "is forced into a patient's consciousness, it seems to him to be a present experience." Only when it is over may he recognize it as a vivid memory of the past. Such a memory is "as clear as it would have been thirty seconds after the original experience." At the moment of stimulation the patient "is himself both an actor and the audience."

Penfield, Jasper, and Roberts [2,3] emphasize the difference between the re-experiencing of such complete memories, that is, the revival of a complete ego state, and the isolated phenomena which occur on stimulation of the visual or auditory cortex, or the memory for speech and words. They stress that the temporal recording carries with it important psychical elements, such as understanding of the meaning of the experience, and the emotion it may have aroused. Penfield himself, however, does not use the term "ego state."

Kubie, in his comments on these experiments,[1] notes that the subject is both the observer and the observed, and that the archipallial, as well as the neopallial, reservoirs are tapped. "The recall is essentially total, involving far more than he is consciously able to recapture, approximating that totality of recall which can sometimes be achieved with patients under hypnosis." The past is as imminent and vivid as the present. What is evoked is a specific reliving of a specific experience. The verbal, or neopallial, memory, seems to serve as a screen memory, which covers the sensory, or "gut," memories of the same experiences. Kubie's implication is that events are experienced simultaneously in two ways, "archipallial" and "neopallial." It is pertinent to note Cobb's statement, in the same symposium,[4] that "the study of the emotions is now a legitimate medical occupation," which he relates to the physiology of the "archicortex."

It is well-known to psychologists, that is, students of the mind, whatever their diplomas, that complete ego states may be permanently retained. Federn[5] is the one who first stressed on psychiatric grounds what Penfield later demonstrated in his remarkable neurosurgical experiments, that psychological reality is based on complete and discrete ego states. He notes that the term "ego state" met resistance when introduced. It was easier for people to continue to think in orthodox conceptual terms than to shift over to a phenomenological approach.

Weiss,[6] Federn's chief exponent, has clarified and systematized Federn's ego psychology. Weiss describes an ego state as "the actually experienced reality of one's mental and bodily ego with the contents of the lived-through period." In this connection, Federn speaks of "day-by-day ego states." Weiss points out exactly what Penfield proved: that ego states of former age levels are maintained in potential existence within the personality. This was already well-established clinically by the fact that such ego states "can be re-cathected directly under special conditions; for instance in hypnosis, in dreams, and in psychosis." He also notes that "two or more separate ego states may struggle to maintain integration and may consciously exist at one time." Repression of traumatic memories or conflicts is possible in many cases, according to Federn, only through repression of the whole pertinent ego state. Early ego states remain preserved in a latent state, waiting to be recathected. Furthermore, in speaking of cathexis of ego states, Federn says that it is the cathexis itself which is experienced as ego feeling. This is related to the problem of what constitutes "the self."

Weiss speaks of "the residual infantile ego state of the adult person, which usually remains cathected but, in any event, is easily recathected," a sort of "child ego." On the other hand, there is another kind of influence which he calls the "psychic presence." This is "the mental image of another ego," sometimes a parental one, which affects the emotions and behavior of the individual. He describes various situations in which (a) the residual infantile ego state, (b) the current ego state, or (c) the psychic presence, respectively, may determine the individual's response.

More recently Chandler and Hartman,[7] working with LSD–25, have demonstrated the striking similarity between the pharmacological reactivation of archaic ego states and that obtained through electrical stimulation of the cortex, although like Penfield, they do not employ the term "ego state" itself. They describe the same simultaneous experiencing of two ego states, one oriented toward the current external and psychological reality, the other a "reliving" (rather than mere recall) of scenes dating back as far as the first year of life, "with great vividness of color and other detail, and the patient feels himself to be back in the situation and experiences the affects in all the original intensity."

There are other authors whose work is pertinent to the subject of ego states, but the observations quoted will serve the purpose of turning the reader's attention to these phenomena. Structural and transactional analysis, the subjects of the present work, are based solely on clinical observation and experience with patients, with previous preconceptions set aside. Under these conditions, the study of complete ego states emerged as the "natural" approach to psychology and psychotherapy. But as Federn implied, since most therapists are trained to think and work in orthodox conceptual terms, the naturalistic approach is not always thoroughly explored. In seeking confirmation in the literature for the findings of structural and transactional analysis the writer was gratified to discover, or re-discover, that he was following in the footsteps of two of the most remarkable of his teachers (Penfield and Federn). The pertinence of the excerpts which have been assembled here will become evident in the course of the ensuing text.

REFERENCES

1. Penfield, W. "Memory Mechanisms," *Arch. Neurol. & Psychiat.* 67: 178–198, 1952, with discussion by L. S. Kubie et al.

2. Penfield, W. & Jasper, H. *Epilepsy and the Functional Anatomy of the Human Brain.* Little, Brown & Company, Boston, 1954, Chap. XI.

3. Penfield, W. & Roberts, L. *Speech and Brain-mechanisms.* Princeton University Press, Princeton, 1959.

4. Cobb, S. "On the Nature and Locus of Mind." Ref. 1, 172–177.

5. Federn, P. *Ego Psychology and the Psychoses.* Basic Books, New York, 1952.

6. Weiss, Edoardo. *Principles of Psychodynamics.* Grune & Stratton, New York, 1950.

7. Chandler, A. L. & Hartman, M. A. "Lysergic Acid Diethylamide (LSD–25) as a Facilitating Agent in Psychotherapy." *A.M.A. Arch. Gen. Psychiat.* 2: 286–299, 1960.

CHAPTER ONE

General Considerations

1 THE RATIONALE

STRUCTURAL and transactional analysis offer a systematic, consistent theory of personality and social dynamics derived from clinical experience, and an actionistic, rational form of therapy which is suitable for, easily understood by, and naturally adapted to the great majority of psychiatric patients.

Conventional psychotherapies may be roughly divided into two classes: those involving suggestion, reassurance, and other "parental" functions; and "rational" approaches based on confrontation and interpretation, such as non-directive therapy and psychoanalysis. The "parental" approaches have the defect of over-looking or over-riding the archaic fantasies of the patient, so that in the long run the therapist too often loses control of the situation and finds himself being surprised or disappointed at the final outcome of the case. The rational approaches are designed to establish controls from within; with the usual methods this may take a long time, and meanwhile not only the patient, but also his intimates and associates are exposed to the results of his injudicious behavior. If the patient has small children, such a prolonged delay may have a decisive effect on the character development of the offspring.

The structural-transactional approach helps to overcome these difficulties. Since it tends to increase rapidly the patient's ability to tolerate and control his anxieties and to circumscribe his acting out, it has many of the advantages of "parental" therapy. At the same time, since the therapist remains fully aware of the archaic elements in the patient's personality, it loses none of the value of rational therapy. It has proven particularly valuable in certain cases where conventional therapies are notoriously difficult to apply effectively. These include psychopaths of various types; latent, remittent, or border-line schizophrenics and manic-depressives; and mentally retarded adults.

From the educational point of view, structural and transactional analysis are easier to teach effectively than most other clinical approaches. The principles can be grasped in ten weeks, and with a year of supervision an otherwise well-qualified clinician or research worker can become quite adept in theory and practice. Formal psychoanalytic training may give rise, initially at least, to a strong resistance to the principles of structural analysis, unless the individual is especially interested in ego psychology.

Self-appraisal in this system is free of some of the difficulties of self-psychoanalysis, making it relatively easy for the practitioner to detect and control archaic or prejudicial elements in his own responses.

2   THE PROCEDURE

In both individual and group work, this method proceeds in stages which can be clearly defined, and which schematically at least succeed one another, so that both the therapist and the patient can at any given moment state the therapeutic position with some precision; that is, what they have accomplished so far, and what the next step is likely to be.

Structural analysis, which must precede transactional analysis, is concerned with the segregation and analysis of ego states. The goal of this procedure is to establish the predominance of reality-testing ego states and free them from contamination by archaic and foreign elements. When this has been accomplished, the patient can proceed to *transactional analysis:* first, the analysis of simple transactions, then the analysis of stereotyped series of transactions, and finally the analysis of long complex operations often involving several people and usually based on rather elaborate fantasies. An example of the last is the rescue fantasy of the woman who marries one alcoholic after another. The goal of this phase is *social control:* that is, control of the individual's own tendency to manipulate other people in destructive or wasteful ways, and of his tendency to respond without insight or option to the manipulations of others.

In the course of these therapeutic operations, traumatically fixated archaic ego states have been segregated, but not resolved. At the end of this program, the individual is in a particularly favorable position, because of the predominance of reality-testing, to attempt the resolution of the archaic conflicts and distortions. Experience has shown that such a sequel is not essential to the therapeutic success of the method, and the decision as to whether or not it is undertaken becomes a problem of clinical judgment and situational freedom.

3 THE LANGUAGE

While the theoretical exposition is more complex, the application of structural and transactional analysis requires an esoteric vocabulary of only six words. *Exteropsyche, neopsyche,* and *archaeopsyche* are regarded as psychic *organs,* which manifest themselves phenomenologically as exteropsychic (e.g., identificatory), neopsychic (e.g., dataprocessing), and archaeopsychic (e.g., regressive) *ego states.* Colloquially, these types of ego states are referred to as *Parent, Adult,* and *Child,* respectively. These three substantives form the terminology of structural analysis. The methodological problems involved in moving from organs to phenomena to substantives are not relevant to the practical applications.

Certain repetitive sets of social maneuvers appear to combine both defensive and gratificatory functions. Such maneuvers are colloquially called *pastimes* and *games*. Some of them which readily yield both primary and secondary gains tend to become commonplace; the game of "PTA" for example is prevalent in this country wherever parents come together in parties or groups. More complex operations are based on an extensive unconscious life plan which is called a *script*, after the theatrical scripts which are intuitive derivatives of these psychological dramas. These three terms, "pastime," "game," and "script," form the vocabulary of transactional analysis.

It will be demonstrated that Parent, Adult, and Child are not concepts, like Superego, Ego, and Id, or the Jungian constructs, but phenomenological realities; while pastimes, games, and scripts are not abstractions, but operational social realities. Once he has a firm grasp of the psychological, social, and clinical meanings of these six terms, the transactional analyst, whether physician, psychologist, social scientist, or social worker is in a position to use them as therapeutic, research, or case-work tools according to his or her opportunities and qualifications.

NOTES

A rigid *classification of psychotherapies* is not possible due to the flexibility of all experienced therapists. The division into "parental" and "rational" types roughly corresponds to the scheme given in 1943 by Giles W. Thomas,[1] who based his classification on that of Merrill Moore (1942). K. E. Appel[2] divides psychotherapy into "Symptomatic or Direct Psychological Approaches," including hypnosis, suggestion, moral suasion (Dubois), persuasion (Déjerine), authority, direction, and will; and "Approaches Involving Reorganization of the Personality," including psychobiology (A. Meyer), "personality study," psychoanalysis and its modifications, and "dynamic growth" therapy, to which nowadays would be added non-directive therapy (Rogers). These two divisions again correspond roughly to "parental" and "rational" approaches, respectively. A third type which is in a special category is play therapy with children; this may be at times neither parental nor rational, but "child-like."

The teachability (or learnability) of the present system is illustrated by the fact that students of transactional analysis are now applying it in individual and group therapy in a variety of settings with general psychiatric patients, as well as with various special categories which will be described or mentioned in the text. (More recently, it is being used by psychiatric nurses, parole and probation officers, clergymen, and Army and Navy personnel.)

Concerning *Self-analysis*, the dictum is that "the trouble with self-analysis is the counter-transference." (There are at least a half-dozen psychiatrists, each of whom will modestly acknowledge that he originated this aphorism.) This difficulty can be handled fairly effectively by structural procedure.

As for the *vocabulary*, "neopsychic" and "archaeopsychism" are found in Hinsie & Shatzky's "Psychiatric Dictionary."[3] "Archipallium" and "neopallium" are well established neurological terms.[4]

REFERENCES

1. Thomas, G. W. "Group Psychotherapy: A Review of the Recent Literature." *Psychosom. Med.* 5: 166–180, 1943.

2. Appel, K. E. "Psychiatric Therapy." In *Personality and the Behavior Disorders*. (Ed. by J. M. Hunt) Ronald Press Company, New York, 1944, pp. 1107–1163.

3. Hinsie, L. E. & Shatzky, J. *Psychiatric Dictionary.* Oxford University Press, New York, 1940.

4. Tilney, F. & Riley, H. A. *The Form and Functions of the Central Nervous System.* Paul B. Hoeber, New York, 1928.

PART I

Psychiatry of the Individual and Structural Analysis

CHAPTER TWO

The Structure of Personality

MRS. PRIMUS, a young housewife, was referred by her family physician for a diagnostic interview. She sat tensely for a minute or two with her eyes downcast, and then she began to laugh. A moment later she stopped laughing, looked stealthily at the doctor, then averted her eyes again, and once more began to laugh. This sequence was repeated three or four times. Then rather suddenly she stopped tittering, sat up straight in her chair, pulled down her skirt, and turned her head to the right. After observing this new attitude for a short time, the psychiatrist asked her if she were hearing voices. She nodded without turning her head, and continued to listen. The psychiatrist again interrupted to ask her how old she was. His carefully calculated tone of voice successfully captured her attention. She turned to face him, pulled herself together, and answered his question.

Following this, she answered a series of other pertinent questions concisely and to the point. Within a short time, enough information was obtained to warrant a tentative diagnosis of acute schizophrenia, and to enable the psychiatrist to piece together some of the precipitating factors and some of the gross features in her early background. After this, no further questions were put for awhile, and she soon lapsed into her former state. The cycle of flirtatious tittering, stealthy appraisal, and prim attention to her hallucinations was repeated until she was asked whose voices they were and what they were saying.

She replied that it seemed to be a man's voice and that he was calling her awful names, words she had never heard before. Then the talk was turned to her family. Her father she described as a wonderful man, a considerate husband, a loving parent, well-liked in the community, and so forth. But it soon came out that he drank heavily, and then he was different. He used bad language. She was asked the nature of the bad language. It then occurred to the patient that she had heard him use some of the same epithets that the hallucinated voice was using.

This patient rather clearly exhibited three different ego states. These were distinguished by differences in her posture, manner, facial expression, and other physical characteristics. The first was characterized by tittering coyness, quite reminiscent of a little girl at a certain age; the second was primly righteous, like that of a schoolgirl almost caught in some sexual peccadillo; in the third, she was able to answer questions like the grown-up woman that she was, and was able to demonstrate that in this state her understanding, her memory, and her ability to think logically were all intact.

The first two ego states had an archaic quality in that they were appropriate to some former stage of her experience, but were inappropriate to the immediate reality of the interview. In the third, she showed considerable skill in marshaling and processing data and perceptions concerning her immediate situation: what can easily be understood as "adult" functioning, something that neither an infant nor a sexually agitated school-girl would be capable of. The process of "pulling herself together," which was activated by the business-like tone of the psychiatrist, represented the transition from the archaic ego states to this adult ego state.

The term "ego state" is intended merely to denote states of mind and their related patterns of behavior as they occur in nature, and avoids in the first instance the use of constructs such as "instinct," "culture," "superego," "animus," "eidetic," and so forth. Structural analysis postulates only that such ego states can be classified and clarified, and that in the case of psychiatric patients such a procedure "is good."

In seeking a framework for classification, it was found that the clinical material pointed to the hypothesis that childhood ego states exist as relics in the grown-up, and that under certain circumstances they can be revived. As already noted in the introduction, this phenomenon has been repeatedly reported in connection with dreams, hypnosis, psychosis, pharmacological intoxicants, and direct electrical stimulation of the temporal cortex. But careful observation carried the hypothesis one step further, to the assumption that such relics can exhibit spontaneous activity in the normal waking state as well.

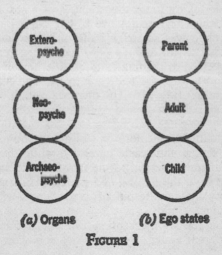

(a) Organs   *(b)* Ego states

FIGURE 1

What actually happened was that patients could be observed, or observed themselves, shifting from one state of mind and one behavior pattern to another. Typically, there was one ego state characterized by reasonably adequate reality-testing and rational reckoning (secondary process), and another distinguished by autistic thinking and archaic fears and expectations (primary process). The former had the quality of the usual mode of functioning of responsible adults, while the latter resembled the way very young children of various ages went about their business. This led to the assumption of two psychic organs, a neopsyche and an archaeopsyche. It seemed appropriate, and was generally acceptable to all individuals concerned, to call the phenomenological and operational manifestations of these two organs the Adult and the Child, respectively.

Mrs. Primus's Child manifested herself in two different forms. The one which predominated in the absence of distracting stimuli was that of the "bad" (sexy) girl. It would be difficult to conceive of Mrs. Primus, in this state, undertaking the responsibilities of a sexually mature woman. The resemblance of her behavior to that of a girl child was so striking that this ego state could be classified as an archaic one. At a certain point, a voice perceived as coming from outside herself brought her up short, and she shifted into the ego state of a "good" (prim) little girl. The previous criteria warranted classifying this state also as an archaic one. The difference between the two ego states was that the "bad" girl was indulging in more or less autonomous self-expression, doing what came naturally, while the "good" girl was adapting herself to the fact that she was being chastised. Both the natural and the adapted states were archaeopsychic manifestations, and hence aspects of Mrs. Primus's Child.

The therapist's intervention brought about a shift into a different system. Not only her behavior, responsiveness, reality-testing, and mode of thinking, but also her posture, facial expression, voice, and muscle-tone took on a more familiar pattern as the Adult ego state of the responsible housewife was reactivated. This shift, which was brought about repeatedly during the interview, constituted a brief remission of the psychosis. This implies a description of psychosis as a shift of psychic energy, or, to use the commonly accepted word, *cathexis,* from the Adult system to the Child system. It also implies a description of remission as the reversal of this shift.

The derivation of the hallucinated voice with its "unfamiliar" obscenities would have been evident to any educated observer, in view of the change it brought about in the patient's behavior. It remained only to confirm the impression, and this was the purpose of turning the discussion to the patient's family. As anticipated, the voice was using the language of her father, much to her own surprise. This voice belonged to the exteropsychic, or parental system. It was not the "voice of her Superego," but the voice of an actual person. This emphasizes the point that Parent, Adult, and Child represent real people who now exist or who once existed, who have legal names and civic identities. In the case of Mrs. Primus, the Parent did not manifest itself as an ego state, but only as a hallucinated voice. In the beginning, it is best to concentrate upon the diagnosis and differentiation of the Adult and the Child, and consideration of the Parent can be profitably postponed in clinical work. The activity of the Parent may be illustrated by two other cases.

Mr. Segundo, who first stimulated the evolution of structural analysis, told the following story:

An eight-year-old boy, vacationing at a ranch in his cowboy suit, helped the hired man unsaddle a horse. When they were finished, the hired man said: "Thanks, cowpoke!", to which his assistant answered: "I'm not really a cowpoke, I'm just a little boy."

The patient then remarked: "That's just the way I feel. I'm not really a lawyer, I'm just a little boy." Mr. Segundo was a successful court-room lawyer of high repute, who raised his family decently, did useful community work, and was popular socially. But in treatment he often did have the attitude of a little boy. Sometimes during the hour he would ask: "Are you talking to the lawyer or to the little boy?" When he was away from his office or the court-room, the little boy was very apt to take over. He would retire to a cabin in the mountains away from his family, where he kept a supply of whiskey, morphine, lewd pictures, and guns. There he would indulge in child-like fantasies, fantasies he had had as a little boy, and the kinds of sexual activity which are commonly labeled "infantile."

At a later date, after he had clarified to some extent what in him was Adult and what was Child (for he really was a lawyer sometimes and not always a little boy), Mr. Segundo introduced his Parent into the situation. That is, after his activities and feelings had been sorted out into the first two categories, there were certain residual states which fitted neither. These had a special quality which was reminiscent of the way his parents had seemed to him. This necessitated the institution of a third category which, on further testing, was found to have sound clinical validity. These ego states lacked the autonomous quality of both Adult and Child. They seemed to have been introduced from without, and to have an imitative flavor.

Specifically, there were three different aspects apparent in his handling of money. The Child was penurious to the penny and had miserly ways of ensuring pennywise prosperity; in spite of the risk for a man in his position, in this state he would gleefully steal chewing gum and other small items out of drugstores, just as he had done as a child. The Adult handled large sums with a banker's shrewdness, foresight, and success, and was willing to spend money to make money. But another side of him had fantasies of giving it all away for the good of the community. He came of pious, philanthropic people, and he actually did donate large sums to charity with the same sentimental benevolence as his father. As the philanthropic glow wore off, the Child would take over with vindictive resentfulness toward his beneficiaries, followed by the Adult who would wonder why on earth he wanted to risk his solvency for such sentimental reasons.

One of the most difficult aspects of structural analysis in practice is to make the patient (or student) see that Child, Adult, and Parent are not handy ideas, or interesting neologisms, but refer to phenomena based on actual realities. The case of Mr. Segundo demonstrates this point fairly clearly. The person who stole chewing gum was not called the Child for convenience, or because children often steal, but because he himself stole chewing gum as a child with the same gleeful attitude and using the same technique. The Adult was called the Adult, not because he was playing the role of an adult, imitating the behavior of big men, but because he exhibited highly effective reality-testing in his legal and financial operations. The Parent was not called the Parent because it is traditional for philanthropists to be "fatherly" or "motherly," but because he actually imitated his own father's behavior and state of mind in his philanthropic activities.

In the case of Mr. Troy, a compensated schizophrenic who had had electric shock treatment following a breakdown during naval combat, the parental state was so firmly established that the Adult and the Child rarely showed themselves. In fact, he was unable at first to understand the idea of the Child. He maintained a uniformly judgmental attitude in most of his relationships. Manifestations of child-like behavior on the part of others, such as naiveté, charm, boisterousness, or trifling were especially apt to stimulate an outburst of scorn, rebuke, or chastisement. He was notorious in the therapy group which he attended for his attitude of "Kill the little bastards." He was equally severe toward himself. His object, in group jargon, seemed to be "to keep his own Child from even sticking his head out of the closet." This is a common attitude in patients who have had electric shock treatment. They seem to blame the Child (perhaps rightly) for the "beating" they have taken; the Parent is highly cathected, and, often with the assistance of the Adult, severely suppresses most child-like manifestations.

There were some curious exceptions to Mr. Troy's disapproving attitude. In regard to heterosexual irregularities and alcohol, he behaved like an all-wise benevolent father, rather than a tyrant, freely giving all the young ladies and men-about-town the benefit of his experience. His advice, however, was prejudicial and based on banal preconceptions which he was quite unable to correct even when he was repeatedly proven wrong. It was no surprise to learn that as a child he had been scorned or beaten by his father for occasional exhibitions of naiveté, charm, and boisterousness, or trifling, and regaled with stories of sexual and alcoholic excesses. Thus his parental ego state, which was protectively fixated, reproduced his father's attitudes in some detail. This fixated Parent allowed no leeway for either Adult or Child activities except in the spheres where his father had been skillful or self-indulgent.

The observation of such fixated personalities is instructive. The constant Parent, as seen in people like Mr. Troy; the constant Adult, as seen in funless, objective scientists; and the constant Child ("Little old me") often exemplify well some of the superficial characteristics of these three types of ego states. Some professionals earn a living by the public exhibition of a constant ego state: clergymen, the Parent; diagnosticians, the Adult; and clowns, the Child.*

The cases presented so far demonstrate the theoretical basis for structural analysis, which comprises three pragmatic absolutes and three general hypotheses. By a "pragmatic absolute" is meant a condition to which so far no exceptions have been found.

1. That every grown-up individual was once a child.
2. That every human being with sufficient functioning brain-tissue is potentially capable of adequate reality-testing.
3. That every individual who survives into adult life has had either functioning parents or someone *in loco parentis.*

The corresponding hypotheses are:

1. That relics of childhood survive into later life as complete ego states. (Archaeopsychic relics.)
2. That reality-testing is a function of discrete ego states, and not an isolated "capacity." (Neopsychic functioning.)
3. That the executive may be taken over by the complete ego state of an outside individual, as perceived. (Exteropsychic functioning.)

In summary, the structure of personality is regarded as comprising three organs: the exteropsyche, the neopsyche, and the archaeopsyche, as shown in Figure 1A. These manifest themselves phenomenologically and operationally as three types of ego states called Parent, Adult, and Child respectively, as shown in Figure 1B.

* (The case histories presented in this book are fragmentary. Different aspects of the same case are used from time to time to illustrate specific points. The references to each individual patient are assembled in the "Patient Index" which is appended for the convenience of readers who may wish to follow a specific case throughout the text.)

NOTES

Psychoanalytic terms such as "primary process," "secondary process," and "reality-testing" are most concisely elucidated in Freud's "An Outline of Psychoanalysis."[1] The relationship of hallucinations to archaic mental contents, specifically to "primal images," has been discussed elsewhere by the writer.[2]

The cases of Mrs. Primus and Mr. Segundo have been previously reported.[3] Since I have had several lawyers in my practice recently, it should be strenuously emphasized, to forestall attempts at identification, that Mr. Segundo is not one of them. In real life, he rests in safe anonymity in another profession 3000 miles from my office.

REFERENCES

1. Freud, S. *An Outline of Psychoanalysis.* W. W. Norton & Company, New York, 1949.

2. Berne, E. "Primal Images and Primal Judgment." *Psychiat. Quart.* 29: 634–658, 1955.

3. Berne, E. "Ego States in Psychotherapy." *Amer. J. Psychother.* 11: 293–309, 1957.

CHAPTER THREE

Personality Function

1 REACTION TO STIMULI

JUST as the various ograns of the brain and of the body react differently to stimuli, so do the different systems of the personality. The exteropsyche is judgmental in an imitative way, and seeks to enforce sets of borrowed standards. The neopsyche is principally concerned with transforming stimuli into pieces of information, and processing and filing that information on the basis of previous experience. The archaeopsyche tends to react more abruptly, on the basis of pre-logical thinking and poorly differentiated or distorted perceptions. In fact, each of these aspects perceives the environment differently, in accordance with its function, and hence is reacting to a different set of stimuli. An over-simplified but illustrative example is the reaction to one of the over popular news stories about embezzlers. In a few people, this arouses a Parental, moralistic reaction. In more people it arouses a more matter-of-fact Adult interest as to how the embezzlement was managed. Possibly the most common reaction is the naive, child-like, though usually unexpressed, thought: "That would be interesting to do." In the language of transactional analysis, the fault-finding Parent plays Blemish, the Adult plays Accountant, and the Child wants to play Cops and Robbers.

The three aspects also react on each other. The Parent may become excited (i.e., distressed) by the Child's

19

fantasies, and the Child is particularly sensitive to inhibitory stimuli from the Parent. This relationship is usually a replica of the original child-parent relationship which the individual experienced.

2   THE FLOW OF CATHEXIS

Mrs. Tettar, a 22-year-old housewife, was referred for treatment of a severe state of agitation following the birth of her second child. One of her most frequent operations during her therapeutic hours was coercive nagging. For she would ask the therapist again and again what to do about her maid leaving, or whether she should go to the hospital. It soon became possible to point out to her that, while on the surface her questions represented an Adult quest for information, at another level they constituted an attempt of her Child to manipulate the therapist in some way. The patient responded by expressing resentment against her mother for babying her. She gave examples of how she had begged her mother to do things for her that she could well do for herself. She felt that her mother should not have given in.

As this problem was worked over during the hour, the patient's demeanor gradually changed. She sat up, her face relaxed, her voice became more assured, and instead of whining and nagging, she was sociable, cheerful, and communicative: just like her old self, as she remarked. But as she was escorted to the door at the end of the hour, she relapsed into her former state of mind and began to whine once more. Then abruptly she pulled herself together, smiled merrily, and said: "There I go again!"

Such shifts in ego state, which can be readily observed in healthy people as well as in patients, may be accounted for by using the concept of psychic energy, or cathexis, on the principle that at a given moment that ego state which is cathected in a certain way will have the *executive power*. In the first instance it will suffice to speak simply of "the flow of cathexis." The data given about Mrs. Tettar, for example, can be explained in this regard by saying that she came in with a highly cathected Child; that cathexis gradually flowed from the Child into the Adult until the Adult took over the executive; that as she departed, cathexis was drained back into the Child, and that when she "pulled herself together" cathexis abruptly flowed back into the Adult. Mrs. Primus's cycles of behavior and attitude can be similarly accounted for.

3   EGO BOUNDARIES

When it was said above that cathexis flowed *from* the Child *into* the Adult, and vice versa, this concept or metaphor implies that there was some sort of *boundary* between the two ego states. While this implication can be thought of in neurological terms, a physiological verification is not yet possible, so that here we shall confine ourselves to considering the psychological phenomena.

In her pre-psychotic state, and during the remissions which occurred in the course of her therapy, Mrs. Tettar was aware of certain obsessions, phobias, and compulsions which were *ego dystonic*. At such times, her obsession with cleanliness, her fear of dirt, and her compulsion to wash her hands a certain number of times in succession were usually perceived by her as not part of her "real self." In this kind of thinking, her mind was divided into two systems: "real Self" and "not real Self." "Real Self" was capable of reality-testing in regard to dirt and cleanliness; "not real Self" was incapable. "Real Self" knew things about sanitation (particularly since her husband was a public health worker) which an infant would be incapable of appreciating, while "not real Self" was guided by magical thinking in a way characteristic of an infant at a certain specific phase of development. Thus "real Self" was characteristically Adult, and "not real Self" was characteristically Child.

Mrs. Tettar's own view of these two different aspects of her personality implied the existence of a boundary between them, since in her mind certain forms of behavior and feeling pertained to one system, which she perceived as her real self, and other forms pertained to a system which was outside of that. The multiplication of such reports justifies the assumption that each ego state is a kind of entity which is differentiated in some way from the rest of the psychic contents, including other ego states which existed many years ago or a few moments previously, or which are active simultaneously. The most convenient and probably the most accurate way to say this is to talk of each ego state as having a boundary which separates it from other ego states. Hence a set of circles, such as that in Figure 1B, may be taken as a fair way of representing the structure of personality.

4   THE PROBLEM OF THE SELF

When it was said that Mrs. Tettar's hand-washing was ego dystonic, this meant specifically Adult-ego dystonic. In her overt psychotic state, however, when her "real Self" was the Child, the hand-washing became *ego syntonic:* that is, at such times she accepted her own farfetched rationalizations for this behavior, which was only to be expected, since the rationalizations themselves came from the Child. In her neurotic state they were heard by the Adult, who disagreed, while in her psychotic state they were heard by the same personality who devised them. In other words, her hand-washing was Adult-ego dystonic and Child-ego syntonic, so whether at a given moment she perceived it as dystonic or syntonic depended upon which was her "real Self" at that moment.

The problem now revolves around what determines "real Self." Evidently this does not depend upon executive power, since when she was reluctantly washing her hands or hunting for specks, in her non-psychotic condition, her Child had the executive power, but the Adult was still experienced as "real Self."

Clinical understanding in this area can be obtained by postulating three states of cathexis; bound, unbound, and free. A physical analogy is offered by a monkey on a tree. If he remains inactive, his elevated position gives him only potential energy. If he falls off, this potential energy is transformed into kinetic energy. But because he is a living being, he can jump off, and then a third component, muscular energy, must be taken into account in order to understand how he lands where he does. When he is inactive, the physical energy is bound, so to speak, in his position. When he falls, this energy is unbound, and when he jumps he adds a third component by free choice. The kinetic and muscular energy together might be called the active energy. Bound cathexis then corresponds to potential energy, unbound cathexis to kinetic energy, and free cathexis to muscular energy; and unbound cathexis and free cathexis together may be called *active cathexis*.

Ego boundaries are conceived as semi-permeable under most conditions. They are relatively impermeable to bound and unbound cathexis, while free cathexis can pass with relative ease from one ego state to another.

The psychological situation may then be summarized as follows: (a) That ego state in which *free cathexis* predominates is perceived as the *Self;* or, as Federn[1] puts it, "It is the cathexis itself which is experienced as ego feeling." (b) The executive power is taken over by that state in which the net sum of unbound plus free cathexis (active cathexis) is greatest at a given moment. These two principles can be illustrated by the case of Mrs. Tettar in her three different clinical states.

1. In her healthy state, her "old self," the Child contains only *bound cathexis* and is therefore *latent,* while the Adult is charged with free cathexis and is therefore experienced as her "real Self." The Adult also has the executive power, since it contains the greatest sum of active cathexis (unbound plus free).

2. In her neurotic hand-washing state the free cathexis still resides in the Adult, while the Child contains *unbound cathexis.* This unbound cathexis predominates quantitatively over the active cathexis of the Adult. The Child therefore has the executive power, while the Adult is still experienced as her "real Self."

3. In her psychotic state, the Child contains unbound cathexis and also the free cathexis which has been drained from the Adult. This leaves the Adult relatively depleted of active cathexis. Therefore the Child both has the executive power and is experienced as the "real Self."

5   SHIFTS IN EGO STATE

Shifts in ego state in such a system depend on three factors: the forces acting on each state; the permeability of the boundaries between ego states; and the cathectic capacity of each ego state. It is the quantitative balance between these three which determines the clinical condition of the patient, and also indicates the therapeutic procedures (or the corruptive procedures of exploiters). In Mrs. Tettar's case, the therapy was planned so as to deal with these factors one after the other.

First, the therapist attempted to activate the Adult, as in the case of Mrs. Primus, by emphasizing reality-testing. The neopsyche, as a system, was assumed to exist intact; the problem was to increase its active (i.e., unbound plus free) cathexis. The transference and social aspects played their part in this mobilization. Secondly, he attempted to clarify and strengthen the boundary between the Adult and the Child so as to "capture" this increased cathexis of the Adult. Thirdly, he attempted to increase the cathectic capacity of the Child both absolutely and relatively by the resolution of infantile conflicts, so that the Child would be less apt to become active at inopportune times in an unhealthy way. The actual techniques used are not pertinent to the present discussion, whose purpose is only to illustrate the importance of studying the factors which influence shifts in ego state. The principles involved are often intuitively recognized by the patients themselves; by which particular aspect will be discussed later.

At this point, two distinctions which often cause difficulty should be clarified. The Parent can function either as an active ego state, or as an influence. In Mr. Troy's case, the Parent was both the executive and the "real Self," and functioned as an active ego state. This meant that he behaved *like father*. On the other hand, when Mrs. Primus pulled down her skirt, her active ego state was that of a compliant Child, while her Parent, in the form of hallucinated voices, functioned only as an influence. She did not behave like father, but rather *as father would have liked*. Thus whenever the Parent is spoken of, it must be understood whether the *active ego state* or the *Parental influence* is meant.

It is the Parental influence which determines whether the adapted Child or the natural Child is active at a given moment. The *adapted Child* is an archaic ego state which is under the Parental influence, while the *natural Child* is an archaic ego state which is free from or is attempting to free itself from such influence. It is the difference, for example, between an obedient child and a child having a temper tantrum. Again, it should be understood which is meant when the Child is referred to.

NOTES

Freud's discussions of "psychic energy" and "cathexis" (*Besetzungsenergie*) are among his most obscure. Some of the difficulties may reside with his translators.[2] Colby[3] has attempted to resolve some of these problems. The simplest course is to accept gratefully the concept of cathexis and attempt to correlate it with one's own observations.

REFERENCES

1. Weiss, Edoardo. *Loc. cit.*, p. 37.
2. e.g., Freud, S. *An Outline of Psychoanalysis, loc. cit.*, p. 44 f.
3. Colby, K. M. *Energy & Structure in Psychoanalysis.* Ronald Press, New York, 1956.

CHAPTER FOUR

Psychopathology

STRUCTURAL analysis makes possible a systematic *general pathology* for psychiatric disorders. *Pathology* is concerned with the reactions of living organisms to injury. The study of specific nosological entities and of particular defense mechanisms belongs to the field of *special pathology*. At the moment we are concerned with more general reactions which involve the whole psychic organization, or which are common to large categories of disturbances.

Structural pathology deals with anomalies of psychic structure, two of the commonest being exclusion and contamination. *Functional pathology* is concerned with the lability of cathexes and the permeability of ego boundaries.

1 EXCLUSION

Exclusion is manifested by a stereotyped, predictable attitude which is steadfastly maintained as long as possible in the face of any threatening situation. The constant Parent, the constant Adult, and the constant Child all result primarily from defensive exclusion of the two complementary aspects in each case. Secondary transactional gains tend to reinforce the exclusion.

The *excluding Parent* is classically found in "compensated" schizophrenics, and in such cases exclusion constitutes the principal defense against the confused

27

archaeopsychic activity. Such people have the greatest difficulty in acknowledging the existence of the Child, since the object of the exclusion is to control and deny that aspect. The stability of such an exclusion was demonstrated by Mr. Troy over a period of six years in group therapy, following his release from a naval hospital. The structure of his highly cathected Parent has already been described. The Adult and the Child showed themselves only under the most favorable circumstances.

Whenever the proceedings became safely commonplace, Mr. Troy's Parent relaxed sufficiently for the Adult to make a timid exhibition. He was then able to discuss in an upstanding way the weather, the news, the times, and the ironies of his personal affairs. His manner was pleasant and safely platitudinous.[1] It was warm enough for him, Negroes were good people but you had to watch them, nobody had learned anything from the last war, and whenever you washed your car it rained. Sometimes, like the Boeotian Oread, he could say little in this ego state beyond echoing sturdily the last words of another: "have to watch them"; "last war"; "rains." But the moment a controversy threatened, the weakly cathected Adult retreated before the fierce dogmatism of the reinstated Parent.

On the other hand, when the therapist spoke, he responded with silent compliance, verging on awe, and a deferential posture. This was the adapted Child behaving in seemly fashion under the watchful supervision of the alert Parent. But if the therapist threatened the Parental hegemony by an indulgent attitude toward any of his child-like peccadillos (non-sexual, such as boisterousness), the Child was quickly excluded from the proceedings and the Parent took over forthwith with his policy of no such nonsense and kill the little bastard. The group was quite convinced that Parent Troy had actually tried to do the latter on one occasion by driving Child Troy over a cliff, unless it was the exasperated Child doing it the other way 'round. In all this he demonstrated the weak (unbound) cathexis of his Adult and Child and the overwhelming strength of the Parent in his "compensated" state. Such a personality is represented in Figure 2A, which was drawn on the blackboard for Mr. Troy's benefit at an appropriate phase of his treatment, about the time he began to distinguish actual children by gender as "he" or "she," instead of referring to the infants in his environment indiscriminately as "it."

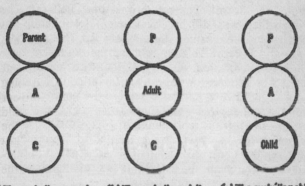

(a) The excluding parent   *(b)* The excluding adult   *(c)* The excluding child

FIGURE 2

The personality of Dr. Quint illustrated another kind of structure. As a social scientist he was at his best with experimental design and the calculating machine. On the one hand he was devoid of the charm, spontaneity, and fun which are characteristic of the healthy child, and on the other he was unable to take sides with the conviction or indignation which is found in healthy parents. The null hypothesis was his favorite device; at parties he was unable to join in the fun, and in time of need he could neither father his wife nor offer his students paternal inspiration. Since he had an *excluding Adult,* he functioned almost solely as a planner, information-collector, and data-processor, building a well-earned reputation as a superior worker in such matters. This Adult was his "real Self," and he had a sincere commitment to data-processing as a way of life.

Thus, in nearly all situations, he managed to keep his Child and his Parent under the iron grip of intellectualization. Unfortunately, the exclusion failed in his sexual activities because there the excluded aspects became so highly charged with unbound cathexis that the Adult lost control. The result was that "he" (i.e., the Adult which was still his "real Self") felt chaotic and helpless in the ensuing battle between the activated Child and Parent. This made clear the defensive function of the exclusion. As he had found to his cost, the slightest relaxation toward the Child ended in impulsive behavior, and any tolerance toward parental attitudes ended in self-reproach and depression. Dr. Quint's personality structure is represented in Figure 2B.

The *excluding Child,* as represented in Figure 2C, is most readily observed socially in narcissistic impulsive personalities, such as certain types of "high class" prostitutes, and clinically in some types of active schizophrenia, where both rational (Adult) and judgmental or nurturing (Parent) ego states are warded off. In many cases there may be weak exhibitions of the Adult or Parent, but these scatter easily in the face of threats, and the seductive or confused Child is reinstated. The latter are the "intelligent" and "helpful" prostitutes and schizophrenics. At other times there may be surprising manifestations of "native" shrewdness and basic morality, but these are essentially child-like in nature, as a comparison with the behavior of actual children, or with the studies of Piaget[2, 3] will show.

The clinical problem presented by such pathological

exclusions demonstrates both the function and the nature of the paramount ego state. Attempts to communicate with the excluded aspects are frustrated by the idiosyncratic response of the defending Parent, Adult, or Child: religiosity, intellectualization, or flattering pseudo-compliance, for example. The operational characteristic of these personalities is that under ordinary conditions all their overt responses come from a single system. The other two systems are *decommissioned*. For a long time it was almost impossible to reach the Adult or Child of Mr. Troy, or the Parent or Child of Dr. Quint. The exasperation of men who attempt to appeal to the morality or rationality of narcissistic impulsive women is a notorious illustration of the difficulties encountered with exclusion phenomena.

It should be emphasized that excluding ego states are not roles. The question of roles will be discussed later.

2 CONTAMINATION

Contamination is best illustrated by certain types of prejudice on the one hand, and by delusions on the other. The diagram in Figure 3A represents the structure of a prejudice. It will be noted that part of the Parent intrudes into the Adult and is included within the Adult ego boundary. The son of a missionary undertook to prove that all dancing is wicked, citing conditions on an island in the Pacific where his father had been in 1890. Eventually he was able to recognize that this Adult-ego syntonic conclusion, which he experienced and defended as though it were rational, was really a Parental prejudice. After treatment this, along with other prejudices, was relegated to the Parent by a realignment of the Adult ego boundary, as shown in Figure 3B. In practice this meant that under ordinary circumstances he was able to discuss dancing and allied activities rationally with his adolescent daughter and her mother, but under certain types of stress the Adult was decommissioned and the Parent took over, thus reinstating his intransigence. When the Adult was reactivated, he was able to look objectively at what had happened. As the Adult became stronger, the clamorous Parental episodes grew less and less frequent. But the pre-requisite for this was the original therapeutic decontamination of the Adult, i.e., the difference between Figures 3A and 3B.

A woman had the idea that she was being spied upon in the bathroom. Her clinical condition pointed to

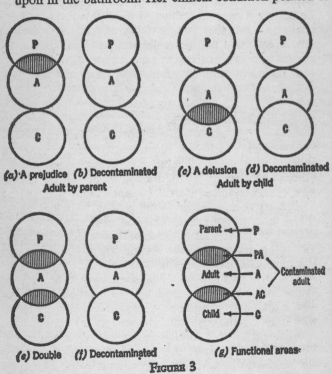

(a) A prejudice (b) Decontaminated Adult by parent

(c) A delusion (d) Decontaminated Adult by child

(e) Double (f) Decontaminated

(g) Functional areas

FIGURE 3

this being a delusion and by chance there was convincing proof that this was so. Meanwhile, childhood material readily offered a genetic background for this idea. Nevertheless she persisted in adducing logical evidence to prove that there was a nest of spies in her back yard. The structure of this delusion is represented in Figure 3C. Here there was contamination of the Adult by the Child. In the course of treatment, she recognized in other connections that there was an archaic aspect of her personality which was not Adult-ego syntonic. In this way the existence of the Child in her was established. At a later date she was able to perceive the archaic nature of her proofs concerning the spies. Thus her Adult could be decontaminated and her delusional system relegated to the Child. After the realignment of her Adult ego boundary, as shown in Figure 3D, the delusions were no longer Adult-ego syntonic. It was now only if the Adult were decommissioned that the delusions could reappear as such. With increasing clarification and strengthening, the Adult ego boundary became more and more firmly established and more difficult to disrupt. Thus she was able to withstand increasing amounts of stress and her lucid intervals became longer and longer.

A *double contamination* is represented in Figure 3E and the result after treatment in Figure 3F. It would appear from these diagrams that the Adult is constricted after treatment, but it should be remembered that the actual situation is more like a three-dimensional diagram. The contaminations are not subtracted from the Adult, but peeled off, as it were. It is metaphorically like scraping the barnacles off a ship so that sailing is less clumsy afterward.

The diagnosis of simple contamination requires the recognition of four areas in the personality, while double contamination involves five, as indicated by the arrows in Figure 3G. An item originating from Area P is recognized by the patient's Adult as a Parental product, while one from Area C is recognized as a product of the Child. Items originating from Areas PA, A, and AC, however, are all experienced by the patient as Adult-ego syntonic, and defended as such. It is here that the therapist renders his service, by correcting the patient's mis-diagnosis and helping him to achieve decontamination and realignment of boundaries. The therapeutic techniques, mechanisms, problems, and precautions involved in changing the situation from that represented in Figure 3E to that represented in Figure 3F will be discussed in their proper places.

3 FUNCTIONAL PATHOLOGY

There are some patients who are capable of either stubborn persistence or of shifting opportunistically and rapidly from one ego state to another. One of these, Mrs. Sachs, was noted socially (on the one hand) for obstinately clinging to certain racial and other familial prejudices at any cost to herself, and maritally (on the other hand) for weeping and whining and accusing and stubbornly punishing her husband by passive aggression until she got what she wanted. Sometimes, after this stubborn Child persisted with such intensity for three or four days and nights, she got migraine.

Yet in treatment the situation was quite different. A word from the therapist could transform her from the indignant bigot into the whining Child, and another word could bring her up short and temporarily fix the rational Adult, who could survey her previous behavior with a considerable degree of objectivity. But a slip on his part might then raise once more the hostile, supercilious Parent or the Child wallowing in her own misery. It appeared as if there were a low viscosity in the flow between bound and unbound cathexis in each state, and the free cathexis was also labile. Thus in treatment the real Self could shift rapidly from one ego state to another, and each could become highly charged and uncharged with considerable ease. But her outside life demonstrated also that each ego state was capable of retaining the active charge and keeping the executive power over a long period in special circumstances, which was taken as evidence of firm ego boundaries. Hence it seems proper to speak of *lability of cathexis*, without defect in ego boundaries, in certain personalities. Indeed, these qualities if properly organized can form the basis for highly effective and adaptable functioning. The complementary type with good ego boundaries and *sluggish cathexis* also exists, the people who are slow to start or to stop playing, thinking, or moralizing.

The *permeability* of ego boundaries also has its two poles. The mechanism of exclusion is only available to people who have *rigid* ego boundaries. Thus, some schizophrenics have difficulty in "compensating," or in maintaining their compensation. Asthenic people who lack identity, who slide from one ego state to another without much intensity, have *lax* ego boundaries. Child and Parent, though both weak, leak into or burst through the ego boundaries of the Adult with little difficulty, and the real Self shifts under small stresses. Mrs. Sachs had a slovenly Child, but the organization of her total personality was by no means untidy. In people with lax ego boundaries, the whole personality gives the impression of being slipshod.

REFERENCES

1. Cf. Harrington, A. *The Revelations of Dr. Modesto.* Alfred A. Knopf, New York, 1955. This is one of those curious satires which can quite easily be taken seriously.

It deals with "Centralism," a platitudinous method of getting along with people.

2. Piaget, J. *The Construction of Reality in the Child*. Basic Books, New York, 1954.

3. Piaget, J. *The Moral Judgment of the Child*. Harcourt Brace & Company, New York, 1932.

CHAPTER FIVE

Pathogenesis

SOMATIC life may be conceived of as a continuum, in which the total state of the body shifts from moment to moment according to the principles of biological fluidity and homeostasis. Clinically, however, it is more expedient to consider the effects of various stimuli on special systems, and to isolate more or less arbitrary epochs from the continuum.

Psychic life may be thought of as a similar continuum, with a single ego state which is modified from moment to moment in an abrupt or plastic way. Here again clinicians usually find it helpful to consider special systems and epochs. Natural psychological epochs are outlined by nature, with bursts of activity intercalated between periods of relative rest. Ordinarily the psyche is bombarded during the day with internal and external stimuli, not all of which can be "assimilated" at the time. The ensuing state of sleep offers an opportunity for this assimilation. Thus a day may be conveniently taken as an "ego unit." From this point of view, the function of dreams is to assimilate the experiences of the day before. The new day then starts with a relatively fresh ego state, and the process is repeated. If something cannot be "assimilated," dreams tend to become repetitive and the waking ego begins to stagnate.* This concept is familiar enough.

* Since this was written, Dement's work on dream deprivation[4] has appeared.

The genesis of pathological personalities may be illustrated by a simple metaphor. Each day's experiences, an ego unit, may be compared to the rough cast of a coin, which is polished during the night. An idealized, trauma-free life would then consist of a pile of such coins, each bearing the stamp of the same personality, but each a little different from the others, and all finished off so that the whole pile stands straight and true, as in Figure 4A. A traumatic ego state, however, would be like a warped coin, which would skew the pile from then on no matter how true all subsequent coins were, as in Figure 4B. If there were periodic traumatic ego states, all of the same nature, then the pile would skew more and more in the same direction until it was in danger of toppling, as in Figure 4C. If they were of different natures, then the pile would zigzag

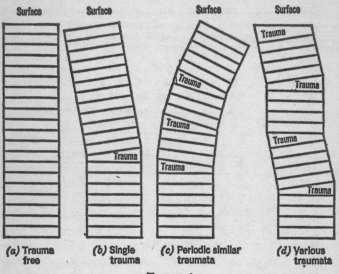

(a) Trauma free   (b) Single trauma   (c) Periodic similar traumata   (d) Various traumata

Figure 4

here and there from time to time, and by chance might end up pointing vertically again, but with an inherent instability, as in Figure 4D. In any case, the warpings would have an algebraic additive effect in changing the balance and direction of the pile.

Translating this metaphor into clinical terms, an early trauma might throw the pile off the true; a later one might throw it off still further; and subsequent traumata might bring it closer and closer to instability, even though the top coin in some cases might not reveal the underlying tilts. The important thing is that in order to correct the situation, it might only be necessary to rectify one or two coins.

It is evident that the lower down the warped coin is, the greater its effect on the ultimate stability. At this point, it would be possible to speak of different kinds of coins: the pennies of childhood, the nickels of the latent period, the quarters of adolescence, and the silver dollars of maturity. Here one bent penny might eventually cause thousands of silver dollars to tumble in chaos. Such a bent penny symbolizes what has been referred to up to now as the Child. The Child is a warped ego state which has become fixated and has changed the direction of the whole subsequent portion of the continuum. More specifically, it is either a single grossly warped ego unit (a really bad penny), or a series of slightly warped ego units (a set of pennies from a poor mold). In the case of the traumatic neuroses, the Child is that confused ego state which was fixated on the day X of the month Y of the year Z in the patient's infancy. In the case of the psychoneuroses, it is the unhealthy ego state which recurred day after day under similar adverse conditions from month A to month B of the year C in the patient's infancy. In either case, the number of fixated pathological archaic ego states (or series of ego states) in any one individual is very limited: one or two, and in rare cases perhaps three. The further exploration of the metaphor of the coins, which is apt in a number of other respects besides those mentioned, will be left to the reader.

A member of the Hept family taught sexual perversions to her three-year-old grandson from his 39th to his 42nd month. Each morning he would lie in bed with her in a state of expectancy and excitement which he had been instructed how to conceal if anyone came into the room, waiting for his mother to leave the house to go to work. This complex ego state was then followed by one of sexual abandon. One day the successful deceiver and lover grew so bold that he made an attempt on his mother as she was drying herself after a bath. This confirmed a growing suspicion which had previously appeared so bizarre to the mother that she had thought herself pre-psychotic. Her horror was so great that the little boy froze in his tracks. His whole highly charged ego state became fixated and split off from the rest of his personality. In this sense, that epic moment marked the birth of his Child.

Here the decisive trauma was not the seduction, but the mother's reaction. When the boy's personality was later analyzed into Parent, Adult, and Child components, the Child, which manifested himself at times both phenomenologically and socially, consisted of an ego state that reproduced in full cathexis all the elements present in the grandmother's bedroom. It was the ego state of that actual child between 38 and 41 months of age who had once really existed. Although the child himself had vanished irrevocably as a unique phenomenon in the universe, his ego state persisted unchanged, to be resurrected in full bloom on certain occasions. His Parent reacted to his own child-like behavior and similar behavior in others, with the specific attitude of horror, as manifested by his mother in the bathroom (Figure 5A). There was no opportunity to observe whether the Child was excluded from the

Adult as well as from the Parent, which would result in traumatic neurosis (Figure 5B), or whether certain elements of the Child were Adult-ego syntonic by contamination, which would constitute in this case a remorseful perversion (Figure 5C). If it had been the mother herself who had seduced him, then some elements of the Child might have been not only Adult-ego syntonic but also Parent-ego syntonic, which constitutes a "psychopathic" perversion (Figure 5D). On the other hand, if the situation with the mother had not arisen, there might have been only an accretion of daily slight traumata, resulting in a psychoneurosis.

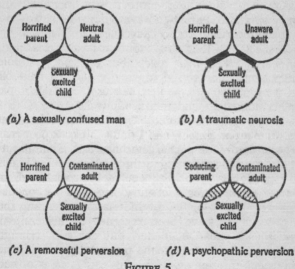

(a) A sexually confused man

(b) A traumatic neurosis

(c) A remorseful perversion

(d) A psychopathic perversion

FIGURE .5

Miss Ogden had been seduced by her grandfather at the age of six, after her Oedipal Parent had been well-established. This Parent had been decommissioned during the event, so that she had co-operated to some extent. She had kept it a secret from her mother because she had anticipated no sympathy from that quarter. The sexual element of the ego state of that day had been excluded (from the Adult), while the secretive elment remained, as it had been at the time, Adult-ego syntonic. When the complete ego state, that is, her total Child, manifested itself in her dreams, it reproduced with little weathering the actual ego state of a real little girl as she existed at 3 p.m. on October 12, 1924, the time of the seduction. In her waking life she was sternly asexual, used no make-up, and dressed as austerely as a nun. Since the secrecy was Adult-ego syntonic, however, she rationalized her pathological secrecy. And since her mother was secretive, the secrecy was also Parent-ego syntonic; thus it was not only pathological, but also "psychopathic." On one occasion she told a long story about a former class-mate in a school 3000 miles away, but referred to her as "this person" and refused to divulge her first name or even mention her sex at first because "you might run into her sometime and then you would know who it was. Anyway," she added, "my mother taught me never to mention names, and I don't think it's proper."

The structure of a character neurosis is similar to that of a "psychopathy," and the evidence so far is that the distinction is probably made by the social environment. A Fijian chief a century ago who ate people, clubbed his wives, or fed ground glass to offending servants, seems to have been regarded by his contemporaries as a mean character, but not as a criminal "psychopath."[1] Nowadays, the psychiatric consultant is often called in by colonial governments in cases of barbaric behavior.

In fact, structural analysis leads to some surprising conclusions concerning "normal" people, which are nevertheless in accord with competent clinical judgment. In structural terms, a "happy" person is one in whom important aspects of the Parent, the Adult, and the Child are all syntonic with each other. A young doctor with marital problems nevertheless felt happy in his work. His father was a physician, respected by his mother, so that his Parent, without internal conflict, approved of his career. His Adult was satisfied because he was interested and competent in his specialty and liked to do a good job. His Child's sexual curiosity was well-sublimated and well gratified in his practice. Hence Parent, Adult, and Child all respected each other and each received appropriate satisfaction in his profession. But since parents and children cannot agree on everything, he was at times quite unhappy when he was away from the office. The moral is that one can define a happy person, but no one can be happy all the time.

It is disconcerting, however, to have to acknowledge that the same analysis applies to the "healthy criminals" of the concentration camps. The myth that these people must fundamentally be tortured souls is a comforting one, but some well-qualified observers feel that the assumption is unwarranted.[2] The following anecdote illustrates the structure of the "happy" personality carried to its logical end:

A young man came home one day and announced to his mother: "I'm so happy! I've just been promoted!" His mother congratulated him, and as she got out the bottle of wine she had been saving for such an occasion, she asked him what his new appointment was.

"This morning," said the young man, "I was only a guard at the concentration camp, but to-night I'm the new commandant!"

"Very good, my son," said his mother, "see how well I've brought you up!"

In this case, just as in the case of the young doctor, Parent, Adult, and Child were all interested in and gratified by his career, so that he met the requirements for "happiness." He fulfilled his mother's ambitions for him with patriotic rationality while obtaining gratification of his archaic sadism. In this light, it is not so surprising that in real life many of these people were able to enjoy good music and literature in their leisure hours. This distasteful example raises some serious questions about certain naive attitudes concerning the relationship between happiness, virtue, and usefulness, including the Greek aspect of "good workmanship."[3] It is also an effective illustration for people who want to know "how to raise children" but cannot specify clearly what they want to raise them to be. It is not enough to want to raise them to be "happy."

There is another kind of "normal" personality which can be described structurally, and that is the "well-organized" person. In these terms, the well-organized person is one with well-defined but not impermeable ego boundaries. He may be subject to severe internal conflicts, but he is able to segregate Parent, Adult, and Child so that each is able to function in a relatively stable way. (Segregation is a more healthy and less categorical relative of exclusion.) A Scottish schoolteacher with an excellent professional record drank a quart of whiskey almost every night for thirty years, yet each morning he arrived at school on time and did his job well. He was able to segregate his Adult completely during the working day, so that his drinking remained more or less a secret through generations of affectionate pupils. At home the Adult was decommissioned and his Child took over while he drank. His Parent remained weakly cathected through all these years, but during a certain phase of his life this aspect took over as completely as the Child had been accustomed to, and he never touched another drop as far as anyone knows. But he became a terror to his pupils because they were now confronted with his Parent instead of his Adult. Because of the Parental disapproval of his drinking, this man was not happy during his whiskey years, but he was well-organized.

The concept of "maturity" has a special connotation in structural analysis. Since everyone is assumed on good clinical grounds to have a completely formed Adult, there is no such thing as an "immature person." There are people whose Child has the executive power so that their behavior is that of an individual who has not yet reached maturity; but if the decommissioned, or uncommissioned, Adult in such individuals can be cathected through therapeutic interventions, then their behavior becomes "mature," as in the case of Mrs. Primus. Thus behavior can be "immature," but an individual (possibly barring organic developmental defect) cannot. A radio which is not plugged in does not play; nevertheless the full potentiality is there and can be brought out by fixing the plug. It is not correct for a patient to assume, just because there is no music in the office during his interview, that the doctor does not have a radio, or only has a broken one. In the writer's experience, not only each neurotic, but each mental defective, each chronic schizophrenic, and each "immature" psychopath has a well-formed Adult. The problem is not that such a person "is" immature, but that it is difficult to find a way to get the Adult "plugged in."

Because of the unfortunate semantics of the words "mature" and "immature" in this country, the best policy is to delete them from the clinical vocabulary. Nowadays only biologists use them in an objective Adult way; in the rest of the population, the Parent seems to have pre-empted these terms to enlarge its own vocabulary.

REFERENCES

1. Derrick, R. A. *A History of Fiji.* Printing & Stationery Dept., Suva, 2nd Ed. Rev. 1950.

2. Cohen, Elie A. *Human Behavior in the Concentration Camp.* W. W. Norton & Company, New York, 1953.

3. Cf. Plato, Aristotle, and Kant on happiness, passim.

4. Dement, W. "The Effect of Dream Deprivation." *Science* 131: 1705–1707, 1960.

CHAPTER SIX

Symptomatology

ONCE more it is desirable initially to have a general view of the subject in order to understand better the special phenomena in this field. Structural diagrams, which are necessarily drawn in two dimensions, would better represent the situation if they could be three-dimensional; or even, if such a thing could be made clinically intelligible, four-dimensional. Nevertheless, there are sufficiently thought-provoking features in the two dimensions.

The Parent was put at the top and the Child at the bottom intuitively. This intuition had good moral origins. The Parent is the guide for ethical aspirations and empyrean esuriences; the Adult is concerned with the earthly realities of objective living; and the Child is a purgatory, and sometimes a hell, for archaic tendencies. This is a way of thinking which has come naturally in all times and nations. Freud prefaced his book on the interpretation of dreams with a quotation from Virgil: "If I cannot bend the Gods above, I shall move the underworld."

This moral hierarchy is reinforced by its clinical significance. The Parent is the weakest member, and Adult is less easily decommissioned, and the Child seems to be almost indefatigable. Under the influence of alcohol, for example, the Parent is first anesthetized, so that the Child, if depressed or inhibited, can express

47

itself in a more buoyant or freer way, which may lead socially to either increased pleasantness or increased unpleasantness. Next goes the Adult, so that social techniques and objective judgments of physical reality begin to fade. It is only with the strongest doses that the untrammeled Child, confused by its own freedom, begins to pass out as unconsciousness supervenes. The saying that people reveal their true selves when they are drinking means that the adapted Child who listens to the dictates of the Parent and Adult, gives way to the natural Child as the upper levels of functioning fade away. On coming out of an anesthetic, the order may, with more or less clarity, be reversed in accordance with Federn's principle of orthriogenesis.[1]

Allowing for certain complexities and idiosyncrasies, the situation is similar in falling asleep. The moral being of waking life gives way in the hypnagogic state to an amoral but practical daydreamer. Instead of thinking of what he *should* do ethically, practically, and pleasurably, the dozer begins to think of what he would like to do without regard to moral problems, but keeping his imagination close to possible realities. When sleep comes, not only ethics and prohibitions, but also the objective world of reality with its limited physical and social possibilities, sinks into oblivion, so that the Child is relatively free to pursue his magic way in dreams. True, certain relics of Parent and Adult functioning may be apparent even before the secondary elaboration,[2] but their occurrence does not violate the hierarchal principle. They are due to the presence in the Child itself of archaic parental influences and awarenesses of reality. This is what differentiates formally the phenomenon of the Child ego state from the concept of the Id. The Child means an organized state of mind which exists or once actually existed, while Freud describes the Id as "a chaos, a cauldron of seething excitement . . . it has no organization and no unified will."[3]

Symptoms are each *exhibitions of* a single definite ego state, active or excluded, although they may *result from* conflicts, concerts, or contaminations between different ego states. The first symptomatic task in structural analysis, therefore, is to decide which ego state is actually exhibiting the symptom. In some cases this is simple, in others it requires a high degree of diagnostic acumen and experience. Mr. Troy's irritable attitude toward boisterousness duplicated that of his father, and was clearly Parental. Dr. Quint's pedantry and Miss Ogden's secretiveness required more careful study. The result of decommissioning Mr.Troy's Parent was heavy drinking and impulsive behavior, both manifestations of the Child, as were Dr. Quint's temper tantrums, and Miss Ogden's somatic anxiety in the face of a threat. This means that certain "characterological" features in each case were exhibitions of one ego state, while certain "symptomatic" manifestations were exhibitions of another.

Bearing these principles in mind, it should be possible to analyze psychiatric symptoms in structural terms, including those which require the simultaneous activity of two different ego states.

Hallucinations are generally exhibitions of the Parent, as exemplified in the voices heard by Mrs. Primus. Two of the commonest types of hallucinations are the obscene epithet and the deadly injunction. Both the accusation "You are a homosexual!" and the command "You must kill him!" may be safely regarded as revived and not very much distorted memories of parental utterances.

While the voice itself emanates from the Parent, the audience consists of the Child and sometimes the contaminated Adult as well. In confusional states, whether toxic or those signifying the onset of an acute schizophrenic episode or a homosexual panic, the Adult is decommissioned, and the frightened Child is left alone to listen. In some paranoid conditions, the active but contaminated Adult agrees with the Child that the voice is really there. In the rarer cases where the voice is that of the Child, it is again the contaminated Adult which agrees that the voice is really there.

This may be clarified by reference to Figure 6A, in which there are only three ego states, but four regions. If "real Self" at a given moment is the Adult, then voices emanating from either the Child or the Parent may be perceived as coming from outside the personality if they are processed by the contaminated area. Reality testing in this region is faulty because the area is experienced as belonging to the Adult whereas it is really an intrusion of the unrealistic Child. Making proper topological allowances, this is a situation which is quite plausible from the neurological point of view. If verbalizations are processed by the clear area of the Adult, then they will not be perceived as hallucinations, but as "the voice of conscience" or as "childish promptings," and will be recognized as internal phenomena. In that case, it will be something else that is processed by the faulty area, resulting in some other kind of psychopathology.

Delusions are generally exhibitions of the Child, but they arise from the contaminated area in Figure 6A, which is included within the Adult ego boundary. Hence they are Adult-ego syntonic, which means that reality testing cannot occur unless and until the boundary between the Adult and the Child can be realigned as in Figure 6B, in which case the delusions become Adult-ego dystonic and will no longer be experienced as delusions, but as strange ideas, as long as the Adult still remains "real Self." The Adult then says in effect: "Part of me thinks it's so, but *I* don't think it's so." But if the Adult becomes decommissioned, and the Child

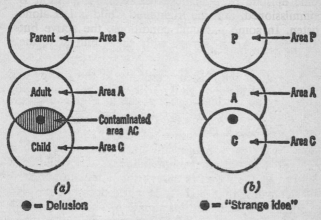

FIGURE 6

becomes "real Self," then once more the individual will say: "*I* think it's really so," since the idea is now syntonic with the "real Self." In the case of Mr. Troy, whose Parent was "real Self," the derivatives of what had been delusions during his psychotic state (because then the Child was "real Self"), were now vehemently repudiated in a characteristically parental way as "silly, foolish ideas," with his usual fatherly implication of "Kill the little bastard who has such thoughts."

Ego boundaries appear to function like complex membranes of highly selective permeability. Lesions of the boundary between the Adult and the Child may give rise to any of a special group of symptoms which may be called "boundary symptoms": feelings of unreality, estrangement, depersonalization, jamais vu, déjà vu, and their analogues, such as the well-known déjà raconté. Their malignance, like that of many other symptoms, depends upon the distribution of the free cathexis. If the Adult is the "real Self," this series of symptoms belongs, for the time being at least, to "the psychopathology of everyday life"; if the Child is the "real Self," they become part of the psychotic array. In any case, they are pathognomonic of boundary lesions, ranging from mild and benign to malignant and intractable.

The patient who listens carefully to the doctor and then says: "But why should I listen to you, since you do not exist?" is manifesting an extreme loss of reality sense. Here "real Self" is the Child, which has excluded the Adult through closure of the Adult-Child ego boundary. Hence neopsychic data-processing, which may still be efficient, cannot influence the Child. The Child treats the Adult as though the latter did not exist, and the feeling that the outside world does not exist is a secondary derivative of this situation. This hypothesis is tested in such cases if it is found that the patient as an actual child cut himself off from communication with the people around him. Now the Adult hears and understands perfectly well what the doctor says, but the Child is not influenced by the information obtained by the Adult, and hence feels justified in saying that there is no such information, i.e., that the doctor does not exist. Hence appeals to reason in such cases, however well they are received by the Adult, cannot usually alter the opinion of the self-isolated Child.

The structure of estrangement, curiously enough, is the same as the structure of insight. Here the outside world loses its previous meaningfulness due to exclusion of the Child by the Adult. The Child's archaic data-processing is cut off and the Adult feels the loss as estrangement. Thus, with feelings of unreality, the Child is "real Self" and with feelings of estrangement the Adult is "real Self"; both are due to a functional sclerosis of the intervening boundary. Insight in the process of psychotherapy comes about when the Adult is decontaminated and the proper boundary between the Child and the Adult is re-established. Thus both es-

trangement and insight are based on a reinforcement of
the Adult-Child boundary, with the Adult as "real
Self," but in one case the reinforcement is pathological,
and in the other it is a re-establishment of normal processes. (Insight may also concern the Parent-Adult
boundary, but this may be disregarded for the present.)

The exclusion of the Child in estrangement was
demonstrated by Mr. Ennat, a 24-year-old unmarried
biologist. He complained that one day while he was
hunting, everything had suddenly seemed meaningless,
and it had been so ever since. He went through the mo-
tions of his daily routine without any conscious incentive or gratification. His Adult sought for explanation
and relief by intellectual means. He began to speculate
about the origins of the universe, of life, and of himself
in philosophical terms. His choice of profession, of
course, had from the first been directed toward answering these questions, and seemed to have been motivated
by child-like sexual curiosity. It appeared that his
monastic life had resulted in a piling up of sexual tension in the Child. Since the Child's sexuality was
oriented around sadism, this was not a healthy
situation. At the same time, the Child's rage against
his father was becoming more intense. His solution
for both tensions was exclusion of the Child, for which
he was paying a distressing price.

Although he felt that nothing was meaningful to him
(i.e., to his Adult) it was evident that the Child still
found plenty of significance in what went on around
him. From time to time, when someone in the group
asked him a question about his feelings, he would
thump his fist violently on his thigh and cry: "I don't
know why I feel that way!" He (i.e., his Adult "real
Self") was quite unaware that he was thumping his
thigh, and expressed great and convincing surprise
when it was pointed out to him. Investigation indicated
that this gesture was a relic connected with his adven-

tures during his early toilet-training. Thus, while the Adult found no meaning in what went on around him, his Child found the same events full of significance. The feeling of estrangement was due to the fact that there was no communication between the archaeopsyche and the neopsyche.

In depersonalization, somatic stimuli may be processed in a matter-of-fact but distorted way by the confused Child, but the distortions are incomprehensible to the Adult because they remain Adult-ego dystonic. If they become Adult-ego syntonic, then they are transformed from feelings of depersonalization into delusions of bodily change, which means that the Adult helps the Child by rationalizing the supposed changes. Protests against the "feelings" are Adult manifestations, while the "delusions" are exhibitions of the Child. The distorted somatic image is not a new phenomenon, but has lain dormant since childhood, until a lesion of the Adult-Child ego boundary allows it to leak through into the neopsychic area, where it causes confusion. The test of this hypothesis is that the prodromal phase should indicate a sclerosis of the boundary, while the symptom should indicate a small rupture whose effects are localized permanently or temporarily by appropriate defensive measures.

The symptoms so far discussed—hallucinations, delusions, and boundary symptoms—are all schizoid in character. In hypomania there is an exclusion of the Parent by the Child with the co-operation of a contaminated Adult, so that neopsychic judgment, impaired though it is, is still influential. If mania supervenes, then the Adult as well as the Parent is overpowered by the hypercathected Child, who then has a clear field for his own frantic activity. The exclusion, however, is like a one-way glass: the outraged but temporarily incapacitated Parent can observe everything that is going on. The Child takes advantage of the Parent's helplessness, but is well aware that he is being watched. Hence the delusions of reference and recording. If a day of reckoning comes, it may be a terrible one. After the Child is exhausted, the Parent may become equally hypercathected and take his revenge.

There is no contradiction here between the structural features of manic-depressive psychosis and the psychoanalytic theory.[4] Psychoanalysis deals with the genetic mechanisms, while structural analysis is concerned with the cathexis of anthropomorphic precipitates: the relics of the infant who once actually existed, in a struggle with the relics of the parents who once actually existed. The struggle is described here in anthropomorphic terms just because it retains its personal quality: it is not a battle between abstract conceptualized forces, but reduplicates the actual childhood fights for survival between real people, or at least that is the way the patient experiences it.

Neurotic symptoms, like psychotic ones, are exhibitions of a single well-defined ego state, although they may result from, and in, complex conflicts. For example, the actual symptom in conversion hysteria is an exhibition of the Child, which is excluded from the Adult by a special selective form of exclusion known as repression. This may enable the Adult to go about his business with a jaunty air. Therapy consists of breaking down the barrier so that the Child and the therapist can talk together in the presence of the active Adult. If the therapist is seduced by the Child into decommissioning the Adult by the use of drugs or hypnosis, they may have an exhilarating hour together, but the final therapeutic result will depend on the ultimate attitude of the Adult and the Parent toward this procedure, which in turn depends on the therapist's skill.

Character disorders and psychopathies are manifestations of the Child. Structurally, they both have the cooperation of the Adult. Whether the parent is in conflict or in concert is shown by the presence or absence of remorse. Impulse neuroses, which may involve apparently similar transactions and have the same social effects, are structurally different, being eruptions of the Child without the co-operation of either the Adult or the Parent.

REFERENCES

1. Federn, P. *Loc. cit.*
2. Freud, S. *The Interpretation of Dreams.* Macmillan Company, New York, 4th ed. 1915, p. 389 ff.
3. *Idem. New Introductory Lectures on Psycho-Analysis.* W. W. Norton & Company, New York, 1933, p. 104.
4. Fenichel, O. *The Psychoanalytic Theory of Neurosis.* W. W. Norton & Company, New York, 1945, Chap. XVII.

CHAPTER SEVEN

Diagnosis

1 PREDISPOSITIONS TO LEARNING

ALTHOUGH Mr. Ennat, the young biologist, thumped his fist on his thigh three or four times in the course of each group meeting, the therapist allowed this phenomenon to pass unnoticed for several weeks. Unnoticed, that is, by his Adult, who may have been preoccupied with the content of what Mr. Ennat was saying; or perhaps the gesture seemed so characteristic of Mr. Ennat that it was carelessly overlooked as a "habit" or an irrelevancy, a mere triviality in the Gestalt of Mr. Ennat's ongoing personality. But evidently the therapist's Child was more alert, for one day, after Mr. Ennat had thumped his thigh and cried in answer to a question from some member of the group: "I don't *know* why I do it!" the doctor asked: "Did you ever soil your bed when you were little?" Mr. Ennat was startled by this question, and said that he had. The doctor inquired whether his parents had ever said anything about it. Mr. Ennat said yes, they used to ask him reproachfully why he did it.

"And what did you say?" asked the doctor.

"I used to say: 'I don't *know* why I do it!'" replied Mr. Ennat, thumping his thigh. It was at this point that Mr. Ennat was surprised to hear that he had been striking his thigh habitually ever since he came into the group.

This anecdote illustrates the task of the therapist in diagnosing ego states. His Adult should quickly have noticed, and generally did notice, convert eruptions of otherwise latent ego states in unnecessary and usually unconscious gestures and intonations. This kind of alertness was part of his professional equipment as a diagnostician. Eventually it led him to perceive that Mr. Ennat's gestures represented spasmodic activity on the part of Mr. Ennat's Child. The unusual feature of the situation was that the therapist's Child, working intuitively and subconsciously,[1] rather than deliberately and consciously like his Adult, was able to perceive accurately the instinctual connections of the gesture,[2] and its origin in Mr. Ennat's childhood.

The diagnosis of ego states is a matter of acuteness of observation plus intuitive sensitivity. The former can be learned, while the latter can only be cultivated. The capacity for this kind of diagnosis, however, does not depend on either professional training or intellectual level, but rather on psychodynamic factors. Those who are not afraid to know, even when they do not know how they know, will do it well, while people who are afraid of cognition without insight[2] will do it poorly.

Mr. Dix, whose I.Q. on the Bellevue-Wechsler Scale was between 85 and 90 on two tests spaced one year apart, became unusually skillful and accurate in diagnosing the ego states of his fellow-pateints. Newcomers to the group were at first inclined to treat him in a patronizing way because of his apparent naiveté and his verbal ineptitude and limitations. This attitude tended to be replaced by one of pity and consideration when they discovered that he was not only of limited intelligence, but was also still a little confused by his receding schizophrenia. On further acquaintance, however, there was a sharp change to a more respectful attitude when they became impressed with his acumen in diagnosing correctly what they were up to in the group. Pretty soon they stopped treating him like fragile glassware, and no longer hesitated to argue with him as though he were an ordinary human being.

A lack of diagnostic insight, after adequate exposure, may be presumed to derive from resistance rather than inability. Dr. Endicott was an intelligent and successful medical practioner who suffered from somatic symptoms. In the group he tended to take the role of a co-therapist, employing the standard terminology and psychological theory he had learned at medical school. He treated the structural approach in a supercilious way, using the terms half sarcastically. Nothing the group could do would move him to examine himself more carefully. The greater the pressure of the other, less well-educated members, the more polysyllabic were his ripostes. On one occasion he broke down under the pressure of these "inferior" people and fled from the room. When he returned two meetings later he was still his old self. It was necessary for him to be parental in a pseudo-adult medical way in order to exclude his frightened Child. (His father also tended to be supercilious.) In short, he exhibited the same kind of resistance against structural analysis as Mr. Troy, but he had more powerful weapons.

Unfortunately, the therapist was unable to play along with his intellectual game of "Psychiatry," which might temporarily have made Dr. Endicott feel more secure. Since this colleague was unwilling to take himself seriously, he had to be sacrificed for the sake of the other members, whose strength soon made them intolerable to him. He refused to consider individual therapy, which might have been used to prepare him to take his place in the group. At length he withdrew from psychotherapy and immediately sought surgical treatment. Intellectually he was perfectly competent to understand structural analysis, but he was driven to sacrifice his viscera rather than his resistances. This was one of the early failures of purely structural analysis, before transactional analysis came into being. Mr. Dix and Dr. Endicott represent extreme cases. In general, it is the Child's attitude toward the therapist or teacher, and toward former therapists or teachers (what is partly subsumed under the term "transference" in psychoanalytic language), which determines the ultimate diagnostic ability of the patient or student, other resistances being equal. Patients who have had previous psychoanalysis or psychoanalytic therapy readily take to structural analysis with tactful handling. Certain types of physicians like Dr. Endicott and of psychologists like Dr. Quint, who have reasons for being defensive against any type of analytic psychiatry, do not do well. Physicians and clinical psychologists who can afford psychodynamically to be interested, do very well as patients since they are accustomed to thinking in diagnostic and psychological terms.

Most interesting are students who have had personal psychoanalysis or psychoanalytic training. For existential reasons, because they have committed themselves to the psychoanalytic approach; or because they may feel that their careers depend upon their psychoanalytic orthodoxy; or because of so-called "dependency needs" which are best met by being in good standing with their local psychoanalytic groups, it is sometimes a hard struggle for them to turn their diagnostic powers to observing total ego states rather than isolating manifestations of super-ego, ego, and id, or conscious and unconscious. In this sense, psychoanalysis may be called a resistance to transactional analysis. (And to group therapy as well, since there is little doubt now that there transactional analysis is the method of choice. Few orthodox psychoanalysts claim that it is possible to psychoanalyze, in the formal sense of the word, a group or an individual in a group. In fact it is just for this reason that many or most psychoanalysts regard the claims of group therapists with some skepticism.[3] Nevertheless, it is understandably difficult for some young psychoanalytic therapists to make the indicated shift from the framework they use in dealing with individual patients to a different framework when they are confronted with a group.) For first year residents and trainees, of course, it is sometimes just too confusing to try to learn two systems at once.

2 DIAGNOSTIC CRITERIA

The characteristics of the Parental ego state can be studied at PTA meetings, whether in the school auditorium or in a living-room corner at cocktail time. The characteristics of the Adult are best seen at a scientific meeting. The characteristics of the Child can be observed in the nursery, or read about in the works of Piaget.[4]

Ego states manifest themselves clinically in two forms: either as completely cathected coherent states of mind experienced as "real Self"; or as intrusions, usually covert or unconscious, into the activity of the current "real Self." An example of the first is the Parental ego state of Mr. Troy, and of the second Mr. Ennat's thigh-thumping, which was an unconscious intrusion of the Child into his Adult ego state. Contaminations represent standardized inclusions of part of one ego state in another, as in the case of the missionary's son whose Parent intruded into his Adult; or in functional terminology, whose neopsychic ego state was contaminated by an exteropsychic ego state; as another alternative, a neurophysiological mechanism might be postulated to account for the observed phenomena.

Since an ego state comprises the total behavior and experience of the individual at a given moment, an active pure ego state of one type or another should have a characteristic influence on each and every element of behavior and experience. Similarly, the intrusion of a single element or a set of elements from a latent ego state into an active one should bear the characteristics of the intruding ego state. It is these characteristics which form the diagnostic criteria between ego states, and it should now be clear that they may manifest themselves in any act, attitude, or way of experiencing. Hence, diagnostic criteria may be looked for in any field of involuntary, voluntary, or social behavior, or may be detected by introspection in any experience. The therapist is principally concerned with the behavioral aspects, since the experimental aspects are not accessible to him until the patient has been educated. In practice, he deals mostly with the patient who is sitting or lying, so that carriage and gait are not readily available as indicators.

Demeanor: The sternly paternal uprightness, sometimes with extended finger, and the gracious mothering flexion of the neck soon become familiar as Parental attitudes. Thoughtful concentration, often with pursed lips or slightly flared nostrils, are typically Adult. The inclination of the head which signifies coyness, or the accompanying smile which turns it into cuteness, are manifestations of the Child. So is the aversion and fixed brow of sulkiness, which can be transformed into reluctant and chagrined laughter by Parental teasing. Observation of family life with parents, school students, and little children will reveal other characteristic attitudes pertinent to each type of ego state. An interesting and instructive exercise is to go through the text and especially the photogravures of Darwin's book on emotional expression,[5] with structural analysis in mind.

Gestures. The exteropsychic origin of the forbidding gesture is established when its prototype can be located among the parental figures in the patient's history. The referential gesture may usually be regarded as autonomous to the Adult, whether he is a professional man talking to a colleague or client, a foreman instructing a workman, or a teacher assisting a pupil. The warding off gesture, when it is pragmatically inappropriate, is a manifestation of the Child. Variations which are not too subtel may be easily diagnosed by intuition. The indicative gesture, for example, may at times accompany either an exhortation by the Parent or a querulous accusation by the Child appealing as if to a Parental figure.

Voice. It is quite common for people to have two voices, each with a different intonation, although in the office or in the group one or the other may be suppressed for very long periods. For example, one who presents herself in the group as "little old me" may not reveal for many months the hidden voice of Parental wrath (perhaps that of an alcoholic mother); or it may require severe group stress before the voice of the "judicious workman" collapses, to be replaced by that of his frightened Child. Meanwhile, the people at home may be quite accustomed to the dichotomy of intonation. Nor is it exceedingly rare to encounter individuals who have three different voices. Thus in the group one may literally encounter the voice of the Parent, the voice of the Adult, and the voice of the Child, all coming from the same individual. When the voice changes, it is usually not difficult to detect other evidences of the change in ego state. This is most dramatically illustrated when "little old me" is suddenly replaced by the facsimile of her infuriated mother or grandmother.

Vocabulary. The therapist can function as an intelligent layman in linguistics in the country where he resides: at least intelligent enough to distinguish certain characteristic words and phrases which are pathognomonic of each ego state. The most pertinent example in this country is the distinction between "childish," which is invariably a parental word, and "child-like," which is an Adult word if used spontaneously, as by developmental psychologists and biologists. It may be pseudo-Adult, however, when it is employed by patients who are playing the game called "Psychiatry."

Typical Parental words are: cute, sonny, naughty, low, vulgar, disgusting, ridiculous, and many of their synonyms. Adult words are: unconstructive, apt, parsimonious, desirable. Oaths, expletives, and epithets are usually manifestations of the Child. Substantives and verbs are intrinsically Adult, since they refer without prejudice, distortion, or exaggeration to objective reality, but they may be employed for their own purposes by Parent or Child. Diagnosis of the word "good" is a simple and gratifying exercise in intuition. With an implicit capital *G* it is Parental. When its application is realistically defensible, it is Adult. When it denotes instinctual gratification, and is essentially an exclamation, it comes from the Child, being then an educated synonym for something like "Nyum nyum!" or "Mmmmm!" It is an especially common indicator of contamination and of unexpressed Parental prejudices which are rationalized as Adult. That is, the word is said as though it had a small *g*, but confrontation may reveal that phenomenologically it had a capital *G*. The speaker may become angry, defensive, or anxious at the confrontation, or the evidence he marshals for his opinion is at best flimsy and prejudiced.

An interesting phenomenon is the use of the hyperbolic sentimental adverb, which for some reason which is not yet clear (to the writer) occurs most prominently with people who have frankly sadistic fantasies. One patient would occasionally interrupt his Adult "morning report" to remark with sentimental tears in his voice: "But I'm so *tremendously* happy!" or "I'm *wonderfully* popular now!" When the therapist enquired: "Who asked you if you were popular?" he answered: "Nobody. But that's a good point. Who did ask me? It must be my Parent." His parents had indeed taught him to be sentimentally grateful for his blessings, to think how lucky he was compared to the starving Armenians, to the boy who had to walk on crutches, and so forth. At other times, instead of interrupting his flow as though to answer a question from an unheard questioner, his Child would slip a word in "in case somebody (i.e., his Parent) might be listening," even though there was no unheard question. He might say: "The woman was enormously pleased—I mean she was really quite pleased." Here the Child slipped in the word "enormously" and the Adult corrected the hyperbole spontaneously, since in his working life he was not given to exaggeration. (One of his early dreams was reaching up to touch an enormous firehose so he could feel "the big squirt.")

The above categories and examples are offered merely as illustrations. There is a very large number of behavior patterns available to the human being. Anthropologists have compiled long lists of attitudes.[6] Pasimologists estimate that some seven hundred thousand distinct elementary gestures can be produced by different muscular combinations.[7] There are enough variations in timbre, pitch, intensity, and range of vocalization to occupy the attention of whole schools of students and teachers. The problems of vocabulary are so complex that they are divided between different disciplines. And these are only four categories out of the almost innumerable types of indicators available to the structural diagnostician. The only practical course for the serious student is observation: to observe parents acting in their capacity as parents; adults acting in their capacity as data-processors, and thoughtful and responsible citizens; and children acting like children at the breast, in the cradle, in the nursery, bathroom, and kitchen, and in the school-room and play-yard. After cultivating his powers of observation and intuition, he can then apply what he has learned for the clinical benefit of his patients.

3   THE COMPLETE DIAGNOSIS—A RÉSUMÉ

The heuristic discussion of structural analysis now comes to a close. Before moving on to the field of social psychiatry, it is advisable to summarize and restate some of the principles at stake.

There are three types of ego states: Parent, Adult, and Child, which reside in or are manifestations of the corresponding psychic organs: exteropsyche, neopsyche, and archaeopsyche. The significant properties of these organs are as follows:

1. Executive power. Each gives rise to its own idiosyncratic patterns of organized behavior. This brings them within the purview of psychophysiology and psychopathology, and ultimately of neurophysiology.

2. Adaptability. Each is capable of adapting its behavioral responses to the immediate social situation in which the individual finds himself. This brings them into the realm of the "social" sciences.

3. Biological fluidity, in the sense that responses are modified as a result of natural growth and previous experiences. This raises historical questions which are the concern of psychoanalysis.

4. Mentality, in that they mediate the phenomena of experience, and hence are the concern of psychology, particularly of introspective, phenomenological, structural, and existential psychologies.

The complete diagnosis of an ego state requires that all four of these aspects be available for consideration, and the final validity of such diagnosis is not established until all four have been correlated. The diagnosis tends to proceed clinically in the order given.

A. A Parental ego state is a set of feelings, attitudes,

and behavior patterns which resemble those of a parental figure. The diagnosis is first usually made on the basis of clinical experience with demeanors, gestures, voices, vocabularies, and other characteristics. This is the *behavioral* diagnosis. The diagnosis is corroborated if the particular set of patterns is especially apt to be elicited in response to child-like behavior on the part of someone else in the environment. This is the *social* or *operational* diagnosis. It is further corroborated if the individual can eventually state exactly which parental figure offered the prototype for the behavior. This is the *historical* diagnosis. The diagnosis is validated if the individual can finally re-experience in full intensity, with little weathering, the moment or epoch when he assimilated the parental ego state. This is the *phenomenological* diagnosis.

The Parent is typically exhibited in one of two forms. The *prejudicial* Parent is manifested as a set of seemingly arbitrary non-rational attitudes or parameters, usually prohibitive in nature, which may be either syntonic or dystonic with the local culture. If they are culturally syntonic, there is a tendency to accept them without adequate skepticism as rational or at least justifiable. The *nurturing* Parent is often manifested as *sympathy for* another individual, which again may be either culturally syntonic or culturally dystonic.

The Parental ego state must be distinguished from the Parental *influence*. Such an influence can be inferred when the individual manifests an attitude of child-like compliance. The *function* of the Parent is to conserve energy and diminish anxiety by making certain decisions "automatic" and relatively unshakable. This is particularly effective if the decisions tend to be syntonic with the local culture.

B. The Adult ego state is characterized by an autonomous set of feelings, attitudes, and behavior patterns which are adapted to the current reality. Since the

Adult is still the least well understood of the three types of ego states, it is best characterized in clinical practice as the residual state left after the segregation of all detectable Parent and Child elements. Or it may be more formally considered as the derivative of a model of the neopsyche. Such a model may be briefly specified as follows:

The neopsyche is a partially self-programing probability computer designed to control the effectors in dealing with the external environment. It has the special characteristic that its energy state at each epoch is determined by how closely the computed probabilities correspond with the actual results. This energy state is signaled as discharge or overload. (E.g., a green light, experienced as pleasure, satisfaction, or admiration; or a red light, experienced as "frustration," disappointment, or indignation.) This characteristic, under various conditions of probability, accounts descriptively for the "instinct of mastery" and for the admiration of the striving toward such qualities as responsibility, reliability, sincerity, and courage. Interestingly enough, each of these four qualities can be reduced to a simple probability statement.

In accordance with the four diagnostic levels, the Adult is noted to be organized, adaptable, and intelligent, and is experienced as an objective relationship with the external environment based on autonomous reality-testing. In each individual case, due allowances must be made for past learning opportunities. The Adult of a very young person or of a peasant may make very different judgments from that of a professionally trained worker. The criterion is not the accuracy of the judgments, nor the acceptability of the reactions (which depends on the local culture of the observer), but on the quality of the data-processing and the use made of the data available to that particular individual.

C. The Child ego state is a set of feelings, attitudes, and behavior patterns which are relics of the individual's own childhood. Again, the behavioral diagnosis is usually made first on the basis of clinical experience. The social diagnosis emerges if that particular set of patterns is most likely to be elicited by someone who behaves parentally. If the diagnosis is correct, it will be corroborated historically by memories of similar feelings and behavior in early childhood. The decisive phenomenological validation only occurs, however, if the individual can re-experience the whole ego state in full intensity with little weathering. This occurs most effectively and dramatically if he can, in the waking state, re-live a traumatic moment or epoch of fixation, and this will best bring about the feeling of conviction on the part of both the therapist and the patient which is one critical step in the therapeutic process.

The Child is exhibited in one of two forms. The *adapted* Child is manifested by behavior which is inferentially under the dominance of the Parental influence, such as compliance or withdrawal. The *natural* Child is manifested by autonomous forms of behavior such as rebelliousness or self-indulgence. It is differentiated from the autonomous Adult by the ascendancy of archaic mental processes and the different kind of reality-testing. It is the proper function of the "healthy" Child to motivate the data-processing and programing of the Adult so as to obtain the greatest amount of gratification for itself.

By this time the conscientious reader will no doubt have many questions about problems and possibilities concerning ego states which first-order structural analysis cannot deal with. It is hoped that some of these will be answered later when structural analysis of the second and third orders is taken up.

NOTES

The intuition about Mr. Ennat and his soiling constituted an *ego image,* a clear picture of a childhood ego state. In most cases (initially at least) the therapist will have to be content with a less enlightening *ego symbol* ("He looks like a puppy who has been caught having an accident on the rug") or a mere descriptive *ego model* ("He is a tense, guilt-laden, anally frustrated young man").[8] The evidence is that an ego model is a product of the observer's Adult, while an ego image is the concern of a special aspect of his Child.[9]

I should prefer to interpret the similarity in the results of Mr. Dix's two intelligence tests as follows. The psychologist, Dr. David Kupfer, is a skillful test administrator. He was able to bring about a re-cathexis of Mr. Dix's Adult during the test period even when Mr. Dix was in a state of schizophrenic confusion. Once the Adult was re-cathected it functioned optimally, regardless of Mr. Dix's clinical "condition." Therefore, he did as well during his schizophrenic period as he did when he was recovered, since his Adult was at all times structurally intact. Whether it functioned or not in a particular situation depended upon its state of cathexis.

Mr. Dix was presented in person at the Monterey Peninsula Clinical Conference in Psychiatry after his treatment was terminated. Those present agreed with the psychologist (1) that Mr. Dix's "I. Q." was below average; with the therapist (2) that Mr. Dix had recently been schizophrenic and (3) that he was now in good remission; and with the patient himself (4) that his recovery was "due to" the therapy and (5) that he had a good understanding of his personality structure. Mr. Dix had previously been to two other therapists without experiencing any improvement. The others had each tried a different variety of "parental" approach, while the writer had adhered consistently to structural analysis. Instead of trying to protect or exhort the confused schizophrenic Child, he had concentrated on trying to decontaminate and re-cathect the intact Adult of the patient.

Two years after stopping treatment, Mr. Dix's Adult still retains the executive power, and he is getting ahead both socially and occupationally, using his intelligence at his previous optimal level as a federally licensed engineering technician.

More recently Myra Schapps, of Aid Retarded Children in San Francisco, has demonstrated that transactional analysis can be understood and effectively applied by grown-ups with "I. Q.'s" ranging from 60 to 80. A group was started in the Sheltered Workshop with the objective of enabling such people to obtain and hold outside employment. At the end of the first year, 91% of the group members had accomplished this aim, and were deliberately and correctly using "social control" in the employment situation as well as analyzing their transactions at the group meetings.[10]

There is a large literature on the relationship between computers and brain function which the interested reader can easily find for himself through the works of N. Wiener and W. R. Ashby, Cf. Ref.[11] By the "energy state" of the neopsyche is implied such manifestations as the Zeigarnik phenomenon.[12]

The relationship between ego states and the Jungian *persona*, which is also a behavioral, social, and historical reality (and is phenomenologically distinct from role-playing) remains to be studied and clarified. As an *ad hoc* attitude, persona is differentiated also from the more autonomous *identity* of Erikson. The differences between these three—persona, role, and identity—seem to depend on the relationships between the Self, the executive, and the people in the environment, and so far appear to be as much transactional as structural problems; perhaps revolving around the distinction between *adaptation* in general and *compliance* in particular.

At present it seems best to treat "the adolescent" as a structural problem rather than as a separate entity or ego state *sui generis*.

Dr. Endicott's attitude illustrates the distinction between roles and ego-states. He was playing the role of an adult, but his ego-state was that of a parent (his father). He adopted the role of a medical co-therapist, but the significant phenomenon was his superciliousness. Hence he is referred to as a Parental pseudo-adult.

Postures, gestures, metaphors, and speech habits have been an important subject of study since the earliest days of psychoanalysis. S. S. Feldman has recently collected and discussed many fascinating clinical examples of the use of clichés, stereotyped phraseology, interjections, gestures, and other mannerisms.[13] There is an interesting discussion of the differences between "childish" and "child-like" in Fowler's *Modern English Usage*.

REFERENCES

1. Berne, E. "Concerning the Nature of Diagnosis." *Internat. Record of Med.* 165: 283–292, 1952.

2. *Idem.* "Primal Images and Primal Judgment." *Loc. cit.*

3. *Idem.* " 'Psychoanalytic' vs. 'Dynamic' Group Therapy." *Internat. Jnl. Group Psychother.* 10: 98–103.

4. Piaget, J. *Loc. cit.*

5. Darwin, C. *Expression of the Emotions in Man and Animals.* D. Appleton & Company, New York, 1886.

6. Hall, E. T. "The Anthropology of Manners." *Scientific American* 192: 84–90, 1955.

7. Pei, M. *The Story of Language.* J. B. Lippincott Company, New York, 1949.

8. Berne, E. "Intuition V: The Ego Image." *Psychiat. Quart.* 31: 611–627, 1957.

9. Berne, E. "Intuition VI: The Psychodynamics of Intuition." *Psychiat. Quart.* (In Press.)

10. Schapps, M. R. *Reaching Out to the Mentally Retarded.* Read at the 86th Annual Forum of the National Conference on Social Welfare, San Francisco, May 26, 1959. 91% is a later figure than that cited (63%) in her paper.

11. Jeffress, L. A., ed. *Cerebral Mechanisms in Behavior.* The Hixon Symposium. John Wiley & Sons, New York, 1951.

12. Zeigarnik, B. "Über das Behalten von erledigten und

unerledigten Handlunger." *Psychologishe Forschung* 9: 1–86, 1927. Discussed at length by K. Lewin, *Field Theory in Social Science,* Harper & Brothers, New York, 1951.

13.   Feldman, S. S. *Mannerisms of Speech and Gestures in Everyday Life.* International Universities Press, New York, 1959.

PART II

Social Psychiatry and Transactional Analysis

CHAPTER EIGHT

Social Intercourse

1 A THEORY OF SOCIAL CONTACT

THE ability of the human psyche to maintain coherent ego states seems to depend upon a changing flow of sensory stimuli. This observation forms the psychobiological basis of social psychiatry. In structural terms, these stimuli are necessary in order to assure the integrity of the neopsyche and the archaeopsyche. If the flow is cut off or flattened into monotony, it is observed that the neopsyche gradually becomes disorganized ("The individual's thinking is impaired"); this lays bare the underlying archaeopsychic activity ("He shows childish emotional responses"); and finally archaeopsychic function becomes disorganized as well ("He suffers from hallucinations").[1] This is the sensory deprivation experiment.

The work of Spitz[2] goes a little farther. It demonstrates that sensory deprivation in the infant may result not only in psychic changes, but also in organic deterioration. This shows how vital it is for the changing sensory environment to be maintained. In addition, a new and specific factor appears: the most essential and effective forms of sensory stimulation are provided by social handling and physical intimacy. Hence Spitz speaks of "emotional deprivation" rather than of "sensory deprivation."

The intolerance for long periods of boredom or isolation gives rise to the concept of *stimulus-hunger*, particularly for the kind of stimuli offered by physical intimacy. This stimulus-hunger parallels in many ways, biologically, psychologically, and socially, the hunger for food. Such terms as malnutrition, satiation, gourmet, gourmand, faddist, ascetic, culinary arts, and good cook are easily transferred from the field of nutrition to their analogues in the field of sensation. Overstuffing has its parallel in over-stimulation, which may cause difficulties in flooding the psyche with stimuli faster than they can be comfortably handled. In both spheres, under ordinary conditions where ample supplies are available and a diversified menu is possible, choices will be heavily influenced by individual idiosyncrasies.

The question of constitutional determinants of stimulation choices is not of present moment. Those idiosyncrasies which are of immediate interest to the social psychiatrist are based on archaic experiences, neopsychic judgments, and particularly in regard to physical intimacy, exteropsychic prejudices. These introduce varying amounts of caution, prudence, and deviousness into the situation, so that eventually it is only under special circumstances that the individual will make a direct gesture toward the most prized forms of stimulation represented by physical relationships. Under most conditions he will compromise. He learns to do with more subtle, even symbolic forms of handling, until the merest nod of recognition may serve the purpose to some extent, although his original craving for physical contact may remain unabated. As the complexities increase, each person becomes more and more individual in his quest, and it is these differentia which lend variety to social intercourse.

The *stimulus-hunger,* with its first order sublimation into *recognition-hunger,* is so pervasive that the symbols of recognition become highly prized and are expected to be exchanged at every meeting between people. Deliberately withholding them constitutes a form of misbehavior called *rudeness,* and repeated rudeness is considered a justification for imposing social or even physical sanctions. The spontaneous forms of recognition, such as the glad smile, are most gratefully received. Other gestures, like the hiss, the obeisance, and the handshake, tend to become ritualized. In this country there is a succession of verbal gestures, each step implying more and more recognition and giving more and more gratification. This ritual may be typically summarized as follows: (a) "Hello!" (b) "How are you?" (c) "Warm enough for you?" (d) "What's new?" (e) "What else is new?" The implications are: (a) Someone is there; (b) Someone with feelings is there; (c) Someone with feelings and sensations is there; (d) Someone with feelings, sensations, and a personality is there; (e) Someone with feelings, sensations, a personality, and in whom I have more than a passing interest, is there.

A great deal of linguistic, social, and cultural structure revolves around the question of mere recognition: special pronouns, inflections, gestures, postures, gifts, and offerings are designed to exhibit recognition of status and person. The movie fan-letter is one of our indigenous products, which enables recognition to be depersonalized and quantified on an adding machine; and the difference between the printed, mimeographed, photographic, and personal reply is something like the difference between the various steps of the greeting ritual described above. The unsatisfactory nature of such mechanical recognition is shown by the preference of many actors and actresses for the live theatre over the movies, even at a considerable financial sacrifice. This is a dramatic example of the extended validity of Spitz's principle.

2   THE STRUCTURING OF TIME

Mere recognition, however, is not enough, since after the rituals have been exhausted, tension mounts and anxiety begins to appear. The real problem of social intercourse is what happens after the rituals. Hence it is possible to speak not only of stimulus-hunger and social hunger, but also of *structure-hunger*. The everyday problem of the human being is the structure of his waking hours. If they are not structured for him, as they tend to be in infancy, then he is impelled to find or set up a structure independently, hour by hour.

The most common, convenient, comfortable, and utilitarian method of structuring time is by a project designed to deal with the material of external reality: what is commonly known as work. Such a project is technically called an *activity*; the term "work" is unsuitable because a general theory of social psychiatry must recognize that social intercourse is also a form of work. Activities are of interest here only insofar as they offer a matrix for recognition and other more complex forms of social intercourse.

The specific social problem takes the form of (1) how to structure time (2) here and now (3) most profitably on the basis of (4) one's own idiosyncrasies, (5) the idiosyncrasies of other people, and (6) the estimated potentialities of the immediate and eventual situations. The profit lies in obtaining the maximum of permissible satisfactions.

The operational aspect of time structuring may be called *programing*. Programing is supplied by three sources: material, social, and individual. Material programing arises from the vicissitudes encountered in dealing with external reality, and does not concern us here. *Social programing* has already been referred to in discussing *greeting rituals*. This is carried farther in what may be called *pastimes,* which generally take the form of semiritualistic discussions of common-places such as the weather, possessions, current events, or family affairs.

As people become less guarded, more and more *individual programing* creeps in, so that "incidents" begin to occur. These incidents superficially appear to be adventitious, and may be so described by the parties concerned, but careful scrutiny reveals that they tend to follow definite patterns which are amenable to sorting and classification, and that the sequence is in effect circumscribed by unspoken rules and regulations. These regulations remain latent as long as the amities or hostilities proceed according to Hoyle, but they become manifest if an illegal move is made, giving rise to a symbolic cry of "Foul!" Such sequences, which in contrast to pastimes are based more on individual than on social programing, may be called *games.* Family life and married life may be centered year after year around variations of the same game.

Pastimes and games are substitutes for the real living of real intimacy. Because of this they may be regarded as preliminary *engagements* rather than as unions; in effect, they are poignant forms of *play.*

When individual, usually instinctual, programing becomes more intense, both social patterning and ulterior restrictions begin to give way. This condition may be denoted *crasis,* a genuine interlocking of personalities; or more colloquially, it may be called *intimacy.*

Thus social contact, whether or not it is embedded in a matrix of activity, may be said to take two forms: play and intimacy. By far the greater part of all social intercourse is in the form of play.

3 SOCIAL INTERCOURSE

The overt manifestations of social intercourse are called *transactions*. Typically these occur in chains: a *transactional stimulus* from X elicits a *transactional response* from Y; this response becomes a stimulus for X, and X's response in turn becomes a new stimulus for Y. *Transactional Analysis* is concerned with the analysis of such chains, and particularly with their programing. It can be demonstrated that once a chain is initiated, the resulting sequence is highly predictable if the characteristics of the Parent, Adult, and Child of each of the parties concerned is known. In certain cases, as will be shown later, the converse is also possible: given the initial transactional stimulus and the initial transactional response, not only the ensuing sequence, but also some of the characteristics of the Parent, Adult, and Child of each of the parties concerned can be deduced with a considerable degree of confidence.

While any type of social intercourse is amenable to transactional analysis, the transactional therapy group is especially designed to elicit the maximum amount of information concerning the idiosyncratic programing of each patient, since this programing is closely related to his symptomatology and also, barring accidents, determines his social destiny. The characteristics of such a group are as follows:

1. Since there is no formal activity and no stated procedure, there is no external source of structuring for the time interval. Hence all programing is narrowed down to an interplay between that provided by the culture and that determined by previous special conditioning of the individual.

2. The commitment is only partial, and withdrawal of a given response, or withdrawal of a patient from the group, is possible without sanctions. The responsibilities

are rarely as serious or as permanent as those involved in such activities as bridge-building, or in such intimacies as impregnation.

In these two respects the group is similar to a social gathering such as a cocktail party, but it is distinguished by the following two criteria:

3. There is, however, a definite commitment to a decisive group structure. The therapist is in one region and the patients in the other, and this is irreversible. The patients pay the therapist or follow the rules of his clinic, but the therapist never pays the patients. (So far, at least not in his capacity as therapist.)

4. The population from which the group is drawn is not of the patient's choosing, although he may sometimes have the privilege of selecting or rejecting members from the population of candidates.

In the two latter respects, the therapy group resembles many activity groups which have a ready-made program, such as business or educational institutions, but it is differentiated by the first two criteria.

NOTES

Structure-hunger. The experimentalists state quite explicitly that it is not merely a quantitative sensory deprivation that causes the disorganization, but some defect in structuring, a "monotony" which gives rise to "boredom."[1] The classical illustration is offered by the struggles of Robinson Crusoe to ward off his oral confusion by structuring time and place on his solitary island.[3] Crusoe exemplifies poignantly not only structure-hunger but also social hunger. The accuracy of this fictional portrait is impressively shown by the experiences of forced isolates in real life: Baron Trenck during his ten years in Magdeburg, Casanova during his confinement in the Leads in Venice, and John Bunyan during his twelve years in the county jail at Bedford. The cathectic drainage of the neopsyche caused by stimulus, social, and structure deprivation can be demonstrated by comparing patients in good state hospitals with those in bad state hospitals. The archaic suggestibility which results from such deprivations has apparently proven to be one of the most powerful weapons available to ruthless leaders in dealing with intransigent personalities.

Play. Play does not necessarily mean "kidding." In fact most human play, as Huizinga[4] makes clear, is accompanied by genuine emotional intensity. This can be observed at any college campus or card-room. The essential point of social play in humans is not that the emotions are spurious, but that they are regulated. This is revealed when sanctions are imposed on an illegitimate emotional display. Thus play may be deadly serious, or even fatally serious, but the social consequences are only serious if the rules are abrogated.

For a discussion of the contract "This is play," see Bateson et al.[5] In human beings, the conscious contract "This is play" often conceals an unconscious contract "This is not play." A variation of this is the true word which is spoken in jest, for which the speaker cannot be held responsible providing he smiled when he said it. Similarly the conscious contract "This is not play" (e.g., the marriage contract) may conceal a covert or unconscious contract "This is play." A good example of this is the game of "Frigid Woman," with its complex but orderly sequence of mutual provocations and recriminations. The overt contract implies a serious sexual union, but the covert contract says: "Don't take my sexual promises seriously." The same applies to the game of "Debtor" occasionally played by certain types of psychiatric patients in regard to money matters. Jackson and Weakland[6] give a verbatim report of what from the present point of view is a sinister game called "Double Bind" played by "schizophrenogenic" families.

It is interesting to note that the findings of modern psychological research and the ideas expressed in this chapter, although arrived at by quite a different route, are similar to some of Kierkegaard's reflections on boredom[7] (1843). In addition, social control, the behavioral goal of transactional analysis, results in just the kind of optional apartness that Kierkegaard seems to have in mind when he discusses such relationships as friendship, marriage, and business. The concept of a slight but significant apartness is opposed to the pressure for "togetherness" that is active on both sides nowadays. In the extreme position, it may be said that there might be small quarrels, but there could be no wars if people did not come together in groups. This is hardly a practical solution, but it is a good starting point for meditations about war and peace.

REFERENCES

1. Heron, W. "The Pathology of Boredom." *Scientific American* 196: 52–56, January, 1957.

2. Spitz, R. "Hospitalism, Genesis of Psychiatric Conditions in Early Childhood." *Psychoanalytic Study of the Child*. 1: 53–74, 1945.

3. Berne, E. "The Psychological Structure of Space with Some Remarks on Robinson Crusoe." *Psychoanalytic Quart.* 25: 549–567, 1956.

4. Huizinga, J. *Homo Ludens.* Beacon Press, Boston, 1955.

5. Bateson, G., et. al. "The Message 'This is Play.'" *Transactions of Second Conference on Group Processes.* Josiah Macy, Jr. Foundation, New York, 1956.

6. Weakland, J. H. & Jackson, D. D. "Observations on a Schizophrenic Episode." *Arch. Neur. & Psych.* 79: 554–574, 1958.

7. Kierkegaard, S. *A Kierkegaard Anthology,* ed. R. Bretall. Princeton University Press, Princeton, 1947. pp. 22 ff.

CHAPTER NINE

Analysis of Transactions

1 INTRODUCTORY

STRUCTURAL analysis proper deals with the mastery (but not necessarily the resolution) of internal conflicts through diagnosis of ego states, decontamination, boundary work, and stabilization, so that the Adult can maintain control of the personality in stressful situations. After maximum therapeutic benefit has been obtained through structural analysis alone, there are three choices open: trial or permanent termination, psychoanalysis, or transactional analysis. Trial termination was tested by mutual agreement in the case of Mr. Segundo. Psychoanalysis, in structural terms, consists of deconfusing the Child and resolving the conflicts between the Child and the Parent. The aim of transactional analysis is *social control,* in which the Adult retains the executive in dealings with other people who may be consciously or unconsciously attempting to activate the patient's Child or Parent. This does not mean that the Adult alone is active in social situations, but it is the Adult who decides when to release the Child or Parent, and when to resume the executive. Thus one patient might think: "At this party, in contrast to last night's formal dinner, I can afford to take a few drinks and have some fun." Later he might think: "Now I'm beginning to get sloppy, so I'd better stop drinking and simmer down, even though they're all trying to encourage my clowning."

Transactional analysis is best done in therapy groups; or conversely, it may be said that the natural function of therapy groups is transactional analysis.[1] Structural analysis, which is a prerequisite for transactional analysis, may also be learned in the group instead of in individual therapy. It is usually advisable, however, to have two or three preliminary individual sessions. The function of individual sessions prior to group therapy, aside from routine matters such as history taking, is to introduce the patient to structural analysis.

Transactional analysis proper is followed by game analysis and that in turn by script analysis. The first is a prerequisite for the other two, otherwise they may degenerate into a kind of pastime instead of being used as rational therapeutic procedures. Game analysis is necessary in order to attain social control. Script analysis, whose aim might be called "life plan control," is so complex that this stage may never be reached in many therapy groups, but ordinary social control is possible without it. In special situations, such as social counseling and marital group therapy, a special procedure called "relationship analysis" may be indicated. Ordinarily formal relationship analysis may be omitted, but every group therapist, in order to be able to do his best, should have a clear understanding of this procedure and some experience in carrying it through.

2 TRANSACTIONAL ANALYSIS

At this point we may consider a group of housewives between 30 and 40 years of age, each with one or more children, who met weekly for an hour and a half at the office of their psychiatrist, Dr. Q. At the end of eighteen months, Daphne, Lily, and Rosita, who had attended from the beginning, were the most sophisticated members; Hyacinth, Holly, Camellia, and

Cicely, who joined later in that order, were less so. A common *seating diagram* and the *schedule* for this group is shown in Figure 7.

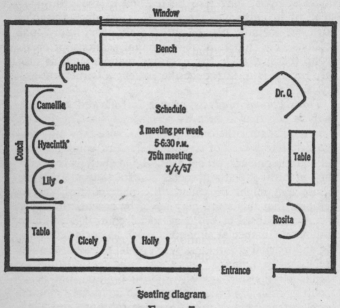

Seating diagram

FIGURE 7

One day Camellia, following a previous train of thought, announced that she had told her husband she was not going to have intercourse with him any more and that he could go and find himself some other woman. Rosita asked curiously: "Why did you do that?" Whereupon Camellia burst into tears and replied: "I try so hard and then you criticize me."

There were two transactions here, which may be represented by the diagrams in Figures 8A and 8B. These were drawn and analyzed before the group. The personalities of the two women are represented structurally as comprising Parent, Adult, and Child. The first transactional stimulus is Camellia's statement about what she told her husband. She related this in her Adult ego state, with which the group was familiar. It was received in turn by an Adult Rosita, who in her response ("Why did you do that?") exhibited a mature, reasonable interest in the story. As shown in Figure 8A, the transactional stimulus was Adult to Adult, and so was the transactional response. If things had continued at this level, the conversation might have proceeded smoothly.

Rosita's question ("Why did you do that?") now constituted a new transactional stimulus, and was intended as one adult speaking to another. Camellia's response, however, was not that of one adult to another, but that of a child answering a critical parent. Camellia's misperception of Rosita's ego state, and the shift in her own ego state, resulted in a *crossed transaction* and broke up the conversation, which now had to take another turn. This is represented in Figure 8B.

This particular type of crossed transaction, in which the stimulus is directed to the Adult while the response originates from the Child, is probably the most frequent cause of misunderstandings in marriage and work situations, as well as in social life. Clinically, it is typified by the classical transference reaction. In fact this species of crossed transaction may be said to be the chief problem of psychoanalytic technique.

The reciprocal of this occurs when a stimulus is directed to the Adult and it is the Parent who responds. Thus anyone who asked Mr. Troy a rational question, expecting a judicious answer, might be disconcerted to find himself being treated to a set of dogmatic, ill-considered prejudices, as though he were a backward child

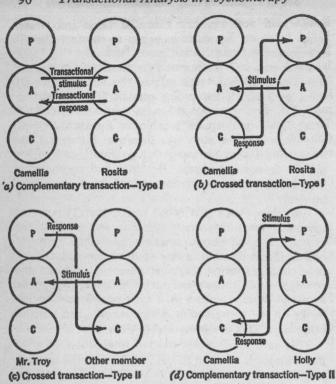

(a) Complementary transaction—Type I

(b) Crossed transaction—Type I

(c) Crossed transaction—Type II

(d) Complementary transaction—Type II

FIGURE 8

in need of correction. This situation is represented in Figure 8C. (The same diagram may be used, *mutatis mutandis,* to represent a countertransference reaction.)

It will be noted that in this scheme, as long as the vectors are not crossed, the conversation proceeds smoothly as a series of *complementary transactions*. As soon as there is a crossed transaction, someone is disconcerted and the *complementary relationship* terminates. In the case of Camellia and Rosita, for example,

Rosita said nothing after Camellia burst into tears. Holly, however, immediately began to comfort Camellia and apologize for Rosita, just as she might talk to a hurt child. A free version of her remarks would read: "Don't cry, honey, everything will be all right, we all love you and that stupid lady didn't intend to be mean." Camellia responded with grateful "self-pity." These transactions are represented in Figure 8D. Since Camellia's Child is now trying to get a Parental response, and that is just what Holly gives her, Rosita's eventual cynical comment: "This love-making could go on forever!" is technically correct. These mutual Parent-Child transactions would go on, if not interrupted from outside, until either Holly or Camellia grew tired of them and changed her ego state, whereupon there would be another crossed transaction and the complementary relationship would terminate.

As it was, it was terminated by Rosita's intervention, which caused the collapse of Holly's Parent and the activation of her hurt and frightened Child. In this state, she was of no more use to Camellia, who then withdrew into a sullen silence. Now it was the therapist's turn to intervene. He gauged the situation carefully, and was able to switch everyone back to an Adult level so that he could proceed with the analysis mentioned above. During this phase, his own transactions with the group reverted back to the original level represented in Figure 8A.

Dr. Q's intervention was motivated by the ultimate aim of establishing social control. Rosita, the most sophisticated of the three members concerned, had already acquired this to a large degree, as demonstrated by her silence when Camellia began to protest and weep; while Holly, being a novice, immediately responded to the overtures of Camellia's Child. Rosita had a clear, rational understanding of the purpose of the group as a learning experience. She knew that Camellia would learn nothing from being comforted, and that Holly would learn nothing from comforting her. Similarly, the other sophisticated members, Daphne and Lily, remained silent because they knew that was the only thing to do; while the other two novices, Hyacinth and Cicely, had kept quiet because they didn't know anything else to do.

The point was that this sort of thing happened regularly to Camellia. As she saw it, people were always misunderstanding her and criticizing her. In reality, it was she who made a practice of misunderstanding people and criticizing them. Rosita perceived correctly that she herself hadn't criticized Camellia and that on the contrary, Camellia had implicitly criticized her by weeping. She retained Adult control of the situation by not allowing herself to be drawn unfairly into the parental role of comforting and apologizing to Camellia. Her Adult was reinforced by the knowledge that to succumb would be to defeat the stated therapeutic object of the meetings. Camellia had demonstrated more than once that she was adroit in eliciting pity and apologies. The educated members were now becoming aware that they were being manipulated into giving her something she did not deserve, and the purpose of this segment of the group at the moment was to make Camellia aware of what she was doing. The most effective way to this was by withholding what she demanded.

They were also becoming aware of how eagerly Holly sought opportunities to be parental. Thus Camellia and Holly complemented each other in certain tendencies, tendencies which in each case promoted marital discord. Holly was about to get a divorce because her husband was exploiting her, and Camellia was having trouble because her husband misunderstood and criticized her. Dr. Q's transactional analysis of this episode, therefore, was pertinent. In the course of repeated analyses of similar situations these two women became more and more aware of what they were up to, and more and more able to control these tendencies both in the group and at home, with corresponding benefits in their marital situations. At the same time, the analyses became increasingly instructive and convincing to the other novices, while the sophisticated members were gaining further understanding and experience in social control, each experience serving to strengthen the Adult. Thus, transactional analysis of the relationship between two members benefited everyone in the group, and these benefits accrued long before any of them was ready to attempt a deconfusion of the Child or a resolution of underlying conflicts.

NOTES

The proceedings of therapy groups are notoriously difficult to present effectively and to follow. A seating diagram should always be used, and a blackboard is a requisite for such discussions. If a seating diagram is dispensed with, no one may be aware of missing it, but if one is supplied, it will soon be observed that everyone present consults it frequently during the discussion, which is sufficient evidence of its usefulness. In addition, it automatically answers innumerable questions about the physical situation of the group, questions which would otherwise be necessarily time-consuming.

The group described had had fifteen members during its eighteen months of life, with a cumulative attendance record of 95%. Two of the members were anomalous. One was transferred out to another group after one session. Another was an alcoholic and the only member who was childless. She was the first alcoholic with whom the writer attempted transactional analysis. She was unable to tolerate the anxiety aroused when the members refused to play her game of "Alcoholic." (See Chapter 10.) After they had steadfastly denied her pleas for them to say something derogatory about her, she did not return; and voluntarily entered a hospital for treatment for the fourth time.

Four of the members, two of them post-psychotic, had moved to other cities, all of them much improved. Another had withdrawn temporarily, well satisfied. Still another, Veronica, had felt benefited enough to make a systematic attempt to improve her marriage, and had transferred to a marital group which she attended with her husband. The other seven felt that the time, money, and effort they were spending to attend was well worthwhile, and could see improvement in themselves and in each other. Of these thirteen, four had had previous experience with one or more other psychotherapeutic approaches, and were able to evaluate more clearly, and to compare with their previous therapy, what they had gained from transactional analysis. Their spontaneous observations confirmed the writer's own experience.

REFERENCES

1. Berne, E. "Transactional Analysis: A New and Effective Method of Group Therapy." *Amer. Jnl. Psychother.* 12: 735–743, 1958.

CHAPTER TEN

Analysis of Games

1 PASTIMES

THE great bulk of social intercourse is made up of engagements. This is particularly true of psychotherapy groups, where both activity and intimacy are prohibited or inhibited. Engagements are of two types: pastimes and games. A pastime is defined as an engagement in which the transactions are straightforward. When dissimulation enters the situation, and the pastime becomes a game. With happy or well-organized people whose capacity for enjoyment is unimpaired, a social pastime may be indulged in for its own sake and bring its own satisfactions. With others, particularly neurotics, it is just what its name implies, a way of passing (i.e., structuring) the time: until one gets to know people better, until this hour has been sweated out, and on a larger scale, until bed-time, until vacation-time, until school starts, until the cure is forthcoming, until some form of charism, rescue, or death arrives. Existentially, a pastime is a way of warding off guilt, despair, or intimacy, a device provided by nature or culture to ease the quiet desperation. More optimistically, at best it is something enjoyed for its own sake and at least it serves as a means of getting acquainted in the hope of achieving the longed-for crasis with another human being. In any case, each participant uses it in an opportunistic way to get whatever primary and secondary gains he can from it.

The pastimes in psychotherapy groups are generally Parental or Adult, since their function is to evade the issue, which revolves around the Child. The two commonest pastimes in such groups are variations of "PTA" and "Psychiatry." The projective form of "PTA" is a Parental pastime. Its subject is delinquency in the general meaning of the word, and it may deal with delinquent juveniles, delinquent husbands, delinquent wives, delinquent tradesmen, delinquent authorities, or delinquent celebrities. Introjective "PTA" is Adult, and deals with one's own socially acceptable delinquencies: "Why can't I be a good mother, father, employer, worker, fellow, hostess?" The motto of the projective form is "Isn't It Awful?"; that of the introjective form is "Me Too!"

"Psychiatry" is an Adult, or at least pseudo-Adult pastime. In its projective form it is known colloquially as "Here's What You're Doing," and its introjective form is called "Why Do I Do This?" In transactional analysis groups, intellectualizers may play "What Part Of Me Said That?" but a sophisticated group will soon call this off if it is evident that it is being prolonged into a diversionary pastime after the learning phase of structural analysis is past.

Some groups are even more cautious, and confine themselves to playing variations of "Small Talk," such as "General Motors" (comparing cars) and "Who Won" (both "Man Talk"); "Grocery," "Kitchen," and "Wardrobe" (all "Lady Talk"); "How To" (go about doing something), "How Much" (does it cost?), "Ever Been" (to some nostalgic place), "Do You Know" (So-and-so), "What Became" (of good old Joe), "Morning After" (what a hangover), and "Martini" (I know a better way).

Pastimes properly belong to the initial phases of group therapy, but if the group is not properly handled the proceedings may never get beyond this stage. The significance of pastimes is well appreciated by sophisticated group members, who soon recognize that they are apt to recur in three types of situations: when a new member enters the group, when the group is avoiding something, or when the leader is absent. In the latter case if they continue to meet with the assistant therapist or observer while the leader is gone, they may report when he returns: "All we did while you were away was play 'PTA' and 'Psychiatry,' and it made us realize more than ever what a waste of time that is." Even a mothers' group, which may initially and understandably have great difficulty in abandoning "PTA," may eventually come to have the same reaction.[1]

Nevertheless, pastimes do have a function initially in the therapy group, serving as an innocuous matrix for tentative excursions of the Child. They provide a preliminary period of non committal observation during which the players can line each other up before the games begin. Many people are grateful for such a trial period, because once the Child is committed to a game he must take the consequences. Some groups, however, elide the pastime phase and plunge right into games. This is particularly apt to happen if there is one rash member who makes the initial move of his or her game without a preliminary survey of the players. Such imprudence usually draws the other members in. This kind of brashness is not necessarily a matter of aggressiveness, but may arise from impulsiveness on the part of the Child, impairment of the Adult, or Parental defect. It is essentially a sign of lack of adaptation. Other members present may be more aggressive, but also more phlegmatic, judicious, or disciplined.

Pastimes may make the group more comfortable in times of stress, but from the analytic point of view they are of little value. They may help to clarify for the patients the properties of the Parent and the Adult, but the therapist's chief task when they occur is to abort them as soon as expediency allows, so that the members can proceed with their games. The banality of pastimes is shown in the following two paradigms, the analyses of which are represented in Figures 9A and 9B.

I. "PTA," Projective Type

Holly: There wouldn't be all this delinquency if it weren't for broken homes.

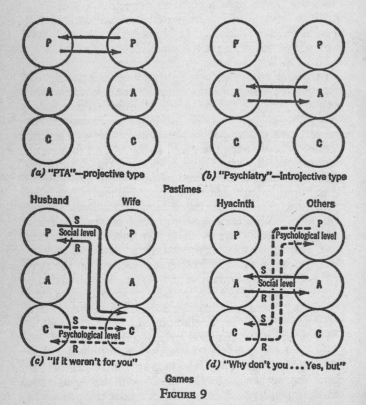

(a) "PTA"—projective type   (b) "Psychiatry"—introjective type

Pastimes

(c) "If it weren't for you"   (d) "Why don't you . . . Yes, but"

Games

Figure 9

Magnolia: It's not only that. Even in good homes nowadays the children aren't taught manners the way they used to be.

II. "Psychiatry," Introjective Type

Daisy: The painting must symbolize smearing to me.

Iris: In my case, it would be trying to please my father.

2   GAMES

The most common game played between spouses is colloquially called "If It Weren't For You," and this will be used to illustrate the characteristics of games in general.

Mrs. Dodakiss complained that her husband would not allow her to indulge in any social or athletic activities. As she improved with treatment, her husband became less sure of himself and withdrew his prohibitions. The patient was then free to enlarge the scope of her activities. Because of her "starved" adolescence, she had always wanted to take swimming and dancing lessons. After she had signed up for her courses, she was surprised and dismayed to discover that she had phobias of both swimming pools and dance floors, and had to abandon both projects.

This exposure partly clarified the structure of her marriage. She had picked for a husband a man who would yield her the maximum of primary and secondary *gains*. It will be recalled that Freud[2] describes how an illness can yield three possible types of gain: external paranosic (primary), internal paranosic (primary), and epinosic (secondary). This concept can be extended to the gains derived from personal relationships. When

Mrs. Dodakiss picked an autocrat for a husband, the *external primary gain* was that he helped her with her phobic avoidances; the *internal primary gain* was that she could turn on him and say "If it weren't for you, I could ... etc.," which was not only gratifying but also helped her handle the underlying guilts and anxieties; the *secondary gains* lay in the material advantages which derived from her position: her "justifiable" resentment gave her leverage in controlling their sex life and other aspects of their marriage, and elicited concessions and gifts which he offered to indemnify her for his severity.

But since we are concerned here with social psychiatry, the most relevant gain is one which is distinct from the other three types, and that is the *social gain*. The question whose answer describes the social gain is as follows: How does the situation contribute to the individual's structuring of time? Mrs. Dodakiss set her game up by seducing her husband (if he needed any seduction) into imposing prohibitions. Besides serving the purposes already outlined, these prohibitions supplied an ever-renewed reservoir of resentment. Whenever activities were lacking or intimacy threatened, this resentment provided a substitute way of filling time with the game of "If It Weren't For You," with its interminable attacks and counter-attacks. In addition, it put Mrs. Dodakiss in an advantageous position in her female social circle, since she could always participate in their conversation with a sense of gratification and accomplishment by playing the derivative pastime "If It Weren't For Him." Thus her marital relationship provided not only protection, control, and perquisites (the Freudian gains), but also the privilege of playing "If It Weren't For You" and "If It Weren't For Him." As an important by-product, the Dodakiss children's emotional education included an intensive field course in playing these games, so that eventually the whole family could and did indulge in this occupation skillfully and frequently.

A fifth type of gain is the *biological gain,* which is derived from the mere fact that the parties are stimulating each other in some way and removing each other's isolation, regardless of the manner or content of the stimulation.

Mr. Dodakiss's gains from this situation can only be guessed, since he did not come for treatment; the male partners in this game are not usually the type who seek solutions in psychiatry. From experience with similar marriages, however, it may be surmised that his internal primary gain was sadistic or counter-phobic; his external primary gain was the same as his wife's, avoidance of sexual intimacy without loss of self-esteem by provoking rejection; his secondary gain was freedom for the hunting-lodge and tavern; and his social gain was the pastime of "Nobody Understands Women."

The transactional analysis of games is most instructive for everyone concerned. Transactions are of three kinds: complementary, crossed, and ulterior. The *complementary transactions* of a well-structured relationship and the *crossed transactions* of a poorly-structured one have already been discussed. In a pastime the transactions are complementary; hence in this situation the relationship is well-structured, relatively simple, and can proceed indefinitely as long as it is well-motivated by gains. In a game the relationship is also well-structured without crossings, but the transactions are ulterior and occur at two levels simultaneously, the social and the psychological. The analysis of "If It Weren't For You" is shown in Figure 9C. At the *social level,* the paradigm is as follows:

H: You stay home and take care of the house.
W: If it weren't for you, I could be having fun.

Here the transactional stimulus is Parent to Child, and the response is Child to Parent.

At the *psychological level* (the ulterior marriage contract), the situation is quite different.

H: You must always be here when I get home. I am terrified of desertion.

W: I will be if you help me avoid phobic situations.

Here both stimulus and response are Child to Child. At neither level is there a crossing, so that the game can proceed indefinitely as long as it is well-motivated. Hence a game can be defined transactionally as a set of *ulterior transactions*. Descriptively, it is a recurring set of transactions, often reiterative, superficially plausible, with a concealed motivation; or more colloquially, a series of moves with a snare or "gimmick."

The most common game in parties and groups of all kinds, including psychotherapy groups, is "Why Don't You ... Yes, But."

Hyacinth: My husband never builds anything right.

Camellia: Why doesn't he take a course in carpentry?

Hyacinth: Yes, but he doesn't have time.

Rosita: Why don't you buy him some good tools?

Hyacinth: Yes, but he doesn't know how to use them.

Holly: Why don't you have your building done by a carpenter?

Hyacinth: Yes, but that would cost too much.

Iris: Why don't you just accept what he does the way he does it?

Hyacinth: Yes, but the whole thing might fall down.

"Why Don't You ... Yes, But" can be played by any number. One player, who is "it," presents a problem. The others start to present solutions, each beginning with "Why don't you . . .?" To each of these the one who is "it" objects with a "Yes, but . . ." A good player can stand off the rest of the group indefinitely, until they all give up, whereupon "it" wins. Hyacinth, for example, successfully objected to more than a dozen solutions before Rosita and the therapist broke up the game.

Since all the solutions, with rare exceptions, are rejected, it is apparent that this game must serve some ulterior purpose. The "gimmick" in "Why Don't You . . . Yes, But" is that it is not played for its ostensible purpose (an Adult quest for information or solutions) but to reassure and gratify the Child. A bare transcript may sound Adult, but in living tissue it can be observed that the one who is "it" presents herself as a Child inadequate to meet the situation; whereupon the others become transformed into sage Parents anxious to dispense their wisdom for the benefit of the helpless one. This is exactly what "it" wants, since her object is to confound these Parents one after another. The analysis of this game is shown in Figure 9D. The game can proceed because at the social level both stimulus and response are Adult to Adult, and at the psychological level they are at also complementary, Parent to Child stimulus ("Why don't you . . .") eliciting Child to Parent response ("Yes, but . . ."). The psychological level may be unconscious on both sides.

It is instructive in view of these interpretations to follow through on Hyacinth's game.

Hyacinth: Yes, but the whole thing might fall down.

Therapist: What do you all think of this?

Rosita: There we go, playing "Why Don't you . . . Yes, But . . ." again. You'd think we'd know better by this time.

Therapist: Did anyone suggest anything you hadn't thought of yourself?

Hyacinth: No, they didn't. As a matter of fact, I've actually tried almost everything they suggested. I did buy my husband some tools, and he did take a course in carpentry.

Therapist: It's interesting that Hyacinth said he didn't have time to take the course.

Hyacinth: Well, while we were talking I didn't realize what we were doing, but now I see I was playing "Why Don't You . . . Yes, But" again, so I guess I'm still trying to prove that no Parent can tell me anything.

Therapist: And yet you asked me to hypnotize you or give you a hypnotic injection.

Hyacinth: You, yes. But nobody else is going to tell me what to do.

The social gain (time structuring) of this game was clearly stated by Mrs. Tredick, whose presenting complaint was erythrophobia. As is commonly the case, Mrs. Tredick could switch roles in any of her games. In the present connection, she was equally adept at playing either "it" or one of the sages, and this was discussed with her at an individual session.

Dr. Q: Why do you play it if you know it's a con?

Mrs. T: If I'm talking to somebody I have to keep thinking of things to say. If I don't, I'll blush. Except in the dark.

Dr. Q: Why don't you blush in the dark?

Mrs. T: What's the use, if nobody can see you?

Dr. Q: We'll talk about that sometime. It would be an interesting experiment if you stopped playing "Why Don't You" in the group. We might all learn something.

Mrs. T: But I can't stand a lull. I know it and my husband knows it too, he's always told me that.

Dr. Q: You mean if your Adult doesn't keep busy

your Child takes the chance to pop up and make you feel embarrassed?

Mrs. T: That's it. So if I can keep making suggestions to somebody, or get them to make suggestions to me, then I'm all right. I'm protected. You know, the blushing doesn't bother me so much any more. As long as I can keep my Adult in control, I can postpone the embarrassment and when it does come it doesn't make me panicky like it used to.

Here Mrs. Tredick indicates clearly enough that she fears unstructured time. The embarrassed, sexually excited Child is prevented from advertising as long as the Adult can be kept busy in a social situation, and a game offers a suitable structure for Adult functioning. But the game must be suitably motivated in order to maintain her interest. Her choice of this particular game is influenced by the economy principle: it yields the maximum internal and external gains connected with her Child's conflicts about physical passivity. She could play with equal zest either the shrewd Child who cannot be dominated, or the sage Parent who can dominate the Child in someone else; or rather who fails to dominate. Since the basic principle of "Why Don't You ... Yes, But" is that no suggestion is ever accepted, the Parent is never successful. The motto of this game is: "Don't get panicky, the Parent never succeeds." Ultimately this refers to an ambivalent bisexual attitude toward the actual parents in early childhood.

Other common games are "Schlemiel," "Alcoholic," "Wooden Leg," "Uproar," "Ain't It Awful?" "You Got Me Into This," "There I Go Again," and "Let's You and Him Fight." The names are chosen (or often bestowed by the patients themselves) so as to have a cogent sharpness which is both technically desirable and therapeutically effective. Each game is descriptively analogous to a formal contest such as chess or football.

White makes the first move, the whistle blows and East kicks off, the ball is thrown into play, etc., each have their analogues in the first moves of social games. X's stimulus is followed by Y's stylized response, whereupon X makes his stereotyped second move. After a definite number of moves, the game ends in a distinct dénouement which is the equivalent of checkmate or a touchdown. Hence a game is not an attitude nor a pastime, but a goal-directed set of exploitative complementary transactions.

"Schlemiel" offers a convincing but dangerous opportunity to see what happens if a game is broken up. In this game the one who is "it" breaks things, spills things, and makes messes of various kinds, and each time says: "I'm sorry!" The moves in a typical situation are as follows:

1. White spills a high ball on the hostess' evening gown.

2. Black responds initially with rage, but he senses (often only vaguely) that if he shows it, White wins. Black therefore pulls himself together, and this gives him the illusion that he wins.

3. White says: "I'm sorry!"

4. Black mutters forgiveness, strengthening his illusion that he wins.

After the cigarette burn on the table-cloth, the chair leg through the lace curtain, and the gravy on the rug, White's Child is exhilarated because he has given vent to his anal aggression and has been forgiven, while Black has made a gratifying display of suffering self-control. Thus both of them profit from an unfortunate situation, and Black is not necessarily anxious to terminate the friendship. It should be noted that, as with most games, White, the aggressor, wins either way. If Black shows his anger, White can feel "justified" in his resentment. If Black restrains himself, White can go on enjoying his opportunites. It is only in these games of life that one can win whichever way events turn out.

"Anti-Schlemiel" is played by a rash and sophisticated player thus:

1. White crushes the baby's rattle with his heel.

2. Black, who has been waiting for this, simply stands expectantly.

3. White, slightly disconcerted by Black's poise, says "I'm sorry!"

4. Black says: "You can pour a highball on my wife's dress, burn the table-cloth, tear the curtain, and spill the gravy on the rug, like you did last time. But please don't say 'I'm sorry!' "

5. Now that White's anal hostility has been publicly exposed, both the internal primary gains from "socially acceptable" messing and the external primary gain of forgiveness have been cut from under him. The problem is whether there will be an immediate burst of rage with a slamming door or worse, or whether he will control himself and take his revenge later. In either case, Black has now made an enemy and White is in peril of a possibly serious disturbance of psychic economy.

Hence it will be seen that while the description of a game is reminiscent of the English humorists,[a] the games discussed here are of a serious nature. Their dynamic function is to preserve psychic equilibrium, and their frustration leads either to rage or to a state which in transactional analysis is called *despair*. (This is clinically distinguishable from depression, and is akin to existential despair.)

"Alcoholic" is complicated because in its classical form it is a four-handed game from which all parties obtain both primary and secondary gains. In its full flower it requires a persecutor, a rescuer, a dummy, and the one who is "it." The persecutor is usually contrasexual, typically the spouse, and the rescuer ipisexual, often a physician. The dummy is a more or less indifferent person who simply offers supplies when needed and may also act as a passive object for instinctual impulses, usually both libidinal and aggressive. These roles may be condensed into a three-handed or two-handed game, and may also be switched. Various organizations print rules for this game and define the roles in their literature. To be "it," one takes a drink before breakfast, etc. To be a rescuer, one believes in a Higher Power, and so on.

The fact that people who play a certain game can potentially play any of the roles in that game explains the success of rescue organizations. Such organizations may be very successful at curing individuals of drinking, but do not cure them of playing the game of "Alcoholic." What happens seems to be that the member switches to the role of rescuer in that particular game, instead of playing the one who is "it." It is known that if there arises a scarcity of people to rescue, those who have been "cured" are likely to relapse,[4] which in the language of game analysis means that they switch back to their original roles of "it" in the alcoholic game. Ex-alcoholics make better rescuers than non-drinkers because they know the rules of the game better and are more experienced in applying them. The game is called here "Alcoholic" instead of "Alcoholism" because in certain cases it can be played without the bottle. That is, there are certain people who are not alcohol addicts who play essentially the same four-handed game.

It is generally agreed that rescue organizations (especially Alcoholics Anonymous) offer the best chance for a cessation of drinking, better than other approaches, including psychotherapy groups. It appears that alcoholics do not find general psychotherapy groups attractive, and the reason is not far to seek. If it is remembered that the basic yield of a group is to help the individual structure his time in such a way as to obtain the maximum gains, it is easy to understand that each person will seek out groups which are most congenial in this respect, groups which initially promise the greatest opportunities for playing his most highly motivated game. If he is frusrated in this quest, he will withdraw from the group. Thus it happens that patients remain in psychotherapy groups if they can play their favorite games there, or if they can see an opportunity to learn "better" ones, and withdraw if they are frustrated. An alcoholic does not find it easy to set up his particular game in a group of ordinary neurotics or psychotics, and since his capacity to tolerate frustration is notoriously low, he will soon withdraw.

On this principle, he can remain in a general group only under two conditions: either the therapist is unaware that the alcoholic is manipulating the group successfully, in which case the patient will obtain no permanent therapeutic benefit; or the therapist is skillful enough to help the alcoholic tolerate his frustrations until the underlying conflicts can be reached. The third alternative is the successful one of having a group made up of people who are all playing the alcoholic game.

One of the most frequent questions encountered after patients have learned social control and have given up their principal games is: "What do I do instead?" i.e., "How do I structure my time now?" Given time, the *vis medicatrix naturae* will take care of this problem by allowing the Child to come up with some more natural and constructive form of expression than the original game, much to the patient's surprise and delight. This is not to say that social control is a cure, but in favorable cases it brings about definite improvement. Certainly it would be inadvisable for the therapist to be so over-zealous as to try to provide new games for old patients; he must adhere to Ambroise Paré's motto: "I treat him, but God cures him." This is a preface to the proposition that some "cured" alcoholics tend to be rather neutral socially. That is because it is hard for them to know "what to do instead." Since in most cases they have shifted roles rather than given up the game, they are not free to seek a new game, and hence find it difficult to engage with people not their own kind.

"Wooden Leg" is an important game in psychotherapy, particularly because it is becoming more and more culturally syntonic. It is the existential equivalent of the legal plea of insanity, which is indeed only a professional version of "Wooden Leg." Like the psychoanalysis of phobias, only much more so, transactional analysis is an actionistic therapy; sooner or later a point is reached where the patient must actually go on the subway, cross the bridge, or take the elevator; the analysis cannot go on forever before such a confrontation is undertaken. Transactional analysis prefers sooner rather than later, and at times approaches the position "Do what is necessary first and we can analyze the problem afterward." The patient may reply with some psychiatric equivalent of "What do you expect of a man with a wooden leg?" such as: "But I can't, I'm neurotic."

Actually, all that the therapist asks is that the patient use what he has learned when he is ready. Many neurotics maintain the illusion that they must wait until the treatment is "ended" and they have some kind of diploma before they can begin to live in the world, and one of the duties of the therapist is to combat this kind of inertia, if that is what it is. People who are accustomed to read popular or technical psychiatric articles may play a more sophisticated version of "Wooden Leg" by saying: "But if I do it, then I won't be able to analyze it," referring to the problem of acting out.

It often requires considerable clinical judgment to determine whether a patient is really not ready, or is playing "Wooden Leg." In any case the therapist should be anti-"Wooden Leg" only under certain conditions: not more than once every three months with the same patient; only when he is sure that the patient will follow his suggestion; and only if the suggestion is made as an Adult, and not as a Parent. In most cases the patient will understand it as Parental, but the important thing is that the Adult quality of the approach be clear to the therapist himself and to the other members of the group, if there is one. Special types of "Wooden Leg" are particularly apt to provoke Parental counter-transference from susceptible therapists: the patient who pleads limited intelligence appeals to their snobbishness; the patient who pleads delicate health may appeal to their sympathy or insecurity; and the one who pleads minority group membership may appeal to their prejudices. The following anecdote illustrates the inconsistency of this game as well as the contemporary sociological implications.

Mr. Segundo boasted that he had won an acquittal for one of his clients by calling in a psychiatrist as an expert witness. The client was being tried for a serious dereliction of duty. The psychiatrist had testified that the man was legally sane, but that he had come from a broken home and had only committed his transgression out of love for his wife because he needed her so badly. His testimony was so convincing, together with Mr. Segundo's plea, that the jury had let the man go.

Mr. Segundo then related how he personally was suing a man who had let him down on a business commitment. On inquiry it developed that this defendant had also come from a broken home, needed the money for his wife's comfort, etc. But this did not deter Mr. Segundo from going ahead with his suit.

In transactional analysis, reliability or commitment is regarded as an inherent social quality of the Adult. Therefore the patient is expected to be reliable insofar as his Adult is functioning and within the limits it is able to function at a given time. This is the rationale for the therapist to be anti-"Wooden Leg" when indicated, and the patients understand this. If the therapist is careful, no difficulties should arise from this maneuver. In the writer's experience, no patient has ever withdrawn from treatment, been damaged, or become involved in a chaotic transference situation because of anti-"Wooden Leg." In structural terms, this position is based on the premise that the Child can learn from experience, therefore the individual should be encouraged early to live well in the world. That premise, together with the one which states that every grown-up, no matter how disturbed or functionally deteriorated, has a fully formed Adult which under proper conditions can be re-cathected, is more optimistic and in practice also seems more productive than the conventional views.

Among the other games specifically mentioned, "Uproar," with its loud voices and slamming doors, is classically a defense against sexual threats, between father and daughter or husband and wife, for example. It is often the terminal phase of the provocation-rejection-projection game of "Frigid Woman" ("All You Think About Is Sex"). "Ain't It Awful?" is played most grimly and poignantly by lonely surgery addicts. "You Got Me Into This" is a two-handed game of money, sex, or crime, played between a gullible one (You) and the one who is "it" (Me); in this game the one who gets caught is the winner. Its inverse is "There I Go Again"; here the gullible one (I) is "it," and the ostensible winner is the *agent provocateur*. In the first, "Me" is typically a man, and in the second "I" is typically a woman. "Let's You And Him Fight" is an essentially feminine opening to a game which may be played with any degree of seriousness from cocktail banter to homicide.

It is evident that games can be classified in various ways. Nosologically, Schlemiel" is "obsessional, "You Got Me Into This" is paranoid, and "There I Go

Again" is depressive. Zonally, "Alcoholic" is oral, "Schlemiel" is anal, and "Let's You And Him Fight" is generally phallic. They can also be classified according to the principal defenses used, the number of players, or the "counters." Just as a pack of cards or a pair of dice or a ball can each be used for a number of different games, so can time, money, words, jokes, parts of the body, and other "counters."

Games must be distinguished from operations, which belong to the sphere of intimacy. A game, by definition, must involve a snare or 'gimmick' through an ulterior transaction. An operation is a direct transaction, simply something that somebody does socially, such as asking for reassurance and getting it. This only becomes a game if the individual presents himself as doing something else, but is really asking for reassurance, or asks for reassurance and then rejects it in order to make the other person feel uncomfortable some way.

Game analysis not only has its rational function, but also lends a lively interest to the serious proceedings of individual or group psychotherapy. While it should not be corrupted to hedonistic purposes, and must be handled with the utmost correctness, the evident pleasure that it gives to many of the participants is a bonus which the conscientious therapist should be grateful for, and is not something to become querulous about.

NOTES

I have often been asked for a *list of games*. Since it takes a long period of observation for the appropriate name, the essential moves, and the motivations of a game to become clear, this is a difficult request to fulfill. The study of games is still at a stage of accumulation and fluidity. Two games which look different at first are often found, when their essences can be extracted, to be the same; and games which sound similar or identical may turn out eventually to be quite different in essence. The inter-relationships of various games are even more difficult to clarify. Even the basic question of whether a certain assortment of games is a necessary accompaniment of a certain script is not yet satisfactorily verified. So far, only the script of the life-plan known colloquially as "Little Red Riding Hood" has been studied in this respect, and as might be expected, all these women play "Let's You And Him Fight," as well as two or three others. But other kinds of women also play "Let's You And Him Fight." In any case it would take another book to describe adequately all the games so far known. The following list, added to those already mentioned, is therefore partial and provisional.

1. "Do Me Something" ("Wooden Leg" with anal stubbornness).

2. "Harass" ("Now that I've made life too complicated, I can give up").

3. "I Am Blameless" (The bland disclaimer).

4. "You Got Yourself Into This" (The fiery disclaimer).

5. "The Stocking Game" ("Look, there's a run in my stocking. . . . I didn't realize I was being provocative"). Here the question of *variations* arises. Some women point to defects in the conformation of their breasts.

6. "Rapo" ("How do you mean, I seduced you, you raped me and I'm complaining"). Here the question of *stages* comes in. In its most socially acceptable form, the gains are obtained from the seduction itself, and the brushoff merely signifies that the game is already over. This is the first stage. In the more malicious second stage of "Rapo," the seduction is secondary to the real kick, which is obtained from the brushoff. In its most malignant form, the third stage, which may end in scandal, homicide, or suicide, the gains are obtained from having actually been "raped."

7. "Now I've Got the Son of a Bitch" (Sometimes a variation of "Debtor" or "Creditor"). This is a question of *hardness*. Its significance as a hard game of "Creditor" is obvious. As a hard game of "Debtor," the gains are derived

from "justification" if the creditor exceeds the limits autistically set for collection by the debtor. ("Collection agency, yes. But I'll get him for calling my employer.")

S. S. Feldman's article on "Blanket Interpretation"[5] is an excellent description of a game of "Psychiatry" in which now the analyst, now the analysand, makes the opening move. In transactional analysis, the therapist or patient would pick out the archaic element in those transactions, and rather than follow Dr. Feldman in seeking the "true interpretation" of the content, would search instead for the genetic origins of the game itself in the early history of the analyst or analysand.

Calling the two levels of an *ulterior transaction* the "social" and the "psychological" may not be scientifically impeccable, but these are the most cogent, clear, and convenient terms available without going through Liddell & Scott to coin neologisms.

The *disintegration* of Alcoholics Anonymous groups when there are no more alcoholics left to rescue was a phenomenon I first noted many years ago.[6] Although Dr. Hendrik Lindt, who is more experienced in this matter than I am, told me privately that he has made the same observation, the conclusion is by no means firm and may still be open to question.

Historically, the most complex game that has ever existed is "Courtier," which is beautifully described by Stendhal in *The Charterhouse of Parma.*

The *biological gain* points in the direction of Spitz's work on emotionally deprived infants, sensory deprivation experiments, and recent studies of masochism as a *faute de mieux*. It is colloquially spoken of in seminars as "stroking." Thus a greeting ritual may be described as "a two stroke ritual," "a three stroke ritual," etc.

REFERENCES

1. Berne, E., Starrels, R. J., & Trinchero, A. "Leadership Hunger in a Therapy Group." *Arch. Gen. Psychiat.* 2: 75–80, 1960.

2. Freud, S. "Fragment of an Analysis of a Case of Hysteria." *Collected Papers*. Vol. III.

3. Potter, Stephen. *Lifemanship*. Henry Holt & Company, New York, 1950. Also his *Theory and Practice of Gamesmanship*.

4. Berne, E. *A Layman's Guide to Psychiatry and Psychoanalysis*. Simon & Schuster, New York, 1957.

5. Feldman, S. S. "Blanket Interpretation." *Psychoanal. Quart.* 17: 205–216, 1958.

6. Berne, E. *The Mind in Action*. Simon & Schuster, New York, 1947.

CHAPTER ELEVEN

Analysis of Scripts

GAMES appear to be segments of larger, more complex sets of transactions called *scripts*. Scripts belong in the realm of transference phenomena, that is, they are derivatives, or more precisely, adaptations, of infantile reactions and experiences. But a script does not deal with a mere transference reaction or transference situation; it is an attempt to repeat in derivative form a whole transference drama,[1] often split up into acts, exactly like the theatrical scripts which are intuitive artistic derivatives of these primal dramas of childhood. Operationally, a script is a complex set of transactions, by nature recurrent, but not necessarily recurring, since a complete performance may require a whole lifetime.

A common tragic script is that based on the rescue fantasy of a woman who marries one alcoholic after another. The disruption of such a script, like the disruption of a game, leads to despair. Since the script calls for a magical cure of the alcoholic husband, and this is not forthcoming, a divorce results and the woman tries again. Many such women were raised by alcoholic fathers, so that the infantile origins of the script are not far to seek.

A practical and constructive script, on the other hand, may lead to great happiness if the others in the cast are well chosen and play their parts satisfactorily.

In the practice of script analysis, transactional (intragroup) and social (extra-group) material is collected until the nature of his script becomes clear to the patient. Neurotic, psychotic, and psychopathic scripts are almost always tragic, and they follow the Aristotelian principles of dramaturgy with remarkable fidelity: there is prologue, climax, and catastrophe, with real or symbolic pathos and despair giving rise to real threnody. The current life-drama must then be related to its historical origins so that control of the individual's destiny can be shifted from the Child to the Adult, from archaeopsychic unconsciousness to neopsychic awareness. In the group the patient can soon be observed feeling out through games and pastimes the potentialities of the other members to play their parts in his script, so that at first he acts as a casting director and then as protagonist.

In order to be effective in script analysis, the therapist must have a better organized conceptual framework than he finds it necessary to communicate to the patient. First, there is no specific word in psychoanalysis for the original experiences from which transference reactions are derived. In script analysis, the household drama which is first played out to an unsatisfactory conclusion in the earliest years of life is called the *protocol*. This is classically an archaic version of the Oedipus drama and is repressed in later years. Its precipitates re-appear as the *script proper,* which is a preconscious derivative of the protocol. In any given social situation, however, this script proper must be compromised in accordance with the possible realities. This compromise is technically called the *adaptation,* and the adaptation is what the patient actually tries to play out in real life by the manipulation of the people around him. In practice protocol, script, and adaptation are all subsumed under the term "script." This is the only one of three words which is actually used in the group, since it is adequate for the intended purpose and is the one which is most meaningful to most patients.

In his quest for characters to fit the roles demanded by his script, the patient perceives the other members of the group in his own idiosyncratic way, usually with considerable intuitive acumen. That is, he tends to pick the right people to play the roles of mother, father, siblings, and whatever others are called for. When his casting is complete, he proceeds to try to elicit the required responses from the person cast for each role. If there are not enough people in the group, someone may have to play a double role. If there are too many, several may be cast in the same role; or new roles may be activated, representing people who played minor parts in the protocol and whose presence is optional and unessential; or else he may just ignore the people who serve no useful function in his adaptation.

The motivation for the patient's behavior is his need to recapture or augment the gains of the original experience. He may seek to bring about a repetition of the original catastrophe, as in the classical repetition compulsion; or he may try to attain a happier ending. Since the object of script analysis is to "close the show and put a better one on the road," it is not too important to determine which of these alternatives applies or to sort out the conflicts in this area. For example, it is regarded as irrelevant whether the woman who failed to rescue her alcoholic father is trying to fail again with her subsequent husbands, or is trying to succeed where she failed before, or is ambivalent. The important thing is to free her from her compulsion to relive the situation, and start her on some other path. This applies to any script which has proven unconstructive.

Mrs. Catters illustrates the problems of script analysis as they appear in practice. For a long time she was unproductive on the couch. Her principal defense was a deliberate manner of speech which effectively insulated the Child so that few indications leaked out which threw any light on her symptomatology. When she was introduced to a therapy group, however, she went into action almost immediately. She took an active part in "How Do You Treat Delinquent Spouses?" (a pastime belonging to the "PTA" family). She also played a steady game of "Let's You And Him Fight," watching with much enjoyment the arguments she succeeded in starting between some of the men. Added to this, when the group played "Ain't It Awful?" she would laugh as she recounted various bloody calamities that had befallen friends and acquaintances. In this manner it happened that a few weeks in the group yielded more information about her than as many months on the couch. Since scripts are so complex and full of idiosyncrasy, however, it is not possible to do adequate script analysis in group therapy alone, and it remained to find an opportunity in her individual sessions to elucidate what had been learned so far.

After a time she complained at one of those sessions that she could not defend herself against male aggressiveness. The therapist, on the basis of previous material, opined that one reason might be that she was so angry at men in general that she was afraid to let go even a little bit for fear that she might find herself going farther than she wanted to. She said it was hard to believe that she could be that angry at men. She went on to report fantasies of the death of her husband, who was a philandering jet pilot. One day he might get into an accident or a fight over another woman and be brought home fatally bleeding and injured. Thus she would become a romantic figure among her friends, the tragic widow.

She then recounted how deeply hurt and angry, in fact enraged, she had been as a child after the birth of her little brother, whom her parents seemed to prefer. She was especially angry at her father, and her thought was: "Daddy deserves to be killed by someone, and it would serve mother right if it happened." She imagined that his death would also give her a special position among her playmates. The picture of her father dying was accompanied by a peculiar kind of laughing pleasure.

There were other complications which are irrelevant to the present discussion. In its simplest form, the protocol was as follows. Her death wishes against her father are realized without any initiative on her part. The death-bed scene has its own special kind of pleasure. This recurs when she goes to notify her mother and observes her mother's grief. Then she becomes a romantic figure to her playmates.

This drama is repeated in her fantasies about her husband, but so far one element is missing: the stunned mother. The therapist therefore asked her if her mother-in-law ever played a part in these fantasies. She replied that it was certainly so, that after the death-bed scene she always pictured herself going to announce the fatal outcome to her mother-in-law.

This protocol contained six principal roles: self, father, mother, rival, assailant, audience. It could be divided into several scenes: e.g., jealousy, assault, death-bed, announcement, romantic threnody.

The script also contained six principal roles: self, male love object, mother-in-law, rival, assailant, and audience; and it could be divided into the same acts or scenes. Her choice of husband had been partly motivated by her morbid need to be jealous, or in the present language, by her need to cast her script.

It will be noted that the gains from the script duplicate the gains from the protocol. The internal primary gain centers around the morbid laughter of the death-bed scene; the external primary gain lies in getting rid of the worrisome love object and simultaneously obtaining revenge on the mother person. The secondary gains come from inheriting the estate, and the social gains from the tragic role she can play in her community.

Her adaptation of this script in her overt behavior in the group was manifested by her three games: "Delinquent Husband PTA" (Scene 1, Jealousy); "Let's You And Him Fight" (Scene 2, The Assault); and "Ain't It Awful?" (Scene 3, The Death-Bed). Reviewing her behavior on the couch, her habit of making "announcements" when something went wrong (Scene 4, The Announcement), and her long discussions about how to appear glamorous at parties (Scene 5, The Romantic Threnody), now fell into place as part of her script. After all this had been worked over at some length (although not in quite such an orderly sequence as it is presented here), the patient understood rather clearly the nature of a script, and could see how she had spent most of her life striving to keep this particular show on the road. Where previously she had been driven with no option by an unconscious archaic compulsion, she was now in a position to exert social control over a large portion of her behavior with people.

Nevertheless, even though her Adult grasped with new understanding the significance of her actions and relationships, the stivings themselves still persisted. But her position was improved not only socially, but also therapeutically, since it was now much clearer to both the patient and the therapist what kind of strivings had to be dealt with. The sexualization of death, which made it her hobby to visit graveyards, was no longer an isolated phenomenon, but could be handled with increased understanding of how it fitted into her whole destiny; and similarly with other characteristics and symptoms.

This is a not atypical script of a neurotic, however morbid it may appear to those unaccustomed to dealing with such archaic dramas. The following represents the actual acting out of a script whose protocol was never completely clarified due to technical difficulties.

Mr. Kinz, a 25-year-old bachelor, went to New York for a week-end of fun. He arrived in the early hours of the morning, tired and somewhat nervous, so he doctored himself with barbiturates and alcohol and found an after-hours bar. There, in the predawn, he fell into conversation with some rough-looking men who he thought might find him a girl. He showed them that he had only ten dollars, but they said that would be enough. They invited him into their car and drove him toward a deserted warehouse district near the river. In the course of their conversation he told them that he carried a hunting knife, and one of them asked to see it. A few minutes later they stopped the car. The man in the back seat threw his elbow around Mr. Kinz's neck while the other men put the blade of the knife against his throat. They demanded his money, and with some difficulty Mr. Kinz managed to reach into his pocket and hand them his wallet. They then released him and drove off, waving a friendly goodbye. Mr. Kinz wiped the blood from his throat and went to find a policeman. He told his story in such a way, however, and his appearance was by this time so disreputable, that the police were quite unimpressed. They took down the required details and then dismissed him with a shrug.

After he had reported the robbery, Mr. Kinz had some breakfast; then without bothering to get cleaned up, he presented himself at the door of his father's club. The doorman did not know him, and with raised eyebrows sent a servant to announce him. His father received him in the library where he was sitting with some of his well-to-do and conservative business associates. Mr. Kinz did not offer to explain his appearance and when his father questioned him he said in a casual way that he had almost had his throat cut. The father offered the use of his room upstairs and the loan of some clean clothes. Mr. Kinz tidied himself up, came downstairs and said a polite farewell to his father and his friends, and went on his way to look for more fun.

It is interesting to note that the two thugs showed no apprehension that Mr. Kinz would raise a really dangerous alarm, or even that he would be very angry or lose his head. Yet when he told the story, Mr. Kinz at first denied that he had invited the assault, or that any of his preceding actions were extraordinary. What interested him more than anything, apparently, was the awareness that he had gone to his father's club as a kind of test, to see if and how his father would reject him.

It is evident that Mr. Kinz chose his cast well. It is not easy to find in real life men who are willing to cut a man's throat for ten dollars. He supplied them not only with an excuse, but also with the actual weapon to murder him while he was looking for a sexually available woman. The protocol for this part of the script is not known. The last act was more familiar. Mr. Kinz was precocious, and once when he was small he had burst into the room where his father sat with some friends to show them his latest achievement. The men were not impressed, and he never forgot his dejection on that occasion. At any rate, Mr. Kinz made a kind of career of a particular sequence: getting himself violently slapped down because of a woman, and then presenting himself to his father. He deliberately exposed himself to the most dangerous possible sexual situations. Between times, when his Adult was in control, he was a gentle, kind, likable, and shy young man.

After some experience, it is possible to acquire considerable diagnostic acumen in script analysis. The following example illustrates the telescoping of a whole script into a few seconds.

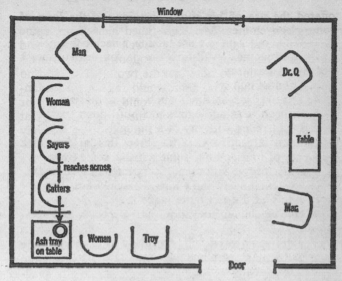

Seating diagram
FIGURE 10

Mrs. Sayers, a 30-year-old housewife, was sitting in the middle of a settee with Mrs. Catters between her and an end-table, as shown in Figure 10. This was a beginners' group, and Mrs. Sayers had just spent considerable time relating her troubles with her husband. Attention had now turned to Mr. Troy. In the midst of an exchange between Mrs. Catters and Mr. Troy, Mrs. Sayers stretched her arm out across Mrs. Catters's chest to reach for an ash-tray on the end-table. As she drew her arm back she lost her balance and almost fell off the settee. She recovered just in time, laughed deprecatingly, muttered "Excuse me!" and settled back to smoke. At this moment, Mrs. Catters took her attention away from Mr. Troy long enough to murmur: "Pardon me!"

Descriptively, this performance may be broken down into the following steps.

1. While other people are talking, I decide to smoke.
2. In order not to disturb the person next to me, I get my own ashtray.
3. I almost fall.
4. I recover just in time, laugh, and apologize.
5. Someone else apologizes too, but I don't answer.
6. I settle back with my own thoughts.

A more subjective view interprets this incident as a sequence of transactions, some autistic, some overt.

1. Other people ignore me, so I pretend to withdraw.
2. I ostentatiously show how diffident I am.
3. As usual, I don't quite make it.
4. Having shown how silly I am, I recover and apologize.
5. I am so covered with confusion at my own ineptness that I make someone else feel uneasy.
6. Now I really withdraw.

The pathos of this situation is the small external yield. All that Mrs. Sayers has to be grateful for as a result of her efforts is Mrs. Catters's murmured "Pardon me!" and that is the story of Mrs. Sayers's life—an attractive, conscientious person working very hard for psychological pennies; or more colloquially and more aptly, for psychological peanuts. And often she might work for nothing. Not everyone would be as polite as Mrs. Catters; engaged otherwise in conversation, some might not give Mrs. Sayers even that trivial recognition.

Her script, in this case adapted within a few seconds by a remarkably efficient integrating mechanism to a special situation in the group, had been repeatedly played out over varying lengths of time ranging from a passing moment to several years, both in Mrs. Sayers's marriage and in her working life, resulting in several separations from her husband, and involving the loss of one job after another. The original drama is based on early experiences. The first, traumatic experience, the protocol, was not recovered within the limited scope of her treatment, but later versions or *palimpsests* can be reconstructed from her history.

1. Since my siblings attract more attention than I do, I pretend to withdraw from family life.

2. But from time to time I try to get some recognition by ostentatiously demonstrating agreement with my alcoholic mother that I am quite unimportant.

3. Because of my clumsiness, mother pushes me. The combination is almost disastrous.

4. My ineffectual but loving father saves me from the disaster. I think how silly I must look to my mother and siblings. Because of that, and because of my pleasure at getting some notice, I laugh. Then I seem to have been too demanding and aggressive, and apologize.

5. What I really want is for them to show that they are sorry for their neglect. But if they do, I cannot afford to acknowledge it for two reasons: first, it makes me feel demanding, as above; and secondly, if I am waiting for it I may be disappointed. So if they so signify, it registers gratefully, but I pretend to overlook it.

6. In any case, the whole situation is so unsatisfactory that now I really withdraw.

There are at least three different early palimpsests of this script: oral, pre-oedipal, and oedipal. The oedipal version reads briefly: "How silly it is to be a girl. I can only get whatever poor satisfactions are available, and then retire and lick my wounds." It was not difficult to see this version being played out every year or so with the disparaging husband she had picked for herself, and in her working life where some slight paranoid distortion was occasionally necessary in order to make her co-workers fit the roles that her script called for.

The striking thing was how much this apparently innocent and simple incident revealed when the lightning fast shifts in attitude were isolated and analyzed. The dramaturgy of this kaleidoscopic thimble theater in six acts is essentially tragic: in spite of the averted pathos, it ends in forlorn threnody, and reflects the quality of Mrs. Sayers's life. The history emphasized and explained the autistic quality of the transactions, and made the structural analysis clear: the wistful Child who is pushed by one intrapsychic Parent and rescued by the other; the momentary breakthrough of the Adult who appraises her behavior; and the ultimate lapse into archaic fantasy.

On the basis of transactional analysis, game analysis, and script analysis, it is possible to state a dynamic theory of social intercourse which complements the biological and existential theory previously stated in Chapter 8. In any social aggregation, including the limiting case of two, the individual will strive to engage in transactions which are related to his favored games; he will strive to play games which are related to his script; and he will strive to obtain the greatest primary gain from each engagement. Conversely, he will choose or seek out associates who promise to yield the greatest primary gains: for casual relationships, people who will at least participate in favored transactions; for more stable relationships, people who will play the same games; for intimate relationships, people who are best qualified to fill roles in his script. Since the dominant influence in social intercourse is the script, and since that is derived and adapted from a protocol based on early experiences of the individual with his parents, those experiences are the chief determinants of every engagement and of every choice of associates. This is a more general statement than the familiar transference theory which it brings to mind because it applies to any engagement whatsoever in any social aggregation whatsoever; that is, to any transaction or series of transactions which is not completely structured by external reality. It is useful because it is subject to testing by any qualified observer anywhere. Such testing requires neither a prolonged period of preparation nor a unique situation.

While every human being faces the world initially as the captive of his script, the great hope and value of the human race is that the Adult can be dissatisfied with such strivings when they are unworthy.

NOTES

Some of the scripts which it has been possible to study adequately so far have had awesome prototypes in Greek literature; while the common script known as "Little Red Riding Hood" is a modern real-life adaptation which follows implicitly certain versions of that folk-tale.

The middle scenes of Mrs. Sayers's script are a good illustration of Berliner's concept of masochism.[1] When Mrs. Sayers returned for further treatment, she retained a very vivid memory of this interpretation.

The necessary qualification for the observer who wishes to test this theory of social intercourse is clinical training, or at least clinical aptitude. A negative finding by an observer who lacks this qualification is of no more significance than a failure to find supernovae by an individual who has not been trained in the use of the astronomical telescope, or a failure to register genes by a person who has not been trained in the use of the electron microscope. In fact it usually requires more training, care, and effort to observe clinical phenomena clearly than it does to use either of those instruments properly.

The standard of worthiness as distinct from self-righteousness or moral prejudice is regarded as an Adult phenomenon rather than a Parental one because of its historical and geographical universality, its apparently autonomous development, and its relationship to probability estimates of behavior.

Of all the statements in the literature concerning *transference neurosis,* those of Glover[2] come closest to the idea of the script. E.g.: "the history of the patient's development, leading up to the infantile neurosis, is re-enacted in the analytic room—the patient plays the part of actor-manager, pressing into service (like a child in the nursery) all the stage property that the analytical room contains, first and foremost, the analyst himself."[3] But Glover is speaking only of what takes place in the analytic room.

REFERENCES

1. Berliner, B. "The Role of Object Relations in Moral Masochism." *Psychoanalytic Quart.* XXVII: 38–56, 1958; and others.

2. Glover, E. *The Technique of Psycho-Analysis.* International Universities Press, New York, 1955, Chaps. VII & VIII.

3. Hinsie, L. E., & Shatzky, J. Loc. cit. Cited under "Transference Neurosis."

CHAPTER TWELVE

Analysis of Relationships

RELATIONSHIP ANALYSIS is principally used in the study of marital relationships and impending liaisons of various kinds. In these situations it may yield some useful and convincing predictions and postdictions. It should be employed sparingly and judiciously in practice, however, because it may too easily represent to the patient an unwarranted intrusion into his autonomy of decision. But as "homework" for the student or therapist, it is a valuable exercise in learning to distinguish more clearly between the three types of ego states.

In Mr. Kinz's case, relationship analysis was undertaken as a specially indicated intervention when he was in the process of forming a new liaison which promised to end even more disastrously than usual. Because of his tendency to re-enact his perilous script again and again, it was deemed advisable from time to time to sacrifice technical rigidity in favor of preventing what seemed imminent tragedy. It seemed better, for example, to have a live patient with a slightly damaged therapeutic relationship than a dead one who had been sacrificed in the cause of aseptic therapy. The situation was analogous to that of the surgeon who has to abandon the neat appendectomy incision in order to administer direct massage to an overanesthetized heart. The relationship between Mr. Kinz and the therapist was clear enough so that real external threats could be distinguished from less sinister attempts to enlist parental protection from the doctor. In this case, Mr. Kinz was not nurturing the liaison for the purpose of alarming the therapist. He had another game in mind, which caused him to overlook the more serious possibilities.

The young lady in question, Miss Ullif, seemed from Mr. Kinz's description to be clinically not very far from suicide, and since Mr. Kinz, because of his underlying severe depression and feeling of futility was a good candidate for suggestions in this direction, the impending affair had an especially unhealthy prognosis. Mr. Kinz himself, however, regarded it in his usual fashion as something which might lead to marriage; this time once more it was the "real thing," and the problem was approached on this basis. At this point he had a good understanding of structural analysis, and the time seemed ripe for him to begin to acquire some measure of social control by applying what he knew. He was also beginning to be aware that relationships between people were not accidental or amorphous but had definite motivation and structure which determined their courses and functions.

Two structural diagrams were drawn on the blackboard as in Figure 11A, one representing Mr. Kinz and the other Miss Ullif. The characteristics of Mr. Kinz's Parent, Adult, and Child were familiar to both himself and the therapist, and the patient was now encouraged to give a free description of Miss Ullif. His thoughts, condensed into one paragraph, proceeded in the following vein.

Wherever she went, men would run after her, oddly enough not for sexual purposes but in order to take care of her. They had gone to Carnegie Hall together. When the concert was half over she said she was too tired to listen any more. For his part, he is just beginning to get interested in good music and does not understand it very well. She is always in need of money and probably would like a man with money, but would not want to talk about how it was made. She is mixed up. She went to a psychiatrist but quit because he was too cold. She wanted to be a musician. Mr. Kinz, like his father, was more interested in business and thought women should be more practical, too. She also wanted to paint. He looked at some of her pictures and felt that they showed her confusion and told her so, which she resented. She cannot stand criticism. She is so sensitive that from time to time she has to shut herself up in her room for a few days and get away from everybody. She expected him to understand that and he told her that he did not think he could go along with it.

At this point it was possible to proceed with the analysis, asking supplementary questions when indicated. The diagram on the blackboard was altered from the form in Figure 11A to that in Figure 11B. Figure 11B represents the non-existent theoretically perfect relationship, in which each aspect of each party is in a *complementary relationship* with each aspect of the other party, so that satisfactory transactions can take place along each of the nine possible *vectors* in both directions. If, for example, the Parent of Kinz gives a transactional stimulus directed to the Child of Ullif, the latter will give an appropriate response, and vice versa. This means in effect that all transactions between the two parties will be complementary.

The first vector investigated was Kinz Parent—Ullif Child. In discussing his Parent, Mr. Kinz was not precise enough at times and mentioned attitudes which properly belonged to his Adult or his Child. These oversights were carefully clarified, and the necessity for taking one aspect at a time was emphasized. If any confusion were allowed to creep in, the purpose of well-defined analysis of the relationship would be defeated.

When this difficulty was taken care of, it emerged

that Mr. Kinz saw Miss Ullif as a kind of waif, a gypsy-like creature in need of protection. Mr. Kinz was notorious for his Parental generosity; in fact many of the scrapes he got into were initiated by this attitude. Miss Ullif on her part was very receptive of such overtures. It was therefore concluded that in general, the vector Kinz Parent—Ullif Child was a *conjunctive* one. But there was a noteworthy exception: when she sequestered herself, his Parent was frustrated because

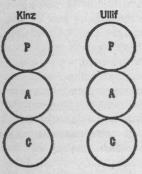

(a) Two unrelated personalities

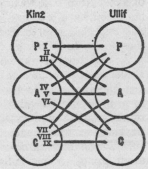

(b) A theoretically ideal relationship

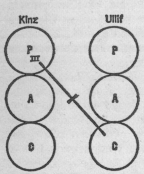

(c) An unpromising relationship

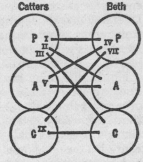

(d) An exceptionally stable relationship

FIGURE 11

then he could not be taking care of her. Therefore, in the long run there were *disjunctive or antipathetic* elements here. The first step in setting up Figure 11C, the actual relationship analysis, was to leave the vector Kinz P—Ullif C[III] as in Figure 11B, but to mark it with a bar.

The available material for studying the vector Kinz Parent—Ullif Adult [II] was mainly concerned with Miss Ullif's desire to be a painter. From the Parental point of view, Mr. Kinz was not very sympathetic, duplicating his father's attitude in this regard. Therefore Kinz P—Ullif A was erased from the relationship diagram. Kinz P—Ullif P[I] was no more promising and was also erased; the two friends had little tendency to moralize together, or to take care of people together.

Kinz Adult—Ullif Child[VI] centered around Miss Ullif's mode of living. On rational grounds he was critical of her sloppy housekeeping, poor eating habits, sequestration, and inability to tolerate criticism, and she resented this. Therefore Kinz A—Ullif C was eliminated as disjunctive. Kinz Adult—Ullif Adult[V] was no better. She was interested in the arts, he in business and aviation, and they could not talk for long with much enthusiasm about each other's projects. Kinz Adult—Ullif Parent[IV] was neutral because she exhibited no perceptible Parental activity at all in the relationship; she offered no maternal advice or backing for his undertakings.

Kinz Child—Ullif Parent[VII] was eliminated for the same reason. She made no attempt to protect him from or censure him for his recklessness; neither did she show any inclination to discuss it rationally, which also eliminated Kinz Child—Ullif Adult.[VIII] This left only Kinz Child—Ullif Child to be settled. Mr. Kinz's script has already been described, and from the woman's point of view it calls for being seduced and then cast aside in some violently unpleasant way involving a third party. On the other hand, Miss Ullif's game had something to do with repeatedly seducing and exploiting the man, and then deserting him by self-sequestration. Since there are strong conflicts here about who is going to do the seducing, the exploiting, and the deserting, Kinz C—Ullif C^{IX} hardly represents a workable relationship.

The end result of this analysis was that only one conjunctive vector was left, Kinz P—Ullif C,^{III} as in Figure 11C. Mr. Kinz decided that the relationship did not look promising, and broke it off.

Mrs. Catters's relationship with one of her woman friends, Mrs. Beth, was also analyzed, for reasons which need not be gone into here. Again, Figures 11A and 11B were drawn at the appropriate times, and the end result is shown in Figure 11D, with the vectors numbered in Roman numerals in the same order as before.

These two women took care of each other in case of illness, and cheered each other up in case of depression, so that Catters Parent—Beth Child^{III} and Beth Parent —Catters Child^{VII} were complementary and conjunctive. They also supplied each other with Parental maxims and encouragement regarding various practical projects, implementing Catters P—Beth A^{II} and Beth P— Catters A.^{IV} Rational discussions of the same problems were mutually satisfactory along Catters A—Beth A.^{V} After they had been to parties together, they delighted in both moralizing and malicious gossip, Catters P— Beth P^{I} and Catters C—Beth C^{IX} respectively. Their quarrels occurred when one tried to reason with the other regarding some impulsive action; this was specifically Catters A—Beth C^{VI} and Beth A—Catters C,^{VIII} since Parental censure from one to the other (P→C^{III}, ^{VII}) was acceptable as part of their game; it was the rational approach (A→C^{VII}, ^{VIII}) which caused the difficulties. Therefore Catters A—Beth C^{VI} and Beth A—Catters C^{VIII} were eliminated.

In this case the relationship had an exceptionally stable structure, which seven of the nine vectors being conjunctive. The history and vicissitudes of their long and happy friendship bore out the results of the analysis.

What has been presented above represents the most elementary type of relationship analysis, and a more advanced form would be attempted with a patient only on the rarest occasions. It is easy to see that there are additional qualitative and quantitative factors to be considered in a more thorough approach. Qualitatively, there are at least four possibilities in "a relationship": some people get along "well" together; some enjoy fighting or arguing with each other; some cannot stand each other; and some just have nothing to say to each other. These alternatives may be characterized respectively as *sympathy, antagonism, antipathy,* and *indifference,* and are easily understood from the viewpoint of game analysis. They represent in that order conjunctive games, disjunctive games, conflicting games or irreconcilable (often identical) roles in the same game, and games which are irrelevant to one another. A qualitative analysis would take account of the nature of the vectors. An example is shown in Figure 12A, in which the qualities are represented by conventional signs: sympathy by a heavy line, antagonism by a zigzag line, antipathy by an obstructed line, and indifference by a light line.

The quantitative aspect is concerned with the *intensity* of each vector, and this can also be represented in a diagram. In this case it would be desirable to have double lines, since complementary vectors might differ in strength: e.g. Catters P—Beth C was stronger than Beth C—Catters P. When Mrs. Beth fell ill, she did not feel as much need to be taken care of as Mrs. Catters did to take care of her, as shown in Figure 12B.

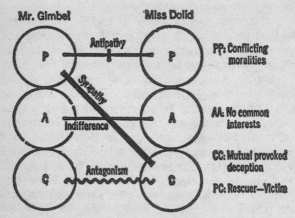

(a) Qualitative relationship analysis

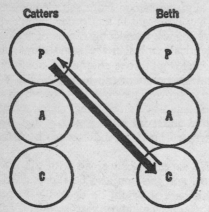

(b) Quantitative relationship analysis

FIGURE 12

A third complication concerns the amount of material available. Analysis of a marriage of long standing requires continual vigilance and re-evaluation as therapy progresses.

These complications, however, are usually significant only from an academic point of view. From that standpoint, relationship analysis may appear to be interminable and indeterminate, and hence of questionable value. In practice, however, the simple type demonstrated in the cases of Mr. Kinz and Mrs. Catters is surprisingly informative, and is a valuable predictive and postdictive instrument with a retrospective accuracy of the order of 80 or 90%. Both what will happen at various times in the course of "a relationship," and the ultimate outcome, can be foreseen with considerable confidence from this procedure. Since in reality there is no such thing as "a relationship" in the popular static sense of the word, but only predominances which vary from time to time among the nine possible vectors, it is necessary to do relationship analysis if the aim is to understand the possibilities.

PART III

Psychotherapy

CHAPTER THIRTEEN

Therapy of Functional Psychoses

1 ACTIVE PSYCHOSES

THE functional psychoses include all those conditions commonly diagnosed as manic-depressive and schizophrenic. For therapeutic purposes, however, they are not classified as different nosological entities, but as structural states. In this respect, psychoses exist in two forms: active and latent. Latent psychoses are variously called compensated psychoses, psychoses in remission, ambulatory schizophrenias, and prepsychotic or borderline personalities. Sometimes schizoid personalities fall into this class.

An *active psychosis* exists when the Child has the executive power and is also experienced as "real Self," while the Adult is decommissioned. In character disorders, psychopathy, and paranoia the Adult is grossly contaminated by the Child and co-operates with it but is not decommissioned, so that the execution, if not the motivation, is subject to reality-testing of a limited kind. The same applies to hypomania and mild depression. Any of these conditions may progress to active psychosis. The situation of the Parent varies and is a strong determinant of the specific form of psychosis. In cyclic manic-depressive conditions, for example, the strongly cathected Parent is at first excluded by a triumphant Child,[1] and later comes strongly to the fore.

The *arrest* of an active psychosis may be defined as the re-establishment of the Adult as the executive and as "real Self." When this has been accomplished, the diagnosis is changed to *latent psychosis,* which requires a different therapeutic approach. This process has already been illustrated in the cases of Mrs. Primus and Mrs. Tettar. Mr. Troy introduces a complication because although clinically his psychosis was latent, it was not, according to the definition, arrested; it would be better to call it, instead, *compensated,* since in his case it was the Parent and not the Adult who controlled the executive and was experienced as "real Self." The distinction is important because even if the psychosis were latent, it could not be dealt with as such. In order to treat a latent psychosis, it is necessary to have a functioning Adult as a therapeutic ally. Such an ally was not available in Mr. Troy's case. For a long time, therefore, the only course was to support the dominating Parent, and nothing could be done systematically for the Child who was "kept locked in the closet." It was several years before the Adult became active enough to assist in the deconfusing of the frustrated Child in the face of the Parent's protests.

Although the "little cures" described in the cases of Mrs. Primus and Mrs. Tettar were not of much clinical value because they were too unstable, nevertheless they exemplify the principles involved in treating active psychoses. These principles are determined by cathectic balances.

The psychosis depends upon the Child retaining cathectic dominance. As long as this prevails the Adult is difficult to reach, since everything that is said is first processed by the Child. The situation is quite analogous to having to reach a grown-up by sending messages through a confused little boy or girl. At best, the outcome will depend upon whether the child is hostile or favorably disposed toward the sender, and is not helped by the fact that however objective they are, the messages are known by the child to concern itself. At worst, the child may be too confused to grasp the situation at all, which is why acute toxic psychoses are rarely amenable to psychotherapy. The patient (namely, at that moment the Child) simply cannot be reached.

This analogy emphasizes again that the social and phenomenological reality of ego states is the primary pragmatic consideration, and it also yields two initial therapeutic rules: (1) Psychotherapy should be initiated only during periods of minimal confusion. (2) No active psychotherapeutic moves should be made until the patient has had a chance to appraise the therapist, and he should be given an opportunity to do this. These rules are known both intuitively and from clinical experience by all good therapists, but their rationale becomes a little clearer in structural terms. The apparent exceptions, such as some of Rosen's cases,[2] are tests rather than contradictions of these general principles, and exceptional procedures are best undertaken by experts.[3] The reason for sitting with the patient for long periods with a reassuring attitude, as Fromm-Reichmann did,[4] is understandable in relation to these rules. It is also evident why it is advisable to change therapists if the patient is unable to relax a hostile attitude toward a certain individual. Because of the Child's acute personal perceptions, it is possibly best to consider in such cases that for some reason the patient is probably justified. The therapist need not feel embarrassed, since not everybody expects to be able to make friends with every little boy or little girl in the world.

After periods of activity, the active (i.e., unbound plus free) cathexis of the Child tends to become depleted, leaving the Adult relatively more accessible. A certain type of child, if he is first given an opportunity to relieve himself of his troubles, is more apt to carry a message correctly. If he is allowed to cry it out first, he may then be your friend, and not only carry messages, but even take you to his grown-ups directly. In fact, if you take the initiative at the right time, he may allow himself to be by-passed. And being nice to a child is often a good way of attracting the attention of his grown-ups if you want to talk grown-up talk with them, especially if you want to talk to them about the child himself. These considerations indicate a third rule for the treatment of active psychoses: (3) Let the Child have his way first. And (4) the initial overture to the Adult should be made in well-timed, firm, and unmistakably Adult language. The Child's cathexis is now relatively depleted and the Adult's cathexis is being suitably reactivated; thus, with good luck the dominance of the Adult may be re-established temporarily. Each time this is done, there is a cumulative effect. But the ultimate outcome will depend upon how the Child views the whole procedure. And if outside influences continue to aggrevate him, then the difficulties may become insuperable. Therefore, in many cases the people in the patient's environment should go into therapy themselves, and group therapy may be the best medium for this.

That is about as far as generalities go in the initial phases of the psychotherapy of acute psychoses, and idiosyncrasies have to be dealt with as they arise. If these rules seem banal, they have become so because of their cogency, and structural analysis may have contributed little to this phase besides a clearer way of talking about it.

The idiosyncrasies, of course, are innumerable, and present varying degrees of difficulty. Mrs. Primus could not go beyond the first stage because further office treatment was not available. But the rules were followed during the diagnostic interview. Nothing was said to her during the more confused seductive phase because it might have been perceived for what it was, a rejection, and this would have increased her confusion. The therapist did not speak until (1) she had had a chance to collect herself in the presence of the voices; she was given time (2) to look him over before he said anything, and his first question, about the voices, was directed to her Child and gave some clues as to his attitude; only after giving her Child these opportunities to appraise him and (3) to express herself, did he attempt to speak to her Adult; when he did so, (4) it was in a firm, objective way which was calculated to attract Adult attention with minimal disturbance to the Child.

Mrs. Tettar's idiosyncrasy was that she was unable to tolerate the termination of an interview. The solution was (3) to comfort and reassure the Child at that time, and then take the matter up at the *beginning* of an interview, (1) after her Adult had become sufficiently well re-established so that it could maintain control during the first half of each session. Her progress has already been reported about midway in her dealing with this problem.

Other idiosyncrasies can also be dealt with according to the rules. If the patient waylays the therapist with a handful of feces, he can only dodge and then (2) let her see how he feels about it. If he doesn't make the grade with her, or she doesn't make the grade with him, he had best retire from the case. If the Child insists that they both sit on the floor before the therapist can talk to the Adult, then it may be best (3) to go along with the Child, but then (4) speak to the Adult, and not to the Child. This means that the therapist does not try to "analyze" why the Child wants it this way, since there is not yet (1) any active Adult to help with the analysis; if he mentions it at all, it can only be in the most matter-of-fact way. He may remark (non-Parentally) that it seems like a strange thing to do, or that he himself will take a cushion and the patient can have one if desired. But if he says: "I like to sit on the floor too," he is playing with the Child; if he says: "Let's sit on cushions," he is talking like a parent to the Child, very likely like one of the patient's own parents. In both cases he is departing from his purpose, if that is to get to the Adult.

While the technique of re-establishing the Adult is relatively simple to state, the theoretical aspect is more complicated. The most useful approach at this point is to say that in an active psychosis the Adult is decathected as it is during sleep, and that it can be recathected by proper sensory and social stimulation. The most appropriate selective stimulation for the neopsyche is a firm objective question or observation, which is calculated to avoid simultaneously stimulating either of the other two systems.

2   LATENT PSYCHOSES

A *latent psychosis,* like anything latent, does not exist, but can only be said to exist. A latent psychosis is said to exist when it can be inferred that the binding capacity of the Child is defective. Depending upon boundary conditions, there will either be areas of pathological activity where the Adult is heavily contaminated, or outbursts when the Adult is temporarily decommissioned, or both. The treatment of latent psychoses involves two aims and is one of the most difficult tests of therapeutic finesse in the field of psychiatry. First, the boundary between the Adult and the Child must be realigned and strengthened. This is a problem for structural analysis. If the Parent is highly cathected, as in manic-depressive conditions, then the therapist, and later the patient's Adult, have the additional task of acting as a buffer between the Child and the Parent when one is being intransigent to the other. The second aim is the psychoanalytic one of deconfusing the Child.

In Mr. Segundo's case, the Parent had comparatively little influence because his father had died when the patient was very young and his relationships with other men had been poorly developed, while his mother was asthenic and paid only scattered attention to him, so that exteropsychic influences were weak. In fact, with some exceptions his Parent was largely factitious and fictitious. Whatever cathexis was in his exteropsychic system centered mostly around representations of property and money. His treatment, therefore, was concerned almost exclusively with the relationship between the Adult and the Child. The first three tasks, which were successfully carried out because his Adult was well-cathected in normal circumstances, were (a) to *decontaminate* the Adult and (b) to clarify and (c) to strengthen its boundary with the Child.

When he said or did something too naively injudicious, or beneath his intellectual capacity, it was proposed to him that this was a rather child-like attitude (*not* "childish") for one of his accomplishments. For example, his idea that the Narcotics Bureau would excuse his saving up morphine which was left with him by some of his clients was at first Adult-ego syntonic, but it was not difficult to confront him with his own legal knowledge when he tried to rationalize this. He also tried to defend his taking an occasional shot of it by giving examples of how strong-minded he was; this meant to him that there was little danger of his getting hooked. Again, from his practice he could see how great the odds were against him, when he was confronted with this in a timely and tactful fashion.

The decontamination process is illustrated in Figure 13. Figure 13A represents his initial state in regard to morphine, in which certain archaic ideas which really belong to the Child are included within the Adult-ego boundary and are therefore rationalized and perceived as Adult. Figure 13B represents the situation after de-

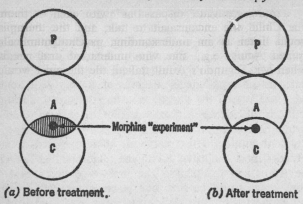

(a) Before treatment.   *(b)* After treatment

FIGURE 13

contamination, in which the blurred area no longer exists. This means that the ideas about morphine are now Adult-ego dystonic, instead of being both Child and Adult-ego syntonic. The decontamination proper stops at this point. Once his Adult understands the situation clearly, he is left to make his own decision as best he can as to whether or not he will save and take morphine. The net therapeutic gain is only that if he decides to do either, he must do it knowing that his position is rationally untenable. He may continue to try to fool authorities, but he can no longer continue to fool himself. This makes it a little harder for him to go ahead, but more important perhaps is that it prepares him for subsequent phases. (Transactionally, his pseudo-stupidity was part of a game, but this aspect was purposefully disregarded, as with all latent psychotics, during the initial structural phase of treatment.)

After as many areas as possible had been decontaminated, Mr. Segundo's Adult was able to appraise much more clearly many of the things he did. The next phase was to clarify and strengthen the boundary between the Adult and the Child. In his case, this was approached by holding separate "discussions" with each of them. The Child was encouraged to talk, and the therapist would listen as an understanding, psychodynamically trained Adult: e.g., one who understood oral needs. When Mr. Segundo's Adult talked, the therapist would listen as an experienced observer of society: e.g., one who understood the narcotics laws. Any crossed transactions which occurred were analyzed within a short time.

For example, the therapist asked the Child: "How do you feel about telling me all this?" The patient answered: "I feel like telling you to go away and not bother me." Then he added quickly: "I don't really mean that!" The therapist asked who had said the latter, and the patient answered: "Both of us!" meaning both the Adult and the Child. The therapist now asked the Adult if he really believed that the therapist would desert him because the Child, in effect, had said "Don't bother me!" Of course he did not "really" believe it. He only believed it when there was a momentary re-contamination of the Adult by the Child, who was panic-stricken by his own boldness and suddenly saw the therapist wrongly as a disapproving Parent instead of as an objective Adult. The patient's Adult–Child boundary could not resist the sudden surge of anxiety and gave way for a brief instant. The ensuing discussion helped to strengthen the still weak boundary. The situation may be clarified by reference to Figures 14, A, B, and C. There was no need to draw this for the patient, since by this time he was quite accustomed to this sort of analysis and could do it in his head quite adequately.

Actionism is an essential feature of structural analysis. The Adult is regarded in much the same light as a muscle, which increases in strength with exercise. Once the preliminary phases of decontamination and clarification are well under way, the patient is expected to

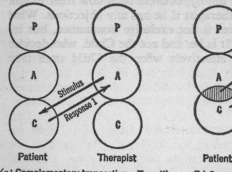

Patient   Therapist

(a) Complementary transaction —Type III
   S. "How do you feel about it?"
   R1. "Don't bother me."

Patient   Therapist

(b) Crossed transaction —Type II
   S. "How do you feel about it?"
   R2. "I don't really mean
      'don't bother me'."

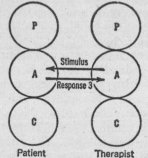

Patient   Therapist

(c) Complementary transaction Type I
   S. "Do you really think I'll desert you?"
   R3. "No."

FIGURE 14

practice Adult control. He must learn to keep the Adult running the show for relatively long periods. The Child is apt to co-operate to a certain extent for three reasons: first, because of the reality gains, which he learns to appreciate, secondly, because he is allowed to have his day under appropriate or less destructive circumstances; and thirdly, because he is now freer to talk it over with the therapist if he has any objections. What the Adult acquires is not exclusive dominance, but increasing *option*. It is he, and not the Child, who decides more and more effectively when the Child shall take over.

In this connection, the Adult and Child are not required to meet Parental demands from the therapist, but only to fulfill the voluntary commitments of the Adult himself. The therapist is not trying to make the patient stop acting out; that is not his business, that is a Parental matter, something for a clergyman or the patient's mother to deal with. He is interested in whether the patient can keep his own Adult commitment: to circumscribe his acting out within economically possible limits; and he tries to help the patient do so by means of his professional techniques. That is an Adult matter; the patient's Adult and the therapist's Adult have agreed to work together on this, without "togetherness" or sentimental "working with" each other; perhaps even better, with dignified "apartness." Both of them are aware that the therapist is a therapist and not a personal manager nor a kindergarten teacher. This objectivity is necessary if the chief barrier is to be eliminated, and that is the game of "Wooden Leg." ("What do you expect of a man with a wooden leg? What do you expect of a neurotic?" Mr. Segundo was particularly apt to play this game because one of his professional duties was to help his clients play it with pleas of insanity when indicated.) The patient has to be reminded if necessary that he is not "a neurotic," but a person with a confused Child on one hand, and a well-formed, if awkward and weakly-cathected Adult on the other, and that his purpose at this stage is to strengthen that Adult and increase its skill by repeated exercises.

It is these exercises which strengthen the now clarified boundary between the Adult and the Child. In Mr.

Segundo's case, they were at first devoted to small, relatively easy matters. He was soon so successful that he was able to postpone the intense and potentially ruinous activities of his Child until they could be indulged in under relatively harmless conditions. His professional and social life during the week was cleaned up; the Child had his day every second week-end or so, when Mr. Segundo would retire to his mountain cabin for "fishing." Thus the Child was tamed, but not frustrated, insulted, or abused, while the Adult was strengthened by his progressively improving reality experiences: more working hours, increased efficiency, more work satisfaction, more cases won, less embarrassment, better social and family life, and reduced rational fear of ruin. Simultaneously, the Child was threatened less and less often by lost cases and other unfortunate occurrences, and he, too, seemed to learn from reality, exerting less and less pressure on the Adult. Just as in an actual situation between a grown-up and a child, when the grown-up can demonstrate that he is able to take care of things better if he is left alone to do it in his own way, the relationship between them becomes better defined and perhaps more distant, but it is improved.

At this point, the goal of structural analysis had been attained. There were now three courses open to the patient, at his option: to terminate treatment, to go on to transactional analysis in a therapy group, or to undertake psychoanalysis. He elected the first. He stayed away for two years, during which he got along well in an increasingly complex situation. He took a law partner and had another child. His indulgences grew less frequent, but their occasional necessity began to trouble him more and more, so that eventually he returned for psychoanalytic treatment. The genetic resolution of the oral conflicts required that the Child speak freely to the Adult and to the therapist, and this sort of communication had already been established. Thus, his previous structural analysis stood him in good stead.

The practical aspect is that the treatment outlined averted the impending ruin which might very well have overtaken the patient during the preliminary phases of orthodox psychoanalysis, if that had been the initial procedure. As it was, the psychoanalytic phase was a luxury rather than a necessity, as the indications were that the patient could have gone on indefinitely living a relatively happy life on the fruits of structural analysis alone.

The therapy of latent psychoses therefore has two aims. The pragmatic cure consists in stabilizing the dominance of the Adult so that exhibitions of the Child take place only in controlled situations. They may consist, for example, of turning a schizoid or borderline personality into a "week-end schizophrenic," to put the worst light on it. The cure in the psychoanalytic sense consists of deconfusing the Child and resolving its internal conflicts and its conflicts with the Adult and the Parent.

The statistical diagnosis of Mr. Segundo's case does not influence the therapeutic approach, which is based solely on structural considerations. It was therapeutically irrelevant whether he was diagnosed as an ambulatory schizophrenic, a border-line schizophrenic, a latent suicidal depressive, an impulsive neurotic, an addict, or a psychopath. The relevant consideration was the structural diagnosis: a weakly cathected and poorly organized, and therefore more or less ineffectual Parent; an Adult with poorly defined boundaries and slightly weakened cathexis, so that contamination and decommission both occurred with facility; and a Child with defective binding capacity.

This diagnosis clarified the therapeutic indications. It was too late to do anything significant about the exteropsyche. The Adult could be strengthened by boundary work, and the Child's relative binding capacity could be ultimately increased by deconfusion and the resolution of infantile conflicts. The optimal prognosis was also clear; since there was no hope of acquiring an adequate Parent, the Adult would have always to cope with the Child without much exteropsychic help. Thus the equilibrium would always be more precarious than in more fortunate individuals whose fathers had made it their business not to die before their sons reached adolescence. Mr. Segundo was fully aware of this difficulty and knew that he would always be more or less on his own, not only in the existential but also in the psychological sense. This knowledge was an added and valuable incentive in his particular case for him to strengthen his Adult.

The position was different in the case of Mr. Disset, who came in because he could not find employment in his field. He felt that prospective employers became prejudiced against him because he was honest and recorded his hospital history on his application forms. He wanted the psychiatrist to do something about it, such as interceding with the employers. Mr. Disset presented typical stigmata of an ambulatory schizophrenic: cold, moist, bluish extremities, downcast eyes, slouching gait and carriage, mumbling speech, fumbling gestures, preoccupation, and startled reaction when he was spoken to. His unemployability was evident on inspection, and the most inexperienced and charitable employer might be kind but not accommodating to such an individual. The psychiatrist listened compliantly for two visits, but on the third explained frankly his view of the situation, not so much with the idea of convincing the patient, as in order to keep the record and his conscience clear. Evidently the patient needed something the psychiatrist had to offer, because he elected to continue treatment even though he said he disagreed with the formulation and made at least a pretense of maintaining his original stand that the problem was purely administrative.

Mr. Disset was introduced to a special kind of group in which the therapist adopted a Parental, rather than an Adult attitude. By various opportunistic procedures, such as intercession with the Veterans Administration when he was sure of success, the therapist tried to make up for the neglect Mr. Disset had experienced at the hands of his actual parents; he also opposed the derogatory attitude of the inner Parent and the actual parents. By doing all this with due regard for the unknown possibilities of masochism, guilt-load, and rebellious rage, and by demonstrating that he was strong enough to prevent the inner Parent and the patient's actual father from getting revenge when the patient was away from the therapy situation, he succeeded in gaining the confidence of the Child. That is, the therapist was able to demonstrate that he was a more powerful and more benevolent parent than Mr. Disset, Sr. As the Child's anxiety subsided, the Adult became relatively stronger until tentative overtures could be made to this aspect of the patient's personality.

At this point, the fact that Mr. Disset simply did not look employable was more firmly broached and the process of decontamination was cautiously begun. Essentially, he had to understand that it was not a question of changing the public attitude toward state hospitalization but of changing his own way of eliciting responses from people. The group was an excellent situation for investigating and experimenting with the latter. The other members were both frank and sympathetic, and just hard-boiled enough to be helpful without being threatening. In addition it was an opportunity for them to learn to distinguish between being helpful in an Adult way and being threatening in a Parental way. They were all in it at the same time and they could all learn at the same time, especially the hyperparental Mr. Troy. Again, at an appropriate phase, Mr. Disset was educated to distinguish the reactions of his Parent, his Adult, and his Child, respectively, to what the therapist and others said to him. (Again, games such as "Wooden Leg" and "Why Don't You . . . Yes, But" were purposefully disregarded in this group of unsophisticated latent psychotics.)

Another approach which is sometimes indicated with such patients was used in the case of Miss Hockett. She was put into a group where the therapist functioned analytically as an Adult and withheld Parental interventions. Concurrently, she was seen individually by a social worker who was trained in structural analysis and who functioned as a Parent. In this way she could have the anxieties aroused in the group by game analysis allayed by the social worker, and have the game she played with the social worker in order to arouse sympathy, analyzed by the group. Thus her Child was reassured and taken care of by one individual, while her Adult was being decontaminated and strengthened by another. The therapist and the social worker discussed the case briefly every few months or when an acute problem arose, but since each of them had a rather clear idea of the division of service, neither of them felt a strong need for that frequent rehashing of everything that had taken place which so often tends to disturb the smooth course of co-operative therapy, and which offers the Child such an inviting opportunity to start a three-handed game. By aborting three-handed games and forcing Miss Hockett to play two separate two-handed games, the situation was much easier to control, and her progress was gratifying to herself, to the group, and to her two therapists, as long as she remained in therapy.

It is, unfortunately, difficult to offer more than a few general suggestions as to how to deal with people who are by definition the epitome and individuality. But by applying assiduously and intelligently the principles outlined above, the therapist will continually add to his knowledge of how to approach such problems, and he may eventually decide that there is no such thing as a boring patient, but only bored therapists, and that this boredom can be alleviated by having a well-planned on going therapeutic program with clearly formulated goals, however modest, and adequate instruments for attaining them. There may be boring hours, and even boring weeks, during periods when forbearance is indicated, but there should no longer be boring months or years.

NOTE

Mr. Segundo was not a morphine addict. This aspect of his problem is chosen as an illustration mainly because the reality factors are uncomplicated and almost self-evident.

REFERENCES

1. Lewin, B. *The Psychoanalysis of Elation.* W. W. Norton & Company, New York, 1950.

2. Rosen, J. *Direct Analysis.* Grune & Stratton, New York, 1953.

3. Sechehaye, M. A. *Symbolic Realization.* International Universities Press, New York, 1951.

4. Fromm-Reichmann, F. *Principles of Intensive Psychotherapy.* University of Chicago Press, 1950.

CHAPTER FOURTEEN

Therapy of Neuroses

THERE are four possible goals in the psychotherapy of the neuroses. These may be stated in conventional language as (1) symptomatic control (2) symptomatic relief (3) transference cure (4) psychoanalytic cure. These goals may be restated in structural terms, and the therapeutic processes are illustrated by the following case histories:

1. *Symtomatic and social control* were attained with unusual rapidity by Mrs. Enatosky, a 34-year-old housewife. Her chief complaint was "depressions" of sudden onset, which lasted two or three days and as suddenly disappeared. They were particularly frightening because she did not know how to account for them. They had begun 15 years previously after her mother got sick. At first she had tried to relieve them by drinking, with the ultimate result that she had had several hallucinatory episodes following prolonged binges. She had then joined Alcoholics Anonymous and had not had anything to drink for the past seven years. During this period she had sought treatment and had found a psychiatrist whose prescription was hypnosis, Zen Buddhism, and Yoga exercises. After three or four years, the patient had become so skillful at the latter that she was appointed a *guru* in the local society. At this point she began to have doubts about the desirability of these

forms of treatment, and sought help with Dr. Q at the recommendation of an acquaintance who was a social worker.

She also complained of periodic insecurity about walking, which she described as "walking high." In addition, she was uneasy about difficulties with her 13-year-old son. He was disobedient and she handled this overtly by "principles of mental health" which she had read about, but while she was "mouthing" the things she thought she was supposed to say, "underneath" she wanted to force him to obey and she felt he must sense that; but she thought her husband would approve more if she handled it "sensibly." When the "mouthings" failed, she would feel depressed, after which her son would become more compliant (about studying, for example). She did other things to gain her husband's approval, such as buying the kind of provocative clothes he seemed to admire, and when he was not appreciative she felt sad and rebellious.

Mrs. Enatosky said several things spontaneously in her second interview which made it easy to introduce her to structural analysis. Some of these were probably based on her previous therapeutic experiences and some were intuitive. "Like a little girl I want approval from my husband even though I rebel against what I have to do to get it. I think that's the way I used to feel with my father. When my father and mother separated, I thought: 'I could have kept him.' I was devoted to him." "Some grown-up part of me know I was acting like a little girl." It was suggested that she might let the little girl out more, at least during her interviews, instead of trying to shut her in. This was a new idea to her, since it was contrary to her previous therapist's advice, and it astonished and intrigued her. "It seems brazen. I like children, though. But I know I can't live up to my father's expectations."

Regarding her covert attitude toward her son, she remarked: "It's just the way my mother treated me, she tried to force me."

With these and other spontaneous productions, there was no difficulty in setting up the structural diagram: the mother she acts like; the grown-up part of her; the little girl who wants approval and the little girl who rebels. At the third interview, it was easy to shift into the usual vocabulary, which was more convenient; these instances then represented the Parent, the Adult, the compliant Child, and the rebellious Child, respectively.

When she discussed her walking symptom, Dr. Q remarked: "That's the little girl, too." (Behavioral diagnosis.) She replied: "Oh, for heaven's sake, that's true, a child walks that way. As you said that I could see a little child. You know how they walk and stumble and get up. It's hard to believe, but that makes sense to me. As you say that, I feel I didn't want to walk: a little girl in rompers who would rather crawl or sit. I feel funny now. They pull you up by your right shoulder and you're outraged and want to cry. You know I still have pains in my shoulder. What a terrible feeling! My mother worked when I was very small and I didn't want to go to the day nursery and I wouldn't walk, and they forced me. And yet I do the same to my own son. I disapprove of his disobedience while I'm thinking 'I don't disapprove, I know just how he feels.' It's really my mother disapproving. Is *that* the Parent part? I'm frightened a little by all this."

In this way the reality of Parent, Adult, and Child as actual ego states (phenomenological reality) was established. When she mentioned being frightened, Dr. Q was mindful of her previous exposure to mysticism and hypnosis, which had contaminated her Adult, and he took pains to assure her that there was nothing mysterious in what they were talking about. He emphasized the derivation of Parent, Adult, and Child from her actual experiences in early life (historical reality), and discussed their selective activation by easily understood current events. He then explained how the Adult could maintain control of the child instead of being merely confused by her, and also how the Adult had to mediate between the Parent and the Child to prevent depressions. All this was gone into in considerable detail.

She began the fourth interview by remarking: "This week I've been happy inside for the first time in 15 years. I've tried out what you said, and I can still feel the depression trying to come out and also the funny feeling while I'm walking, but I can handle these things and they no longer bother me even when I know they're there." At this time the games she played with her husband and son were formulated in a preliminary way. With her husband the sequence was: she complies seductively, he reacts with indifference, she is disappointed and depressed, he then tries to make amends. With her son it went: she uses seductive reasoning, he reacts with indifference, she is disappointed and depressed, he then makes amends by tardy compliance. Although it was not pointed out to her at this time, these are both masochistic-sadistic family games in which, as usual, both parties win primary and secondary gains. In the obedience game, for example, one primary internal gain for her son was that he caused his mother distress, and one primary external gain was that he avoided scholastic competition; secondarily, he often managed to win material advantages when he complied. It was explained that in this case it might be worth trying an Adult—Adult approach instead of a Parent—Child approach, good reason instead of sweet reason.

These are some examples of the problems dealt with, and how they were dealt with. Because of her evident aptitude for structural and transactional analysis, she was judged ready to enter a relatively sophisticated therapy group after only five individual interviews.

At her third group meeting, she remarked how comfortable she now felt after being miserable for 15 years. She went on to attribute this to the fact that she was learning to exercise Adult control over her symptoms and relationships. She also related how much better her son was behaving and feeling and how well she was getting along with him. There were several professional people as patients in the group, and one of them asked: "How long have you been coming to Dr. Q?" Dr. Q smiled at this, and Mrs. Enatosky thought he was laughing at her. Dr. Q explained carefully that he was not laughing at her, but was smiling because he knew what the professional people would think when she answered the question. This explanation satisfied her, and she said: "I've been coming a month." The doctor had allowed himself to smile for reasons which concerned the other patients rather than Mrs. Enatosky, and his self-indulgence was successful, since it influenced the expected reaction of scepticism from the patients who were themselves professional psychotherapists, and who were also beginners in structural analysis. It resulted in a more serious curiosity about the possibilities of this procedure.

Very few patients are able to understand and appreciate the principles of symptomatic and social control as rapidly as Mrs. Enatosky did, and her case is selected for its dramatic illustrative value. Since her Child had been heavily traumatized, this was only the beginning of her treatment and there were difficulties to be met later. But the initial phase promoted a high degree of therapeutically valuable hope and understanding and served to establish a satisfactory and workable relationship between the therapist on one hand, and both the Adult and Child of the patient on the other. It also started the process of establishing the therapist in place of the original parents, which was thought desirable in view of the schizoid elements in the Child. Most important, perhaps, was the fact that the patient continued her therapy much more comfortable than she had been originally, and the path was made smoother for her son during a decisive period of his development. Through her ability to exercise social control while her therapy proceeded, life was made happier not only for herself, but also for the other members of her family.

The further reinforcement of symptomatic and social control in this case, and the steps taken to deconfuse Mrs. Enatosky's Child, are described in the Appendix at the end of the book.

2. *Symptomatic relief* was obtained through structural analysis by Mrs. Eikos, a 30-year-old housewife who had been to many specialists over a period of years for treatment of pains which were repeatedly suspected of being based on organic changes. It was only when everything else failed that she had come to a psychiatrist. It was apparent from the beginning that the initial phase would be the critical one, since her marriage was being precariously maintained only by overlooking certain obvious defects in her husband's behavior.

The structural analysis of this situation was as follows. Her husband's neurotic behavior was highly attractive to Mrs. Eikos's Child, since it yielded her large primary and secondary gains. From an Adult point of view, however, it was outrageous. But by contamination the Child kept the Adult from protesting; she offered all sorts of pseudological excuses and explanations for what he did. Decontamination might be a threat to her marriage because an autonomous Adult might not long tolerate his behavior if it continued unchanged. Also, if she stopped playing the game which constituted one of their chief marital bonds, her Child would feel the deprivation keenly as despair. These dangers were formulated to her on three different occasions, each time in terms which were currently intelligible to her. Each time she reasserted her determination to proceed with the therapy. These tests of motivation not only clarified the responsibilities of the therapist and of the patient, respectively, but also initiated the strengthening of the Adult by making the decision hers on the basis of a realistic appraisal of the treatment situation. The transference aspects of this procedure, that is, the Child's reactions to the therapist's formulations, were segregated to be dealt with at an appropriate time. As she became able to feel and express the autonomous Adult anger and disappointment at her husband's behavior, the pains gradually disappeared.

This symptomatic relief was not the result of banal blind expression of indignation, based on the pious axiom "Expressing hostility is Good," but was carefully planned. The patient's own Adult was able to appreciate the precision and usefulness of the preparatory steps. Besides being grateful for the therapeutic effect, she was also in a position to understand its three principal structural aspects. First, the fact that the disappointment and resentment came out into the open signified that her Adult was now to some extent decontaminated, and she was able to test and exercise her newly found autonomy in other situations. Secondly, now that her Adult was available as a therapeutic ally, the treatment could proceed at a different level. The first hurdle was safely passed, and her marriage survived. She could see that she was actually in a better position than before to ensure its permanence on an improved foundation, if she wanted to, and this gave her new courage. Thirdly, the resentment was itself suspect, since there were in it some elements of child-like ambivalence, and since she had selected Mr. Eikos to be her husband from among several candidates, and since it was apparent at this point that her Child had covertly encouraged his behavior. For all these reasons her expression of "hostility" was not simply accepted as "good," but was viewed critically by both the therapist and the patient.

At this point her Child, deprived of some of the gains she had formerly obtained in her marriage, began to turn her attention to the therapist. She tried to manipulate him as she had previously successfully manipulated several parental figures, including some friends of her father's and an earlier therapist. The analysis of this game disconcerted her, and her productions became less genteel. It was then possible to analyze some of the family games of her childhood, as well as more of her current marital games. As her Child began to experience more and more unbound cathexis, her script came into view and her hours became increasingly stormy. Meanwhile the Adult grew stronger and stronger in her outside activities, while at times it was almost completely decommissioned during her therapeutic sessions. Since she no longer played the marital games, her husband's Child became confused, anxious, and depressed, and he also sought treatment (with another therapist).

Eventually she began to carry on her life with more energy, satisfaction, and equanimity, to the benefit of their three children as well as herself. She was able to discontinue treatment under the following conditions. Changes in ego state were accompanied by tonic and postural changes in her intimate and skeletal musculature. In her Adult ego state she was now symptom-free. If her Child took over, the symptoms recurred, though less severely. By exerting social control and Adult option over incipient games in her family and social life, she was able to abort the dominance of her Child. In this way she could extend almost voluntary control over the occurrence of symptoms. As a kind of bonus, her marriage was, and still is, much improved, in the opinion of everyone concerned.

In this case, symptomatic relief preceded symptomatic control. The partial resolution of her script by deconfusing the Child to some extent, permanently allieviated the severity of some of the symptoms, leaving the remainder subject to Adult option.

Sometimes, symptomatic relief can be offered in another way by teaching the patient to play his game better. In fact the principal motivation that brings the Child of the neurotic to the psychiatrist's office is usually just that: the Child wants the therapist to teach him to play his game more successfully. Thus, if the motivations for seeking therapy are analyzed structurally, they generally line up something like this: Parental—one is supposed to be well, to support one's children, to do the housework, etc.; Adult—one would be happier and more efficient if the Child could be kept under control or have its conflicts resolved, or if the Parental influence could be tempered; Child—one would be happier if one could play one's game better, that is, derive more primary and secondary gains from archaic transactions with other people. A variant of the last is the hope that the therapist will be willing to play when no one else is, and thus give the Child some degree of satisfaction. One witty patient expressed the difference between the Child and Adult motivations for coming to therapy by asking another patient: "Did you come for a treat or a treatment?" This has been expressed in another form in the familiar epigram: "The neurotic comes for treatment in order to learn how to be a better neurotic."

Marital counseling is a common form of offering symptomatic relief by coaching. What sounds like teaching about abstractions such as "marriage" or "human nature" is often actually coaching in how to get more satisfaction out of specific marital games such as

"Frigid Woman," "Budget," or "Mental Health for Children."

Mr. Protus was an example of successful symptomatic relief by coaching. He was in the pyjama game, as he expressed it, and wanted to make a killing. But his social anxiety manifested itself symptomatically during his sales work and impaired his efficiency. He came for treatment for the express purpose of making more money. For various reasons, this goal was accepted by the therapist. Over a long period symptomatic and social control was established so that Mr. Protus could play the sales game better. This was accomplished by laying bare the Child's anger which underlay the businesslike metaphor "making a killing." His inefficiency, parapraxes, and symptomatic outbreaks during his daily work were partly derived from a highly charged Parental conflict (father vs mother) about violence, so that his Child always avoided actually making the killing. Soon the Adult became aware of what it was he had to control, and he succeeded in doing this during working hours. In addition, analysis of the sales game as played in his business made him bolder and more skillful in dealing with the Child in his customers, and in maintaining his Adult against their attempts to manipulate his Child. As a result, he did not make a killing, but he did begin to make more money. Since his Child's rage was never analyzed, however, he still remained an "evening and week-end neurotic." But the original limited goal was attained, and those of his symptoms which were due to his not being able to get sufficient satisfaction for his Child because he played his game badly, were diminished.

In order to permit a fair appraisal of this technique, it should be said that this account represents a synthesis of two similar case histories. Mr. Protus$_1$, who came to treatment specifically to increase his earning power, would never admit that therapy had anything to do with augmenting his income, although the fellow-members of his therapy group were convinced that it did. Mr. Protus$_2$, who came for more conventional reasons and increased his income as a by-product of game analysis, freely gave credit to the treatment for his improved handling of his business contacts. The elations, depressions, compulsions, and impulsions of gamblers are particularly amenable to treatment through game analysis. The card player who learns to deal better with the Child in others, to resist manipulation of his own Child, and not to give way to impulsive temptations, has an advantage at the table. In particular, the innumerable cunning devices contrived by professionals to weaken the Adult and appeal to the Child, lose their effectiveness. The result is more successful, symptom-free gambling through game analysis. This is of some technical interest because the therapeutic effects are not esoteric and can be measured by simple arithmetic.

3. *Transference cure* in structural terms means the substitution of the therapist for the original parent, and in transactional terms signifies that the therapist either permits the patient to resume with him a game that was broken off in childhood by the untimely death or departure of the original parent, or else offers to play the game in a more benign form than the original parent did or does.

Mrs. Sachs, the migrainous woman with the labile cathexis mentioned in Chapter 4, was treated for some time according to these principles. The active transference was based on the fact that her parents, and especially her mother, treated her like dirt during her early years. It was their policy to shame her unmercifully from an early age whenever she wet or soiled herself. One of her most poignant memories concerned a beloved uncle who picked her up to hug and hold her one day, and after she wet herself continued to hold her nevertheless; whereupon her mother remarked: "How

can you hold her when she's in that filthy condition?"
After she reported this, the treatment situation became
clearer. The therapist had only to respond decently
when she related things that seemed shameful to her.
He had to pass many tests in this respect. After a while
it was evident that she was verbally "urinating" and
later "defecating" on him to see whether he would
"push her away" as her mother had done, or "hold on
nevertheless" as her uncle had. As long as the therapist
responded appropriately things went smoothly for her.
Later, when he began to interpret, difficulties recurred.
Even the most carefully worded intervention served to
switch the situation from the uncle–niece game to the
mother–daughter game in her mind. The first was a
permissive game of testing, the second one of provocation and counter-provocation.

In this case, the transference cure occurred when she
was convinced that the therapist would play the role of
the uncle, one of her original parental figures. Even
when she perceived him as a mother, the Child found it
more convenient and less threatening to play the
mother–daughter game with the therapist than with
her husband, so that although the treatment then became stormy, things still went better on the outside.
(The father did not enter the situation actively here.)
The therapist permitted her on one hand to resume the
game that was broken off by her uncle's death, and on
the other to continue the mother–daughter game in a
more benign form. In both cases the Child obtained
sufficient satisfaction to feel some relief, and indeed,
had more freedom from Parental prohibitions than she
had had in the original situations.

A female patient neatly represented her transference
cure in the following dream: "While I was taking a
bath, you took away my clothes and all you left me
was a bathrobe. But somehow it felt better." She de-
coded this dream as follows: "You have taken away all

my fancy games in this treatment, but what you have given me instead is better." By this she meant that the therapist was more benevolent than her own parents. The bathrobe, of course, represents the remaining game, the one she is playing with the therapist.

4. *Psychoanalytic cure* in structural terms means de-confusion of the Child with a largely decontaminated Adult as a therapeutic ally. The therapy may be regarded as a kind of battle involving four personalities: the Parent, Adult, and Child of the patient, with the therapist functioning as an auxiliary Adult. In practice, this conception has a simple but important, even decisive, prognostic significance. As in any battle, numbers are critical. If the therapist is alone, dealing with an *entente cordiale* of all three aspects of the patient, the chances are three to one against success. This is often the case with psychopaths in psychoanalysis. If the patient's Adult can be decontaminated by preliminary structural analysis and enlisted as a therapeutic ally, then it is two Adults against a Parent and a Child, and the odds for success are even.

If the therapist can appeal not only to a decontaminated Adult, but also to the patient's Child, then it is three to one against the Parent, with a corresponding outlook for success. With neurotics, generally speaking, the Parent is the prime enemy. Occasionally, with schizophrenics, the optimal line-up is Parent, Adult, and therapist against the Child, in which case the therapist must appeal to the patient's Parent rather than to his Child. From the structural point of view, electroshock therapy seems to be in effect such an appeal, with the result that both the Parent and Adult of the patient are determined to prevent the Child from again getting all three of them into such an unpleasant predicament with the black box. Mr. Troy was an excellent example of this position, which he actively and verbally maintained for more than seven years, severely reprimanding both *ex cathedra* and rationally any exhibition of the Child. The moment of truth came when he began to see the actual children in his environment as individual personalities with their own rights.

Psychoanalysis is based on free association, with its suspension of censorship. This means in the first instance that the Child will speak freely without interference from either the Parent or the Adult. In practice, however, especially at the beginning, the Child may be kept out of the way, and it is often the Parent who speaks freely without interference from the Adult. Hence it may require some technical skill to bring the Child out and sidetrack the Parent. In this situation, however, while the Child is speaking both the Parent and the Adult are listening and are aware of what is going on. This differentiates psychoanalysis from such devices as hypnosis and narcoanalysis, in which the Parent and usually also the Adult are temporarily decommissioned. When the Adult is recommissioned, the therapist tells him what the Child said. This is not as convincing or effective as if the Adult were functioning throughout, and therein lies the superiority of psycho analysis. In hypnosis, the mother and the governess are metaphorically sent out of the room and later the therapist tells them what the Child said. In psychoanalysis, the Child speaks in their presence and they hear it first hand. Regression analysis, which will be discussed later, retains this advantage, while at the same time appealing more directly to the Child. The recent therapeutic application of the drug LSD–25 appears to hold a similar promise.[1]

The use of structural analysis to decontaminate the Adult as a preparation for psychoanalytic treatment has already been mentioned in the case of Mrs. Eikos; and it is apparent how transactional analysis, game analysis, and script analysis were a good foundation for subsequent psychoanalytic work with Mrs. Catters. The unfolding of the script is the substance of the psychoanalytic process. The transference consists not merely of a set of interrelated reactions, a transference neurosis, but of a dynamically progressive transference drama, usually containing all the elements and subdivisions of a Greek tragedy. Thus, as previously mentioned, Oedipus comes to life in script analysis not only as a characteristic personality, but as one moving inexorably toward a pre-ordained destiny.

NOTES

It is apparent that an adequate annotation of this chapter would involve a great deal of the vast literature on psychotherapy. A selected list is given in the Chicago book, *Psychoanalytic Therapy*.[2] Alexander's description of the "corrective emotional experience" clarifies further the case of Mrs. Sachs, and even more aptly, that of Mrs. Eikos.

In structural terms, Alexander's principle is a psychoanalytic one, since its aim is to deconfuse the Child, to get him, in the language of script analysis, to "close the show and put a new one on the road." As Alexander expresses it: "The old pattern was an attempt at adaptation on the part of the child to parental behavior. . . . The analyst's objective, understanding attitude allows the patient . . . to make a new settlement of the old problem. . . . While the patient continues to act according to outdated patterns, the analyst's reaction conforms strictly to the actual therapeutic situation." (Pp. 66 & 67.) Transactionally, this means that when the patient's Child attempts to provoke the therapist's Parent, it is confronted instead by the therapist's Adult. The therapeutic effect arises from the disconcertion caused by this crossed transaction. In terms of game analysis, the patient's Child is brought up short by the therapist's refusal to play. This is well illustrated by the case of Jean Valjean. (Pp. 68–70.)

Fenichel[3] gives a technical discussion of the concept of "transference improvement," with bibliography.

REFERENCES

1. Chandler, A. L. & Hartman, M. S. "Lysergic Acid Diethylamide (LSD-25) as a Facilitating Agent in Psychotherapy." *Loc. cit.*

2. Alexander, Franz, & French, T. M. *Psychoanalytic Therapy*. Ronald Press Company, New York, 1946.

3. Fenichel, O. *Loc. cit.*, p. 559 ff.

CHAPTER FIFTEEN

Group Therapy

1 OBJECTIVES

TRANSACTIONAL analysis is offered as a method of group therapy because it is a rational, indigenous approach derived from the group situation itself. It relies neither on the concept of "The Group" as a metaphysical entity or entelechy, nor on the opportunistic use of techniques not primarily designed for the group situation.

The objective of transactional analysis in group therapy is to carry each patient through the progressive stages of structural analysis, transactional analysis proper, game analysis, and script analysis, until he attains social control. The attainment of this goal can be validated by observing changes not only in his own responses, but in resultant, independently observed changes in the behavior of intimates who have not been exposed to psychotherapy, as in the cases of Mrs. Enatosky's son and Mrs. Dodakiss's husband. It can also be tested and exercised through his mastery of his responses to everyday manipulative attempts on the part of others, as in shopping situations and in the business transactions illustrated by Mr. Protus. The assumption is made, usually correctly, that the resulting improved social experiences will lead to a diminution of archaic distortions and anxieties, with some relief of symptoms which is predictable, controllable, and intelligible to the patient as well as to the therapist. In more intensive therapeutic situations, it is also a useful preparation for and concomitant of psychoanalytic therapy.

2 METHODS

At nearly all stages it is possible, appropriate, and apparently desirable, for the patient to be aware of what he has accomplished, what he is trying to accomplish, and when his education is sufficiently advanced, what he hopes to accomplish in the future. Thus, there is at almost every phase a complete understanding between the patient and the therapist regarding the therapeutic situation. The patient is as well informed concerning the specific factors at issue as a student therapist is at a corresponding stage of learning, and experience shows that he is able to comprehend them even when he is of very limited "intelligence" (as measured on psychometric scales), since every step is well documented with clinical situations in which he himself has been or is involved.

With patients who begin simultaneously, the whole procedure can be carried out in the group. A late arrival requires some preparation in individual sessions so that he will be able to understand to some extent what is going on in the group when he enters it. Usually a clinical grasp of structural analysis is sufficient initial equipment for a patient entering even a very advanced group. If he has had an opportunity meanwhile to test and engage the therapist, so that he has some confidence in the way his game will be handled, this may help to carry him through the anxiety of his first experiences in the group. If he is overly cautious about engaging the therapist because of past traumata, his entry into the group may be profitably postponed until he has overcome his initial inhibitions.

Once he is in the group, he becomes subject, with

due prudence on the part of the therapist, to the various analytic procedures whose technique has been described in previous chapters. Concurrently, the therapist may opportunistically employ borrowed techniques, such as psychoanalytic interpretations and maneuvers, in the customary fashion. Thus transactional analysis is not intended to replace psychodynamic[1] group therapy, but offers a primary matrix within which other therapeutic operations can find their place according to the therapist's personal inclinations. It is not an exclusive substitute for, but a powerful addition to, the usual psychotherapeutic arsenal.

3 STARTING A GROUP

This and the following section on the selection of patients are empirical, and the material is based on repeated and extensive discussions concerning a large variety of groups with many different group therapists from different types of therapeutic facilities. These ideas have been most critically argued at the San Francisco Social Psychiatry Seminars, and the principles stated represent in most cases the majority consensus there, tested by actual clinical experience.

First, it has been found most profitable for the prospective therapist to spend at least one long session (two hours or more) discussing the projected group before any practical steps have been taken. The following topics have been found to be the most cogent and relevant.

1. The *organizational aspects* of the therapeutic situation are discussed: as the therapist sees them, as the patients are likely to see them from their situation, and as the discussants see them. The "authority" situation is broken down into its elements as completely as possible by drawing an "authority diagram." This starts with the

patients and is carried to its logical conclusion, which may terminate in the President of the United States and ultimately the voters. The putative fantasies of each individual in each echelon, as they pertain to the project, are argued. If the project is being sponsored by an establishment which receives federal funds, for example, the chain might go from patients, their relatives, and their physicians, through the therapist, his supervisor, the agency head, the governing board, the Secretary of Health, Education, and Welfare, and the President of the United States. To each individual in this chain may be attributed a set of assumptions as to what might be "Good" and what might be "Bad" in the therapeutic project. The therapist is consciously or pre-consciously aware of these assumptions, and their possible influence on his behavior is brought out.

Thus it is quite conceivable that something could happen in the therapy group which would disturb any or all of the individuals in this chain, to the extent of causing not only local anxiety, but even a national interest. The Veterans Administration, for example, is particularly susceptible to and continuously aware of such remote influences, each of which constitutes a potential inhibition on therapeutic freedom. Foundations, universities, and other interested official agencies also have to be taken into account in respect to the private plans and interests of the therapist, as well as in regard to the welfare of the parents. Groups in private practice are usually least contaminated by such influences. Since many therapists have known patients in public agencies to write to the Governor of the State or the President of the United States, it is of more than academic interest to carry this type of analysis to its logical conclusion.

2. The *aims* of therapy are discussed. It is often a surprise to the prospective therapist himself to find how difficult it is for him to formulate what he is really trying to do. What is he trying to cure the patients of,

what changes is he attempting to effect in their behavior, and how will he and the patients know when these ends have been accomplished and when they have not? In this connection, ill-defined, pious, or purely conceptual goals are vigorously questioned in an attempt to have them replaced by operational formulations. Curiously enough, psychiatrists, in spite of their medical training, are often just as soft-boiled as non-medical therapists in this connection, and it is sometimes necessary to temper the dull edge of sentimentality in the scorchbellows of criticism.

3. A structural analysis is undertaken of the therapist's own *motivation* and fantasies concerning the proposed group. Initially, he will naturally present his Adult formulation. From these, the Parental elements are then carefully dissected out, with any additions that come to him spontaneously. Finally, any of his Child motivations that he is aware of and cares to discuss are stated. Both autonomous and learned games of the therapist are reviewed, and their possible effects on the prospective patients are discussed. Thus the beginner may have an "advisory" attitude, a tendency to play "Why Don't You . . . Yes, But," and he may have learned to practice psychotherapy according to the rules of Professor K, or group therapy according to the rules of Mr. Y.

4. The *selection* of patients is discussed, with particular attention to autistic, phobic, or snobbish attitudes on the part of the therapist.

It is not easy for a prospective therapist to go through such a rigorous examination of his project with complete insouciance. The situation is softened by the fact that the group is not yet started, so that nothing he says represents a commitment or a *fait accompli*, and everything is open to further consideration. In practice, it is found that most therapists are grateful for such a preliminary survey, and find it helpful when they eventually sit down before the patients.

4 SELECTION OF PATIENTS

The conventional attitude about selection is epitomized in the general form: "Criteria for selection are Good." The word "good" is written with a capital initial because this assumption is implicit and is nearly always taken on faith; it is rarely questioned by unsophisticated therapists. Careful examination of its meaning, however, has resulted in a reversal to the position: "Criteria for selection are hardly ever good." They can usually be reduced to personal prejudices of the therapist, and as such they can be legitimately applied until he gains more confidence, changes his attitude, or learns more; but they are best regarded as symptoms of professional inadequacy.

Since transactional analysis has been adequately tested with groups of neurotics, character disorders, remittent psychotics, borderline cases, sexual psychopaths, married couples, parents of disturbed children, and mental retardates, the formation of groups comprising one of these classes can be undertaken with some confidence. In addition, it has proved effective in groups which included a "random" assortment of the first five categories, without regard to age, severity of symptoms, psychiatric experience, social class, or intelligence; therefore, such a mixed group may also be regarded as a practical undertaking. The method has not yet been sufficiently proved with groups of acute psychotics, alcoholics, narcotics addicts, prisoners, and other more specialized cases, but neither is there any reason for hesitation in attempting it with such patients. (Pilot groups are well established for all of these classes at various public facilities, and it is also being tested with "psychosomatic" patients.)

In general, the behavior of a patient in a group cannot be reliably predicted from his behavior in daily life or in individual interviews. A retarded depressive will not necessarily remain retarded in a group, nor will a deluded paranoid necessarily bring his delusions into the group as an unmanageable, disturbing factor. The only way to settle this in a given case is to try it.

Transactional analysis is a particularly fruitful approach in dealing with two problems which are recurrent topics at scientific meetings and in the literature:

1. The "problem" of the "monopolizer" will be handled with startling competence by a group familiar with game analysis.

2. Silence becomes transformed in such a group from a "problem" to be solved into a phenomenon to be investigated. The question here is not *"Interactio verborum gratia verborum,"* but what *is* "interaction."

The fewer criteria for selection the therapist has, the more likely he is to learn. Such criteria usually mean: "I only want patients who will play games I feel comfortable with or like to play." By inviting "unsuitable" patients into his groups, he may learn about new games. At worst, criteria may be based on mere snobbishness.

The selection of a particular group for a particular patient, however, offers criteria which may be rationally stated in structural terms. With certain remittent schizophrenics, or psychotics following shock treatment, a purely analytic, Adult approach on the part of the therapist may be contraindicated, at least initially. Such patients may be put into a special type of group in which the therapist elects to function primarily as a Parent rather than as an Adult. So far, this is the only rational criterion which has emerged as applicable to transactional groups.

5   THE INITIAL STAGE

Two clinical examples will now be offered, one to illustrate the introductory phase of transactional analysis,
the other to demonstrate the establishment of social
control.

Dr. Q was invited to act as consultant to a state hospital where nearly all of the 1000 or so patients were in
group therapy. A variety of approaches was being used
by different therapists: moralistic, analytic, reminiscent,
"interaction," "supportive," "hot seat," and abreactive.
Most of the patients were sexual psychopaths, and the
object was to rehabilitate them for safe release. One of
Dr. Q's first steps was to sit in at a group meeting
which took place at a convenient hour. There were
about twenty patients in the group, none of whom he
had ever seen before. They had met six times previously, and the meeting was scheduled to last for one
hour. His initial object was merely to become acquainted with the general procedure followed at the hospital,
such as the physical arrangements; to observe the general attitude of the men; and to find out what they
thought about the group therapy program so that he
could see where his services might fit in. A seating diagram is shown in Figure 15.

Dr. Z, the regular therapist, introduced Dr. Q as the
consultant and then unexpectedly abdicated, stating
that since Dr. Q knew more about group therapy than
he did, he would let Dr. Q take charge of the meeting.
Dr. Q then stated that he was there to help with the
group therapy program and might do better if he had
some idea what the men thought about it.

They reacted with great enthusiasm, various members saying that it was the best thing that had ever happened to them, for the first time they knew what living
was, formerly each had lived in a little world apart,
they had thought everyone was against them, or that

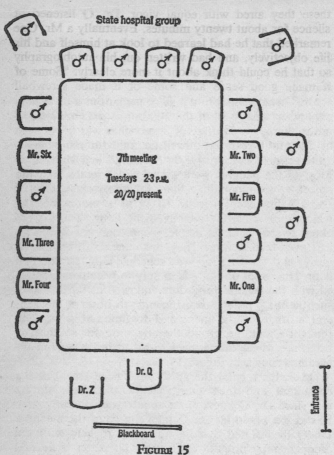

State hospital group

7th meeting
Tuesdays 2-3 P.M.
20/20 present

Mr. Six

Mr. Three

Mr. Four

Mr. Two

Mr. Five

Mr. One

Dr. Q

Dr. Z

Entrance

Blackboard

FIGURE 15

everyone was looking out for himself, whereas now they knew that when you got to know people you could like them and they would accept you; and other such laudatory statements. They also had some complaints against specific group therapists and procedures, and these they aired with equal vigor. Dr. Q listened in silence for about twenty minutes. Eventually a Mr. One remarked that he had learned to look at himself and his life objectively, and had written out his autobiography so that he could think about it more clearly. "Some of it made good sense and some of it made screwball sense," was his summary. The men discussed this in general terms for a few minutes, and then Dr. Q asked Mr. One:

"What did you mean when you said some of it made good sense and some of it made screwball sense?"

"Well," replied Mr. One, "some of it figured straight and some of it figured like you do when you're a kid. I used to disconnect the speedometer from my dad's car when I borrowed it so he wouldn't know. That's kid stuff. That's the way my father used to make me feel, like a kid. Even after I was grown-up."

"I used to feel the same way," said another member, Mr. Two. "Even after I was earning my own living, when I walked into the house and saw my old man sitting there I felt like a kid again."

The men now began to fill the time with a lively round of "Me Too." Several of them described their difficulties in feeling grown-up in the presence of their fathers, who somehow always made them feel like children. With the older men, this was in the form of reminiscence, but with some of the younger ones it was more immediate. The youngest man present, Mr. Three, who was barely 21, made a switch when he said that with him it was his mother, and there were some "Me Too's" for this as well.

Although Dr. Q had not come into the room with any idea of introducing the structural framework, he felt that this was too good an opportunity to be missed. He went to the blackboard and drew three separate circles, as in Figure 16A.

"It seems as though you're telling about three differ-

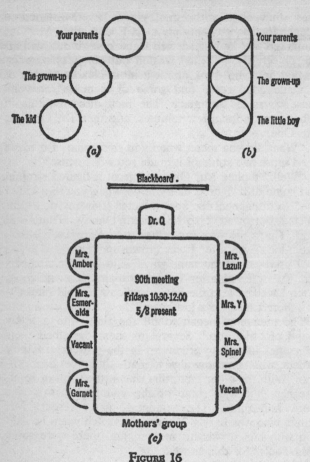

FIGURE 16

ent things here," he ventured. "Just like these circles. One is the kid you feel like at home, one is the grown-up you want to be and are on the outside, and the third is your parents who make you feel like kids."

"That's just about the way it is," agreed Mr. One.

"You've got something there," said Mr. Two. "I remember when I was a kid one time...." He launched into a long, detailed anecdote about his early years. Dr. Q got the impression from the way he talked that he was trying to "dig up significant material," and that this game of "Archaeology" was what the group was accustomed to play under the leadership of Dr. Z, their regular therapist. After listening for a few minutes, he interrupted.

"Since I'm only going to be in this group one time," he explained, "it might be better if we stuck to the subject of how you feel about all this, rather than going into detail."

"The funny thing about it is," said Mr. Four, "that even when you're living your own life as a grown-up, sometimes you act like a kid anyway."

"That's what got us in here in the first place," said Mr. Five.

"One thing about me," said Mr. Six, "even when I'm away from home, I act like I know they want me to."

After some corroboration of these two observations, Dr. Q intervened again.

"It seems to me it's more like this," he pointed out, drawing Figure 16B, the structural diagram, on the blackboard. "It seems as though you carry that little kid around inside of you somewhere even when you're being grown-up, and every once in a while he pops out."

"You may not even know he's there, for years," said Mr. Four with considerable feeling. "And then one day Bingo! You've had it."

"And even when your parents aren't anywhere around," continued Dr. Q, "some of you seem to carry them inside of you too, wherever you go, and that has something to do with the way you act, as one of you already said. So if the big oval is your personality, the top circle could be your mother and father that you carry around with you in your minds, the middle circle could be the grown-up that you want to be and are, and the bottom circle could be the little boy that comes out in you when you go home, or that pops up anyway and may get you into trouble. But, remember, even if he gets you into trouble sometimes, there's lots of good in him that could be brought out, and he's a good kid to have around, so don't call him 'childish' and try to get rid of him. The thing to do is try to understand him, just the way you wanted your parents to try to understand you when you were really that kid."

"That makes good sense," said Mr. Six.

"Well," said Dr. Q, "I guess the time is up now. I think I've found out what I wanted to know. Is there anything you want to tell them, Dr. Z?"

Dr. Z shook his head.

"Thank you all for coming," said Dr. Q, "I hope I see you again."

"Thank *you*, Doctor," said the men as they filed out.

Dr. Z and Dr. Q now repaired to the staff room, where Dr. Q was scheduled to lecture on his approach to group therapy. Dr. Q first asked Dr. Z to tell the staff about the meeting which had just ended. After Dr. Z had given a rough outline, including the men's complaints, Dr. Q asked:

"Would you mind if I fill in some more of the details?"

"Not at all," said Dr. Z.

Dr. Q then recounted more fully what had occurred, much as it has been presented here. When he had finished, he asked Dr. Z:

"Is that a pretty fair account of what actually occurred, or do you think some of it is my fantasy of what happened?"

"It sounds exactly right to me," said Dr. Z.

The first of the anticipated opposition came from Dr. A.

"You must have given them unconscious cues."

"In this case we have Dr. Z as a qualified observer to answer that," said another staff member, Dr. B.

Dr. Z shook his head. "It didn't seem that way to me."

"They certainly handed you what you wanted on a platter," remarked Dr. C, who had read a paper on elementary structural analysis.

"I don't think it was because of unconscious cues," said Dr. Q. "My experience is that if you listen carefully to any patient or group of patients during the first hour or any other hour, you will almost invariably find them bringing up something about two ways of thinking, two states of mind, or two forms of behavior, in one of which they are puzzled, worried, or disapproving concerning the other. This, to my mind, is the most regularly occurring feature of all psychiatric interviews with a large variety of patients and is one of the few things, if not the only thing, that they have in common. Furthermore, the patients themselves will nearly always in some terms or other refer to one of these systems as being child-like, usually with implied disapproval.

"In any case, there's no need to argue about whether I did or didn't give them unconscious cues. It's all right with me if I did. The point is that if I gave them unconscious cues, so do other therapists. In my language, every therapist, whether he knows it or not, teaches his patients how he wants them to play group therapy. The problem is then whether one way of playing it is better than another, and I think that my way gives the best results so far, and not only for me. One thing I did do was hedge them in a little when they wanted to play it the way they're accustomed to do with Dr. Z, by talking in some detail about childhood incidents. In that case I told them explicitly what not to do, but I told them very little about what *to* do. They just did what came naturally."

Curiously enough, whenever Dr. Q sat in on a fresh group in this hospital, as elsewhere, such words as "childish," "immature," "playing around," and "playing games" occurred regularly more than once during the proceedings.

6   SOCIAL CONTROL

The next example illustrates the establishment of social control, particularly in regard to "family games." It is an account of the ninetieth meeting of a group of mothers of disturbed children. The group had been started 21 months previously, when the intake social worker of the Children's Section of the Psychiatric Out-Patient Clinic of a large metropolitan hospital selected eight mothers who she felt would benefit from group psychotherapy. This worker was psychoanalytically oriented, and had little or no acquaintance with transactional analysis, which in any case was still at that time in an embryonic state; nor was she experienced in group therapy. No criteria for selection were offered to her, and the therapist accepted without objection or preliminary interviews whichever patients she chose to send. During the life of the group, a succession of trainees in group therapy, comprising four senior social workers, one social psychologist, and one practicing psychiatrist, sat in as observers. The group met regularly around a table, and a blackboard was freely used when indicated.

The therapeutic plan was built around the following phases: structural analysis, transactional analysis, game analysis, social control. This ninetieth meeting included four patients who had been with the group since its inception, and one who had started fifteen months later. Briefly:

1. Mrs. Esmeralda, aged 30, had had some previous

interviews with a psychoanalytic social worker, but had no individual therapy after she entered the group.

2. Mrs. Garnet, aged 40, was in individual treatment with another therapist during the whole period.

3. Mrs. Lazuli, aged 45, the same.

4. Mrs. Spinel, aged 35, had had no previous treatment.

5. Mrs. Amber, the late comer, aged 40, the same.

All five lived with their husbands. Their children suffered from a variety of behavior disorders, such as belligerence, isolation, and destructiveness, with symptoms such as insomnia, phobias, and in the Amber case, asthma. Throughout the whole course of the treatment, none of the patients was seen individually by the group therapist, nor did any of them request individual interviews, although nothing was said by way of interdiction.

As might be expected, the first few weeks were occupied in playing "PTA." Once the women had grasped the principles of transactional analysis, however, they understood the wastefulness of playing pastimes and concentrated on analyzing the transactions which took place in the group. When something outstanding occurred at home which one of them felt a need to bring up in the group, they also treated this transactionally, and spent little time playing "Why Don't You . . . Yes, But," something they had all been addicted to in the beginning. That is, instead of making redundant suggestions when someone brought up a personal problem, they preferred to analyze the structural origins and motivations of the stimuli and responses involved in the incident.

The seating diagram for this meeting is shown in Figure 16C. The original account was dictated by the therapist after discussion with and in the presence of the observer, immediately following the meeting. The present version has been condensed and trimmed of irrelevant matter in order to clarify the points which are being demonstrated. According to the observer, it represents fairly what happened and has not been influenced in any detectable way by distortions on the part of the therapist. The group has now proceeded to a more advanced phase, but because this particular meeting marked the attainment of the more modest goals, the therapist was more active than usual on this occasion.

Present, clockwise: Lazuli, Mrs. Y (observer), Spinel, Garnet, Esmeralda, Amber, Dr. Q (therapist).

Esmeralda: Something that's been bothering me since Friday. I bought a table, and when I got home I wasn't satisfied. I thought with what I've learned here I should have been able to buy what I wanted to buy instead of what the salesman wanted to sell me. The Adult knew what she wanted but the Child just couldn't resist the salesman.

Q: That's the salesman's job. He's a professional at by-passing the Adult and appealing to the Child in the customer. If he weren't good at it he wouldn't hold his job very long. If he is good, he learns every method to get the Child to do what he wants.

Lazuli: I'm ashamed not to buy something after wasting their time.

Q: Well, that weakness of your Child is one of the things that other people can use to their advantage, as you know already. You people have learned a lot here, and you're just going to have to use your knowledge more on the outside, and shopping is a good place to start. Nobody in this group should be sold anything; you should all be able to buy what you want to buy. You're going to have to keep the Adult in control and realize that the salesman is a trained professional trying to get to your Child. But you also have to know your own limitations. If you know that your Adult can hold out against a salesman for only ten minutes, then at the end of ten minutes, if you haven't made your mind up, you should walk right out of the store rather than run the risk of letting your Child take over. You can always go back later. If you do it that way, you might end up getting back your financial investment in your treatment, which is a pretty good way to tell that it's really working. But the main point is, you have to use your knowledge more. Just talking about it isn't enough, and I think you're all ready to go ahead now.

Esmeralda (initially a shy, confused woman who rarely spoke in the group): My daughter Bea is getting depressed, and I think I know what it is because last week she said to me: "Mommy, Brenda and I notice that you and daddy aren't fighting any more and we think there's something wrong." I think that since I've changed my game my husband and I don't play "Uproar" any more. The children expect us to, and when we don't they're disappointed. I've got to help her do something about it.

Q: You mean that her script calls for two quarreling parents?

Esmeralda: Yes, it wasn't a very constructive script, but it was a comfortable one for her with no surprises, and now that it's gone she doesn't know what to do.

Q: Just as we've noticed here, when someone's script is disrupted she feels confused and depressed and maybe a little angry.

Esmeralda: Yes, I think that's what it is, and I think I can help somehow to find her a more constructive script.

Lazuli: You know I noticed that I have to fight with my son and then complain to my husband about it, or else fight with my husband and complain to my son about it. That's what I have to do after a while when everything has been going well.

Q: Maybe some day we'll find out why your Child

has to make trouble when things are going well. In the meantime, what you're describing is a switchable script in which there are three parts: the one who is "it," the one she fights with, and the one she complains to. The one she fights with and the one she complains to are switchable. I think maybe the third part is switchable too. Maybe Mrs. Lazuli sometimes plays one of the other parts, instead of being "it." Maybe she plays the one who is complained to, or the one who complained about. In other words, maybe this is a script for the whole family, and any of them can play any of the parts, and that's what an important part of their family life consists of. I think Mrs. Lazuli should watch to see if that's what's going on.

Amber: I have something to tell you today. I like to fight too. That's why I fight with my daughter.

Q: (laughing): I'm glad that you finally admit that you like to fight.

Amber: I have to fight with somebody to keep interested.

Q: Something like Mrs. Lazuli?

Up to this time, Mrs. Amber had confined her activity in the group entirely to disputation, and subsequently defending herself against the group's accusations that she was disputatious. She had been particularly vehement in defending the exclusively allergic origin of her daughter's asthma. At this point, by tactful handling and careful questioning, the course of her "fights" with her daughter was elicited, and was set up for Mrs. Amber and the group as her daughter's script, analyzed as follows:

First the child becomes hyperactive. This annoys the mother, who scolds her. When the mother is sufficiently annoyed, the child goes into an asthmatic attack. This makes the mother even more angry. After this, the mother becomes upset at herself, remorseful, and apologizes to the child. This is the end of the script, after which the attack takes its normal course toward recovery.

Q: There are several points here where Mrs. Amber could experiment to test whether this is really a script. If she does not follow her daughter's script, the daughter should become anxious, if it is really a script, and this is the best way to find out. For example, what would happen to the daughter if Mrs. Amber didn't get angry at her hyperactivity, but handled it some other way?

Amber: In other words, I should overlook it.

Esmeralda: That's not what he means. He means don't do what her script calls for.

Q: Exactly. You can overlook it, or go along with it, or encourage it, whatever suits you best, as long as it isn't what she expects. Another point where you can experiment is not to get angry when she gets asthma, and a third point is not to feel regretful if you get angry, or at least not to let her see or know that you're regretful. If this is a script and you disrupt it, then she will either become depressed because she can't go on with it, or she'll try harder by getting more hyperactive or worse asthma, or best of all, she may simply bring herself up short and think about it, and then you'd really be getting somewhere.

Esmeralda: But it's no use doing it once, you have to do it differently again and again until she gets the idea that you aren't going to play it her way.

Spinel: I don't play my son's game any more, and it works, too. He came in the other day and said: "I'm going to play Dalton, the outlaw," and put on his guns and a handkerchief over his face. Instead of making an uproar the way I used to, I just ignored it, and finally he threw the handkerchief down and went out.

Q: This is a very nice example of how a game works. The Adult of Mrs. Spinel's boy says: "I'm going to play Dalton," but what his Child really wants to play is "Uproar." When she won't play "Uproar," he gives up the other game as well.

(This was, transactionally speaking, quite a different Mrs. Spinel from the one who for a whole year had insisted desperately on demanding advice as to how to handle her "delinquent" son.)

Q: Mrs. Garnet, you haven't said much to-day.

Garnet: My husband is just like a child, and up to now I've been playing along with it.

Q: Maybe more than that. Maybe sometimes you even provoke him into it. You must, if that's what the game is between you and him. If you and he are playing "House," you must need to as badly as he does.

Garnet: I always broke his soft-boiled eggs into a cup, but then I decided to stop playing mother to him and didn't break them for him and he got very upset, and that made me angry. That's the first time I've realized that it made me angry to go along with him. Now I'm refusing more and more to play mother to him and he gets more and more upset, and I get angrier each time.

Spinel: You seem to have discovered something too.

Q: But we'd better think about it. If his script is disrupted it will be depressing to him, and he may want to leave, unless he has somewhere to turn. Maybe you shouldn't push it too far.

Garnet: Well, he has somewhere to turn because he used to come to the clinic for treatment, and he knows he can always come back.

Q: Then he has an out other than leaving, so it will probably be pretty safe for you to refuse to play along. You know, this session is particularly interesting to me and that's why I'm doing more talking than usual. You've now all learned exactly what I set out to show you. You know something about the Parent, Adult, and Child in each of you, and can tell them apart, and you can see some of the games you play at home: the same games you've been watching yourselves play in the group here. And as Mrs. Esmeralda has shown us to-day, the whole family is involved in these games, and if one person stops playing that throws all the others off, including the children. So now for the first time there's some profit in talking about your children, because now we know what we're talking about, what the real questions are and how we can talk about them in a way that gives some understanding. As you can see, it's quite different from the way you talked about them at the beginning. You may remember when I was away a few months ago and you met without me; at that session you went back to playing "PTA" to fill in the time, and you decided yourselves it was a waste of time.

Spinel: You know, now I think my husband might be willing to come to the clinic too. Would that be possible?

Q: You mean to turn this into a marital group, with husbands and wives sitting in together?

Lazuli: My husband might come too, if it's possible.

Q: Well, if you have your husbands get in touch with Miss (Intake social worker), we'll see.

Lazuli: My husband wouldn't do that. I'd have to do it for him.

Q: Oh. Well, if anybody wants to do anything about it, Miss (Intake social worker) is the person to speak to.

Post-group discussion.

Present: Mrs. Y, observer; Q, therapist.

Y: You did talk more than usual.

Q: I was really quite excited about this meeting. It's the culmination of twenty-one months' work. And I think the therapy group can take a good deal of the credit for it; although two of them are in individual therapy, the orientation is quite different.

Y: They do seem to have acquired some rather precise and technical knowledge and they seem to be applying it to some extent. What impresses me most though is their enthusiasm after they leave the room. I've heard them express it in the coffee-shop, and some of them have mentioned it to Miss (Intake social worker). I'm surprised at how Mrs. Amber came through. I know you've had doubts about whether she'd stick it out. One thing Mrs. Lazuli is holding on to is her relationship with her husband.

Q: Yes, that's going to be a tough one to deal with. She's taken everything in her stride up to now, but when we get around to dealing with her protecting him, I'm afraid it's going to shake her. She plays two kinds of "House": one where I'm her father, and the other where her husband is a little boy.

Y: One thing I've been wondering is whether the change in their behavior is really influencing their actual children—but there are so many variables there it doesn't seem fair to go into that aspect.

Q: Let somebody else go into that, if he wants to. The fact that some of the women say it's so should be enough for us at this stage of the proceedings.

7 FURTHER PROGRESS

It is apparent from the protocol that these women (with the exception, perhaps, of Mrs. Amber, the late-comer) have a fairly clear idea of what they are doing in many situations and what they are trying to accomplish in group therapy. In some cases, there is evidence of social control of everyday and family dynamics. Clinically, there was a diminution of phobic avoidance, more living in and of the world, and a diminished incidence of symptoms through control (not avoidance) of social involvements. Behavior patterns were more optional. Formerly, there had been an inexorable, unrecognized, and sterotyped progression toward a fruitless or undesirable dénouement, with preciptiation of clinical symptoms related to mutual acting out with their intimates (games). This could now be stopped by conscious intervention and foreknowledge of the outcome: either at the first move, or at any subsequent critical point, as suggested in Mrs. Amber's relationship with her daughter. The Adult was treated as a kind of muscle which grew stronger with exercise. Their progress justified this attitude. As treatment continued, the Adult was better and better able to control the Child, and to intervene not only in external relationships, but also in conflicts between the inner Child and the inner Parent. The therapeutic effects on the Child as well as on the Adult of improved social experiences should not be underestimated. Concurrently, there was social and symptomatic improvement among the patients' intimates, including the children who were their primary interest in first coming to the group.

Even if these improvements are not regarded as striking in themselves under the circumstances, they were of great interest to the therapist because they signified that he had attained his initial goals with predictability, precision, intelligibility, and control; and particularly because he was able to share the last three with his patients at every step of the way.

At the ninety-first meeting, the patients themselves, without any suggestion from the therapist, began to shift the emphasis from the study of external gains (primary, secondary, social, and biological), to the study of internal gains.

Garnet: I noticed the other day that I was happy and singing while I was washing the bath-tub, and all of a sudden the thought came to me: "What if my son should be killed?" I stopped and asked myself why I had that thought, and then I realized that I just couldn't bear to be happy and had to spoil it. Then I looked back and realized that I had done the same thing many times before, and that it was a real problem with me. I never realized it before.

Lazuli: I do that too.

The other members then joined in the discussion, and thus the attention of the whole group was diverted from their previous projections and preoccupations to a real interest in their own individual psychodynamics. Games and scripts, such as those presented by Mrs. Lazuli and Mrs. Amber, were now seen from another point of view. Instead of being regarded as social operations designed to yield the maximum of external gains, they could be investigated as attempts to deal with internal conflicts for internal gains, and their functions as covert sexual gratifications, reassurances, and defenses came to the fore. (What popularly are called "defenses" or "security operations" have the equally or even more significant function of providing and eliciting instinctual satisfactions. Otherwise people would hardly talk to each other at all, since in most cases the best "defense" is to remain silent.) The knowledge and experience these women had gained in the group during the first ninety meetings had not only served its own therapeutic purpose, but had also prepared them for this new undertaking.

Although a "psychoanalytic" group therapist might have felt an itch (and might even feel it on reading this account) to proceed along conventional lines, the writer's experience is that this is not the most fruitful approach even at this stage. Therefore, the subsequent therapy has consisted of advanced transactional analysis, with particular attention to the following points:

1. The emergence of more games in each case, which superficially appear to differ among themselves,

but are eventually found to have a similar core specific to each patient.

2. The fact that a game, which the patient at first recognizes that she plays occasionally, soon emerges as something that she plays almost continuously with the same people all day long every day.

3. The pertinence of such a game to a true long-term script, with all three aspects of protocol, script proper, and adaptation.

4. Second-order structural analysis. (See Chapter 16.)

For example, the subtle game which Mrs. Amber played in the group was not recognized for a long time, but once it was, it soon became apparent that she played it again and again all through the hour, and it was not difficult for the other mothers to imagine the effect of this on a twelve-year old girl such as Mrs. Amber's daughter. The game was "Corner," which might be summarized: "Well, I've answered your question, and you see you're speechless, there is absolutely nothing you can say." She played this in so many different ways that the common element of leaving her opponent speechless was not noticed for a long time. This was connected with an Oedipal protocol, she and her father against her mother, or she against both parents to get the upper hand on her sister. It was soon possible to pin this down structurally to her "Professor," the shrewd (second-order) Adult component of her Child. In this case it was a Jesuitical or Talmudic Professor, a Doctor of Sophistry and Casuistry.

8   WITHDRAWAL

Withdrawal from a therapy group (or any other group) depends on the progress of the individual's games. There were seven members who withdrew from the Mother's Group because for various reasons their games did not proceed satisfactorily and they could not tolerate the resulting anxiety. This phenomenon may be illustrated by two simple examples.

Mrs. Hay, an experienced clinic patient, wished for herself and the psychiatrist to play "Psychiatry" with the rest of the group as subjects. The therapist, without knowing in those early days what he was doing, declined, whereupon she said she could not longer afford a baby-sitter, and announced her withdrawal. She was never heard from again.

Mrs. Vahv was a bigot who tried to play "Ain't It Awful?" She was psychologically a Parental lyncher and child-beater. She left tightlipped when the group refused to play.

NOTES

My indebtedness to the staff of Atascadero State Hospital for inviting me to participate in their therapeutic community program has already been acknowledged. The observer during the ninetieth meeting of the Mothers' Group was Miss Elsa Zisovich, then of the Adult Guidance Clinic in San Francisco. The observer during the later phase was Miss Barbara Rosenfeld, of Contra Costa County Social Service.

The physical aspects of group therapy are extraneous to the subject under discussion, but may be briefly mentioned. For the past two years the Mothers' Group has met sitting in a small circle without any table, and the transactions have perhaps been more direct than with the old arrangement. The optimal size for a psychotherapy group was empirically set at ten by Trigant Burrow, the first dynamic group psychotherapist, in 1928.[2] Nowadays most therapists seem to prefer eight, and some would rather reduce this to six. For a group of eight, a one hour session is a little short, and a two hour session is unnecessarily long. I have discussed these problems at greater length elsewhere.[3]

Seventeen women have entered the Mothers' Group during its present four years of life, and seven of these withdrew without gaining any insight, which is slightly less than the expected proportion.[4]

Bach, one of the most perceptive and creative writers on group therapy, independently observed some of the principles relating to games in therapy groups some years ago. In particular, he emphasizes the gratificatory yield rather than the defensive function of what he calls "set-up operations." What he calls "contact operations" correspond closely to what are here called "engagements."[5]

REFERENCES

1. Berne, E. " 'Psychoanalytic' versus 'Dynamic' Group Therapy." *Internat. J. Group Psychother.* X: 98–103, 1960.

2. Burrow, T. "The Basis of Group-Analysis." *Brit. J. Med. Psychol.* VIII: 198–206, 1928.

3. Berne, E. "Principles of Group Psychotherapy." *Indian J. Neurol. & Psychiat.* 4: 119–137, 1953.

4. *Idem.* "Group Attendance: Clinical & Theoretical Considerations." *Internat. J. Group Psycother.* V: 392–403, 1955.

5. Bach, G. R. *Intensive Group Psychotherapy.* Ronald Press Company, New York, 1954.

PART IV

Frontiers of
Transactional Analysis

*The reader may be well advised to
postpone his onslaught on this
section until the preceding material
has been thoroughly subjugated.*

CHAPTER SIXTEEN

Finer Structure of the Personality

IT IS quite possible that the personality structure so far given might be adequate for a therapeutic lifetime, just as it served the writer well during the first phase of the clinical formulation of these ideas. The observer of more than average curiosity, however, after he has mastered the clinical application of elementary structural analysis, will begin to notice complexities which indicate that further elaboration is desirable.

Mr. Deuter[A], a 23-year-old patient, reported the following dream: "I dreamed that I was a little boy[C] sucking my thumb, though I felt I was too old to do it, and worried about what my mother would say if she saw me. You know, I've always felt guilty[P] about deceiving her."

It is evident that it is the Adult[A] who relates the dream, the Child[C] who appears in it, and the disapproving Parent[P] who makes him feel guilty about deceiving his mother. The dream itself poses a structural problem which can be solved by observing actual children.

A little boy began sucking his thumb after the birth of a baby sister when he was four. His mother said that Aaron had been a thumbsucker up to the age of two years, but had then given up the habit until the new baby appeared on the scene. Aaron himself felt that it was wrong, and thought he was too old to do it, but whenever things went badly that is what he did. The sister was now three, and when things were going well the two children played together in a friendly way. Aaron would show her how to build things with blocks and play games. If she became too exuberant, untidy, or careless, he would say: "You're not supposed to do that. You have to put things back where you took them from," etc. The mother would tell these things to visitors, and when they went to greet the children in the play-room they would usually find Aaron in one or other of these three states: either sulking, playing with his sister, or rebuking her *in loco parentis*.

It was not difficult to diagnose these three states of Aaron as Child, Adult, or Parent, respectively. In fact the little girl too, perhaps in imitation of her brother, exhibited a similar trichotomy, with tattling as the anlage of the Parental ego state. By observing infants, the distinction of neopsychic from archaeopsychic functioning can be observed at a very early age when the breast or bottle begins to be treated as a separate object with an external reality of its own. Later, parentalism begins to appear in imitation of or in alliance with the actual parents.

Aaron exhibited the child-like qualities appropriate to his age: an appealing protectiveness toward his little sister; a shrewdness in dealing with people and things, together with various reactions which were his currently available ways of dealing with pleasure and frustration, and in addition, a regressive phenomenon: the resumption of a previously abandoned, archaic mode of reaction by thumb-sucking. These classes of behavior make it possible to draw a structural diagram for this child as in Figure 17A: the Parental ego state he maintained when he was behaving *in loco parentis;* an Adult ego state which mediated his handling of blocks, games, and people, together with the emotional reactions appropriate to his age; and a Child ego state in which he re-

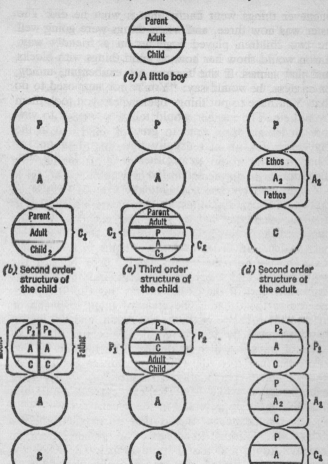

(a) A little boy

(b) Second order structure of the child

(a) Third order structure of the child

(d) Second order structure of the adult

(e) Second order structure of the parent (vertical & horizontal)

(f) Third order structure of the parent (horizontal)

(g) Complete second order structural analysis

FIGURE 17

gressed to previously abandoned forms of behavior. It was the Parent who made him feel uneasy when he was sucking his thumb, and the Adult who, surveying this behavior, realized that somehow it was out of place. In short, the structure of his personality was similar to that of a grown-up. Aaron resembled in many respects the way Mr. Deuter saw himself in some of his dreams.

What had happened to Mr. Deuter was this: when he was in the situation and the state of mind represented by his dream, about the age of six, his big sister had burst into the room to tell him that his mother had been hurt in an accident. This whole psychological structure had become traumatically fixated. Thus when his Child became manifest in later years, usually in situations where he had been caught cheating in some way, it was this whole psychological structure which was revived. In order to represent this in a structural diagram, not only the thumb-sucking urge, but also the guilt feeling and the objective appraisal must be included as part of the Child. It was this Child who appeared in the dream. The state of mind in which he related the dream constitutes the Adult, and the Parent is represented by his current guilt feelings about all sorts of ways in which he deceived his mother. In Figure 17B, therefore, the Child reproduces Figure 17A, the complete personality structure of a regressive thumb-sucker, while Mr. Deuter's current Adult and Parent may be represented in the usual way.

The significance of this is that on detailed analysis "the Child" is found to consist of an archaic Parent, an archaic Adult, and a still more archaic Child. At the moment "the Child" was traumatically fixated, it already comprised a complete personality which included all three elements. Clinically, it suffices in most cases to treat the Child as though it were an undifferentiated entity, but special indications may make it advisable to do a more detailed analysis of this aspect. This internal

structure is what decisively differentiates the phenomenological Child from the conceptualized, unstructured psychoanalytic id. Figure 17B may be called a
second-order structural analysis.

In rare cases it is even possible to do a third-order
structural analysis. The actual child who is sucking his
thumb at the age of two or three may already have a
primitive Parent (the anlage of a Parental ego state)
and Adult, and at times he too may regress to an ego
state which represents, say, an earlier weaning trauma.
Thus we may find (Figure 17C) Child$_3$ (weaning
trauma) present in Child$_2$ (regressive thumb-sucking)
who is the archaic aspect of Child$_1$ (the six-year-old).
This is the well-known situation which is intuitively
represented by the girl on the baking-powder tin who
holds a baking-powder tin, ad infinitum. Figure 17C
represents a *third-order* analysis of such a developmental series.

Turning now to the Adult, it appears that in many
cases certain child-like qualities become integrated into
the Adult ego state in a manner different from the contamination process. The mechanism of this "integration" remains to be elucidated, but it can be observed that certain people when functioning *qua* Adult
have a charm and openness of nature which is reminiscent of that exhibited by children. Along with these go
certain responsible feelings toward the rest of humanity
which may be subsumed under the classical term "pathos." On the other hand, there are moral qualities
which are universally expected of people who undertake grown-up responsibilities, such attributes as courage, sincerity, loyalty, and reliability, and which meet
not mere local prejudices, but a world-wide ethos. In
this sense the Adult can be said to have child-like and
ethical aspects, but this remains the most obscure area
in structural analysis, so that it is not possible at
present to clarify it clinically. For academic purposes

and in order to explain certain clinical phenomena, however, it would be defensible to subdivide the Adult into three areas. Transactionally, this means that anyone functioning as an Adult should ideally exhibit three kinds of tendencies: personal attractiveness and responsiveness, objective data-processing, and ethical responsibility; representing respectively archaeopsychic, neopsychic, and exteropsychic elements "integrated" into the neopsychic ego state, perhaps as "influences" in the manner described in Chapter 20. This tentative formulation is represented in Figure 17D. This "integrated" person *is* charming, etc., and courageous, etc., in his Adult state, whatever qualities he has or does not have in his Child and Parent ego states. The "unintegrated" person may *revert to* being charming, and may feel that he *should* be courageous.

Mr. Troy illustrated the finer structure of the Parent. His father, like other human beings, exhibited all three types of behavior: exteropsychic, neopsychic, and archaeopsychic; and Mr. Troy in his usual Parental ego state duplicated those. Like his father, he exhibited violent, irrational prejudices, especially in regard to children. Along with this, he showed a superficial shrewdness in dealings with "women," which also duplicated his father's behavior. (It was different, for example, from his anxious, child-like compliance in the presence of "ladies.") And with certain types of women he indulged in a kind of sadistic playfulness of the same sort which had led the mother to divorce the father. Similarly, in the group, Magnolia exhibited her mother's "traditional" bigotry, her mother's "superior knowledge" of grammar and diction, and her mother's petulance. The other members reacted to these manifestations with considerable irritation. They perceived clearly that it was not Magnolia, but her mother, who sat with them, and who, as they expressed it, put a "ceiling" on the proceedings. They did not want any "parents" in the group. When "the real Magnolia," that is, her Adult and Child, emerged in the course of therapy, she was quite different, and was well received.

These details are represented in Figure 17E, where for the sake of completeness both the "horizontal" segmentation of the Parent into Child, Adult, and Parent$_2$, and the "vertical" separation of paternal and maternal influences are shown. Parent$_2$ the "Parent in the Parent," signifies of course the influence of the grandparents, the custodians of the "traditional" family attitudes, which may concern anything from colonic irrigations or virtuosity in vice, to social, military, commercial, or Stoic pride. A third-order analysis, as shown in Figure 17F, would subdivide Parent$_2$ into Child, Adult, and Parent$_3$, the last representing the great-grandparents.

With good genealogical material, the fine structure of the Parent might be carried back even farther. Theoretically, on the baking-powder principle, it could be carried back to the first ancestor of man.

A complete second-order structural analysis is represented in Figure 17G. If such a diagram is built up step by step in the course of prolonged therapy on the basis of clinical material, the patient may be fully equipped to cope with it and to understand the personal significance of each region. Such advanced structural analysis may be desirable in working with character problems. Of particular interest there are the Child segment of the Parent, and the Adult part of the Child.

One further illustration will show how second-order structure can emerge in the clinical situation. A 25-year-old woman, Miss Zoyan, described a distressing period in her life when she was about 10 years old. She came of a very pious family, and at that age she began to think obsessively about the question of whether Jesus had a penis. When these thoughts occurred, she would say to herself: "You're not supposed to think about such things, that's wicked." She would then cast about for some way to "occupy her mind," such as building a doll house. She told this story in the group with considerable objectivity, and then added: "I must say I'm not proud of myself for having such thoughts, but at the time they forced their way through in spite of my efforts to control them."

The structural analysis of this passage may be understood with reference to Figure 17B. The 25-year-old woman who sat in the group and related these happenings objectively was talking in her Adult ego state, represented by the middle circle A. The serious but not abject apology at the end implied an alert but not very severe first-order Parent, represented by the upper circle P, and reflected the actual quality of her current Parental judgments when they were exhibited. What she was describing was a complete childhood ego state, represented by the whole of the lower circle C_1. This is the first-order structural analysis.

Her state of mind at the age of 10, as she reported it, comprised three components. Initially, there was the archaic component which forced its way into consciousness, and this is represented by the second-order Child C_2. C_2 was met by the second-order Parent (P in the lower circle) with the injunction "You're not supposed to think about such things," which historically proved to be the internalized voice of her mother. The conflict was resolved opportunistically by the second-order Adult (A in the lower circle) by engaging in outside activities. This is the second-order structural analysis.

She was able to remember and recount these things because her first-order Adult was highly cathected and her first-order Parent was relatively lenient. The other members of the group were unable to remember or recount such early conflicts because of the persistent stringency in their first-order Parents and the relatively poor cathexis of their first-order Adults.

What remained in Miss Zoyon's case was to solve

the enigma of the second-order Child, C_2. Some of the indications were as follows: during her fourth or fifth year she had been told that Jesus was a man who lived a long time ago. The intent of this information was religious-historical, but the inquiring (third-order) Adult of the four-year-old had received it anatomically, in all innocence. When she had tried to discuss her conclusions, in all innocence, she had been traumatically reprimanded. Thus the four-year-old child's ego state had become fixated, and had re-appeared as a blasphemous foreign body (C_2) in the mind of the ten-year-old. The complete ego state of the ten-year-old (C_1) in turn functioned as the Child of the grown-up woman.

NOTES

This chapter attempts merely to illustrate phenomena whose consistent clinical demonstration would require a volume to itself.

The clinical material about Mr. Deuter has been modified for the sake of clarity. Dr. Robert Wald, of the Langley Porter Neuropsychiatric Institute, has advanced some interesting and original ideas about this type of dream.

The baking-powder problem is stated by Korzybski as the map problem, which corresponds structurally to the present instance. An ideal map would contain the map of the map, the map of the map of the map, and so on, as discussed by the logician, Josiah Royce.[1]

The id was described by Freud as "a chaos, a cauldron of seething excitement . . . it has no organization and no unified will . . . the laws of logic . . . do not hold for processes in the id. There is nothing in the id which can be compared to negation."[2] Since the Child ego state reproduces the ego state of the actual child, the difference is immediately apparent. A child has organization, unified will, logic, and, certainly, negation. Also, unlike the id, he knows good and evil. Considerable confusion has arisen from the fact that the word "id" is used colloquially and improperly by psychoanalysts themselves.

The characteristics of the Parent, Adult, and Child in the actual child are just what Piaget discusses in some of his well-known studies.[3, 4, 5] The anlage of the Adult in the Child is the subject of one of Spitz's most interesting works.[6] The work of Melanie Klein[7] and her school on "the early stages of the superego" deals to a considerable extent with what is called here "the anlage of the Parent."

The second-order structure of the Adult raises problems which are similar to those concerning the "autonomous ego," and these are by no means settled. The present position is based on anthropological as well as clinical considerations, namely, that people are the same all over the world. It would be rash to discuss such problems as "autonomous satisfactions" in the present limited state of knowledge. It can be demonstrated, however, that the formal description of the neopsyche already given, as a partly self-programing probability computer with specified feedback characteristics, would result in a "reliability-seeking," "candid" data-processing system with special signals representing an "instinct of mastery." The "primary" programing for such a system could be arranged to vary between internal ("archaic") sources and external parametric factors, representing archaeopsychic and exteropsychic influences respectively.

REFERENCES

1. Korzybski, A. *Science and Sanity*. Science Press Printing Company, Lancaster, Pa., 1941, p. 751.

2. Freud, S. *New Introductory Lectures on Psychoanalysis. Loc. cit.*, p. 104 f.

3. Piaget, J. *The Moral Judgment of the Child. Loc. cit.*

4. Piaget, J. *The Construction of Reality in the Child. Loc. cit.*

5. Piaget, J. *Play, Dreams and Imitation in Childhood*. W. W. Norton & Company, New York, 1951.

6. Spitz, René A. *No and Yes*. International Universities Press, New York, 1957.

7. Klein, Melanie. *The Psycho-Analysis of Children*. Hogarth Press, London, 1949; Grove Press, New York, 1960.

CHAPTER SEVENTEEN

Advanced Structural Analysis

ADVANCED structural analysis is particularly useful in dealing with character disorders and psychopathy. Because of its complexity, no attempt will be made to present its systematic application in a single case. Instead, some brief examples of special structural characteristics will be offered in order to illustrate some of the possibilities.

1 ANALYSIS OF PARENTAL STRUCTURE

Mr. Troy's Parental ego state, which reproduced his father's attitude toward his environment, has already been described. This included a tough attitude toward children (Parent in Parent, transmitted from paternal grandfather); a set of poorly tested propositions about women and their behavior (Adult in Parent, transmitted from father); and an enterprising attitude about promiscuity (Child in Parent, derived from father's attitude and behavior). In the Parental state which he maintained in the group, Mr. Troy reproduced the attitudes of all these three aspects of his father, as illustrated in Figure 18A.

At the time he came to Dr. Q, Mr. Troy functioned well as an autonomous Adult in his nightly work as usher at a public dance-hall. He enjoyed his job because it was congenial to all three aspects of his personality and in this situation he was free of conflicts. His

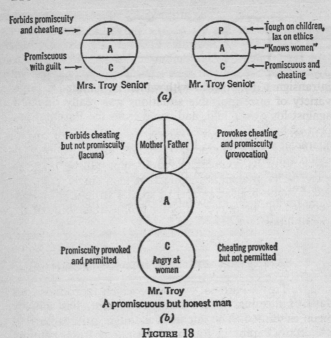

Forbids promiscuity and cheating →

Promiscuous with guilt →

P
A
C

Mrs. Troy Senior

P
A
C

→ Tough on children, lax on ethics
→ "Knows women"
→ Promiscuous and cheating

Mr. Troy Senior

(a)

Forbids cheating but not promiscuity (lacuna)

Mother | Father

Provokes cheating and promiscuity (provocation)

A

Promiscuity provoked and permitted

C
Angry at women

Cheating provoked but not permitted

Mr. Troy
A promiscuous but honest man

(b)

FIGURE 18

own Adult could handle the material problems, his Child enjoyed the rowdy atmosphere, and there was nothing in his Parent which disapproved; in fact, the Child in his Parent encouraged the loose living which the environment made available.

Some of the habitués, however, soon found that Mr. Troy responded to teasing. On such occasions, he would revert from his Adult ego state to his Parental one as a defense against the rage which they aroused in his Child. Specifically, when he was disturbed, his geniality would vanish. He would become pompously harsh and say something like: "I don't have to listen to that kind of childish nonsense. Get away! Get away!" This reproduced a censorious attitude of his father's, derived from his grandfather.

Mr. Troy's case illustrates the structure of both certain kinds of character defenses and certain types of psychopathic behavior. The characteristic reaction of intransignet disapproval with which he handled a large variety of uncomfortable situations was really directed against his own Child, and came from the Parental aspect of his Parent. This was the structural origin of his character defense. On the psychopathic side, his own Child's interest in loose living was not only permitted, but actually encouraged by the Child in his Parent. It was not through parental oversight that he could play games with women; his father had actually through his boyhood years given him demonstrations and field discussions in this area. In structural jargon, it was not simply a question of "a hole in his Parent," similar to what Johnson and her colleagues[1] call a "Superego lacuna," but of positive parental "unwitting" provocation.

His father had offered him "courses" in other games, such as those based on financial irresponsibility, but Mr. Troy's Child had rejected them because in this area the Mother side of his Parent was still effective. By her own behavior, however, she had abdicated as a Parent in the field of man-woman relationships and had also wounded Mr. Troy's Child so that he had a special interest in exploiting women. His promiscuity, therefore, was based on three structural factors: a Child who had an idiosyncratic interest, encouragement from the Father Parent, and a lacuna in the Mother Parent. This is represented in Figure 18B.

The transmission of cultural "psychopathies" illustrates dramatically the principles of advanced structural analysis. Stealing among gypsies, head-hunting on the Amazon, piracy on the Barbary Coast, criminality in the Mafia, and malicious gossip among certain classes

in civilized countries, probably all have the same structure as Mr. Troy's promiscuity, according to the evidence offered by popular books. This is epitomized in
the epigram: "To make a lady, start with the grandmother," that is, the parent's Parent.

Cannibalism and cruelty among the Fijians is a good
example to study since the history of Fiji is well
documented.[2] The cruelty of Fijian chiefs was transmitted from generation to generation because not only
was there no parental prohibition against it, but the activities of the chief's ancestors actually encouraged by
example this exhibition of the unadapted Child. When
the chiefs became converted to Christianity, the inner
Parent was replaced by an external Parental authority. At first there were sporadic outbursts of cruelty,
but now, a few generations later, the Fijians are among
the kindest and most sensitively polite people on earth.
The inner Parent of a contemporary Fijian youth includes a second- and even third-order Parent who
prohibits cruelty, where a hundred years ago, before
the *lotu* conversions, it included an indefinite sub-order
of Children who gloried in such activities. The tremen-
dous psychic upheaval which may occur as an inner
Parent is replaced by a new exteropsychic influence is
beautifully described by Margaret Mead in her follow-
up study of the Manus Islanders.[3] An understanding of
such broad historical and cultural changes makes it
easy to comprehend structurally the woman who follows in the footsteps of her gossipy, promiscuous
mother, and the professional murderer whose mother
aggressively defends his criminal behavior when he is
brought to trial.

The case of the Triss sisters illustrates the structural
situation in families where the siblings turn out differently. Of all the factors involved in such outcomes, the
structural position is the one which can be expressed
most cogently, succinctly, and precisely, although it

leaves many questions unanswered. When other factors are clarified, they can usually be fitted quite neatly into the structural analysis.

Grandfather Triss became wealthy in his middle years, and soon took on the role of a dictatorial patriarch who demanded complete submission from his clan, using the power of money as a sanction to enforce his demands. Everybody complied except one son-in-law, who rebelled unsuccessfully for several years and finally deserted his wife, leaving her with two daughters, Alice and Betty, aged eight and four. The mother was so compliant to the grandfather's will that she dropped her married name at his behest and raised the two girls under the name of Triss.

Mrs. Triss, however, managed to find one escape from the grandpaternal strictness: in adolescence she was an overt homosexual, an aberration of her Child which Grandfather Triss was inclined to treat indulgently so long as she was obedient in other respects. She apparently suspended these activities after her marriage, except for some sexual play later with the older girl.

After a year or two, by the time Alice was nine, her mother became more cautious in the face of the girl's increased understanding of what was going on, and desisted from further seductive activities. Alice's presence also protected Betty from becoming the object of such attentions. Alice became a fixed homosexual. In later years, the chief blemish on her happiness was the fear that her divorced father might find out what she was, and for this reason she never visited him, even though he lived only a short ride on the subway from Alice's apartment in Greenwich Village. Like her mother, she was compliant in most other respects. Although she succumbed somewhat to the Bohemian way of life with her contemporaries, she was prim and proper in the presence of her elders.

Betty, on the other hand, although she was heterosexual, was in active revolt against the middle-class standards of her mother and grandfather, and was regarded by them as impudent and irrevocably corrupted. She had the same feeling of guilt toward her mother as Alice did toward her father.

These two divergent outcomes in the case of two individuals with the same actual parents, were not difficult to understand from the structural point of view. Alice's position and guilt feelings regarding sex were determined by mother's Child and father's Parent, while her social attitude complied with mother's Parent. Betty's social attitude and the resulting guilt were influenced by father's Child and mother's Parent, while her sexuality complied with father's Parent. This may look simpler than it sounds. The Parental structure is shown in Figure 19A.

Because of Grandfather Triss's attitude, Mrs. Triss had no Parental protection from homosexual impulses. Therefore her Child was free to indulge in these activities, and her Child seduced Alice's Child. The father aspect of Alice's Parent made her feel guilty, but not guilty enough to desist. This is represented in Figure 19B. Since Alice was mother's girl, she felt the influence of mother's strong Parental prohibition against impudent behavior, and in effect complied with Grandfather Triss's wishes in other than sexual activities.

Betty was father's girl. If she somehow sensed the possibilities for homosexual satisfaction in the household, her Child adapted herself to father's influence, and she resisted these possibilities. But her father's own rebellious Child, which caused him to leave the clan, seduced Betty into rebellion also against the clan mores. This rebellion, however, made it difficult for Betty to face mother's disapproval, transmitted from Grandfather Triss via mother's Parent. This is represented in Figure 19C.

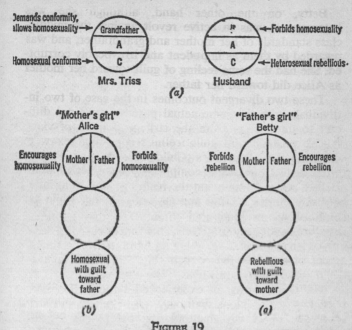

Demands conformity, allows homosexuality → Grandfather A / C — Homosexual conforms → Mrs. Triss

→ Forbids homosexuality A / C ← Heterosexual rebellious — Husband

(a)

"Mother's girl" Alice — Encourages homosexuality Mother Father Forbids homosexuality — Homosexual with guilt toward father (b)

"Father's girl" Betty — Forbids rebellion Mother Father Encourages rebellion — Rebellious with guilt toward mother (a)

FIGURE 19

2 ANALYSIS OF CHILD STRUCTURE

The operational Child as observed clinically among outpatients or in private practice manifests itself in four different ways.

1. It may take the form of a characterological attitude. Common is an awestruck naive receptivity known colloquially as "The Peasant," or "Gee, you know everything, Professor!" In this state, the patient asks questions and gives the impression of marveling at the virtuosity and omniscience of the therapist. A similar manifestation is the helpless coquetry known as "Little old Me."

2. There may be brief episodic intrusions of the

Child into Adult activity, as when Mr. Ennat interrupted his judicious discussions with excited thigh-thumping.

3. The Child may be active alongside the Adult, and show itself in unconscious gestures and intonations. The movement of a single group of facial muscles no more than a few millimeters may suffice to betray this form of activity.

4. The Child may be carefully observing the progress of a game and never show itself openly unless something goes wrong. If that happens, there may be a single shrewd observation which can easily pass unremarked. An example of this revealing phenomenon will be given shortly. In the first three cases, the Child is exhibited as an integrated totality, so that its finer structure is not easy to detect. This fourth case is a second-order manifestation, being an exhibition of a single aspect of an early fixated ego state, the Adult in the Child, colloquially known as "The Professor."

Mrs. Quatry was an experienced patient. She had been to three previous therapists, all of whom she had succeeded in grossly manipulating before she terminated treatment with them. She co-operated with Dr. Q, but remarked periodically: "I'm stupid. I just don't get it." Dr. Q suspected that she had stupefied her Adult by contamination, but that her Child was not as stupid as she wanted to appear and that she was playing a game whose origin and motivation were not yet clear.

After she had been in weekly treatment for some time, she offered a dream one day, and as was her custom after speaking for a while, she waited expectantly for Dr. Q to make some comment. He remarked encouragingly: "That's interesting." Mrs. Quatry looked disapproving, and said: "You're supposed to say more than that. You're supposed to tell me that it has a sexual meaning."

On another occasion, she recounted a household incident, evidently wanting Dr. Q to tell her that she was right and her husband wrong. Dr. Q asked her what would happen if he told her just that. "Oh, then I'd feel better," she replied. "And what if I said your husband was right and you were wrong?" he asked. "Oh, I knew that all along," she answered.

It was evident that some aspect of Mrs. Quatry was observing the progress of her games with considerable care. When she rebuked Dr. Q for handling her dream wrongly, she was performing the function of a teacher or professon of psychiatry, a remarkable position for someone who consistently maintained that she was the stupidest person in the group. The discussion of the household incident showed the same shrewd appraisal of what was going on. She had previously shown herself with some experienced psychotherapists to be unusually adept at eliciting "therapeutic support" in her domestic arguments, and now she was attempting to involve Dr. Q in the same three-handed game with her husband. But as she made it clear, some part of her personality knew what she was up to all along.

This kind of shrewdness in appraising and manipulating personal relationships is an important aspect of the growing child's personality, and is part of his neopsychic functioning, since it requires sensitive and objective data-processing based on experience. For this reason, it is probably correctly diagnosed as coming from the Adult in the Child. It often has a disconcerting and sometimes withering accuracy, as shown in many anecdotes about children. After three or four exhibitions, the group generally finds "The Professor" an appropriate name for this sub-aspect of the personality. It is true, as Erikson[4] says, that a child analyst is not a child who practices psychoanalysis, but is also true that there is a great deal to learn from the psychiatrist in the child, who observes our "therapeutic" efforts and responses with the keenest insight. As Ferenczi pointed out,[5] a large measure of such capacities is lost through education.

In hospitalized patients whose first-order Parents and Adults have been decommissioned so that they are openly psychotic, the finer structure of the Child is easier to see. In the hospital are found people who are once more enduring the agonies of morbid early ego states: the torments of feeling that their minds can be read, that their secret hostilities and sexual confusions cannot be hidden from the penetrating regard of their harsh and intuitive parents, and that their every word will be marked and thrown back at them. Or the agony of feeling their own wickedness so keenly in the face of deprivations and tyranny that the only solution is abject self-abasement. And if the tyrant can be put out of commission, who can curb the wild elation as of a little child possessing the whole world? And so the Child, who sees his parents not distorted, but only with highly cathected primal imagery so that they stand before him with almost eidetic clarity, becomes what grown-ups call paranoid, depressed, or manic. The thoughtful observer who calls forth his own primal imagery and primal judgment[6] can see those parents as clearly as the patient does. Thus, in many psychotic patients the archaic second-order Parent, the Parent in the Child, becomes visible, though indescribable.

The well-known intuition about people which is attributed to schizophrenics is a manifestation of the same Professor, the Adult in the Child, that was exhibited in the case of Mrs. Quatry. And the manifestation may take the same form: the benevolent, "accepted" psychotherapist may be told by the schizophrenic that he has made a therapeutic error, and that he should conduct the treatment in another way. Whether this injunction is given by hints and tentative gestures, or by imperatives, the wise therapist will listen with serious regard, and often find that he has made a "discovery." The cardinal principle which led to the discoveries of psychoanalysis, for example, was enunciated to Freud by his first classical patient, Frau Emmy von N., who repeatedly pointed her finger at him and cried: "Keep quiet—don't speak—don't touch me!" The impression these words made on the therapist may be judged from the frequency with which he includes them in his case report.[7] The patient later explained that she was afraid of being interrupted in the stream of thought, because that would make everything more confused and worse. At this time, therefore, the Adult in the Child of Frau Emmy von N. was a better technician than Freud, and anyone that competent is well deserving of the title "Professor."

The Child in the Child, when laid bare by psychosis, is manifested by the archaic intensity of its reactions to its own imagery. This intensity may seem inappropriate to the naive observer, but it is justified by the intensity of the primal images themselves, and in this way it is not at all out of line. The flavor of these images was well recognized by Breuer and Freud, who called them "plastic" images.[7]

NOTES

Johnson and Szurek[1] speak of "unwitting seduction" by the parents resulting in "superego lacunae" in the child. Structural analysis differentiates in transactional terms between "unwitting seduction" (into promiscuity) as in Mr. Troy's case, passive sanction (for rebellion) as in Betty Triss's case, and active seduction (into homosexuality) as in Alice Triss's case. Second-order structural analysis of the Parent permits a precise etiological statement. It distinguishes between paternal and maternal influences, and provides a systematic framework for tracing these back to the grandparents and to the childhood activities of the actual parents. Szurek[8] broadens Johnson's concepts with a variety of clinical material to strengthen his con-

clusions. What is offered here is a comprehensive theoretical statement which helps in generalizing such findings
with increased clarity and effectiveness. Structural analysis
also offers a useful framework for generalizing the results
of Fisher and Mandell[9] and others.

In practice, the situation with Mrs. Quatry was handled
by having her and her husband come together to a marital
group. There she again tried to get support by describing
her husband's "misbehavior." This is the commonest game
played in marital groups, and is there called "Court-room."
Since the other members of the group were familiar with it,
they declined to play it with her, and instead encouraged
her to analyze it, which she did with some success, and
after a while she no longer played it. The key, of course,
was the depressive position: "I knew all along it was I who
was wrong," and the game of "Court-room" was an attempt
to ward off the depression by getting people to tell her again
and again that it was really her husband who was wrong.
The refusal of the other members to play made it possible
to shift the focus from the domestic scene to her infantile
depression.

The structural situation itself was noted from the beginning by Breuer and Freud (1895). In "Observation I"
(Miss Anna O.), Breuer remarks: "There were two entirely
separate states of consciousness, which alternated very
frequently and spontaneously, moving farther apart during
the course of the disease. In one of them she knew her
environment, was sad and anxious, but relatively normal;
in the other, she hallucinated, was naughty." In this "Second Condition" on one occasion, she could not talk at all
until she remembered a nursery rhyme. Breuer later notes
the persistence of the Adult even in the depths of the
psychosis. "But no matter how distinctly the two states
were separated, the 'second state' not only mixed with the
first, but as the patient expressed it, that at least frequently
during her worst states 'there sat a keen and quiet observer
somewhere in a little corner of the brain, who watched all
this crazy stuff.' "

Thus the two "conditions," "states," or "states of consciousness," (as Breuer's translator calls them) in "Obser-

vation I" were respectively a "normal" ego state and a "childish" ego state, or as they are called here, an Adult series and a Child series, and the former could sit quietly by and watch the latter. In "Observation II" (Emmy von N.), the psychotic ego state was itself split, so that while she was talking about her plastic, primal images, she could simultaneously give instruction to Freud in the art of psychotherapy, which was an activity of the Adult portion of her unmasked Child. For reasons which were completely cogent at the time, Freud's attention was diverted from structural considerations into the area of psychodynamics, and this eventually resulted in a structural scheme which was conceptual rather than clinical.

Nowadays the emphasis in the Fiji Islands has shifted from religious to racial and economic factors, as evidenced by the recent riots (December 1959).

REFERENCES

1. Johnson, A. M., & Szurek, S. A. "The Genesis of Anti-social Acting Out in Children and Adults." *Psychoanalytic Quart.* 21: 323–343, 1952.

2. Derrick, R. A. *A History of Fiji. Loc. cit.*

3. Mead, Margaret. *New Lives for Old.* William Morrow & Company, New York, 1956.

4. Erikson, Erik H. *Childhood & Society.* W. W. Norton & Company, New York, 1950.

5. Fenichel, Otto. *Psychoanalytic Theory of Neurosis. Loc. cit.*, p. 229.

6. Berne, Eric. "Primal Images and Primal Judgments." *Loc. cit.*

7. Breuer, J., & Freud, S. *Studies in Hysteria.* Nervous and Mental Disease Monographs, New York, 1950, pp. 14–76. (Trans. by A. A. Brill).

8. Szurek, S. A. "Concerning the Sexual Disorders of Parents and Their Children." *J. Nerv. & Ment. Dis.* 120: 369–378, 1954.

9. Fisher, S. & Mandell, D. "Communication of Neurotic Patterns over Two and Three Generations." *Psychiatry* 19: 41–46, 1956.

CHAPTER EIGHTEEN

Therapy of Marriages

1 INDICATIONS

It is generally considered bad practice to treat two marital partners simultaneously. Under such conditions it is extremely difficult for the therapist to avoid interventions which can with only slight distortion be exploited to damage the therapeutic relationship, or at least render it inordinately complex. So much so, that successful treatment in such cases is considered an event unusual enough to report in the literature.[1] In the present language, if both parties are in treatment with the same therapist, it is difficult for him to avoid becoming involved in a three-handed game. If there are two therapists, it is much simpler for them to resist attempts to play a four-handed one.

"Marital counseling," as distinct from therapy, according to all accounts is set up from the beginning as a three-handed game, and may be successful with couples who are unable to play by themselves and need a third player. The counselor, at the social level, may act as a coach, telling the couple how to play their game better, or he may perform the functions of an umpire. At the psychological level, he tends to become a third party to the marriage itself, usually in a Parental capacity.

Thus among conservative therapists there is a strong tendency to avoid either marital therapy or marital

230

counseling because these difficulties are recognized and formulated in some terms or other, and make those procedures uncongenial to many conscientious and sensitive clinicians. A common practice is to tell the couple that therapy is designed to treat individuals rather than situations or relationships.

Conventional group therapy with married couples is usually open to the same objections because it too often takes the form of many-handed games, some of which will be described presently. For this reason, before game analysis was available, the writer followed the conservative policy in both individual and group therapy, with an occasional experimental exception. These experiments did not always end happily, and their course could not be followed or controlled with adequate precision or intelligibility. When the principles of transactional analysis had become sufficiently clear, a pilot experiment was tried to test their usefulness in the marital situation. This consisted of taking a "group" consisting of one couple. The results were so gratifying, from both the therapeutic and scientific points of view, that it was decided to form a full-fledged marital group.

The most comfortable population for such a project seems to be four couples. Two couples is risky because for game analysis an "unselected" audience of divergent personalities is desirable, and married couples tend to react alike to too many things. In many situations a group of two married couples presents the same difficulties as a group of two members. Three couples is almost equally risky because whenever one couple is absent, the therapist is faced with the rather stultifying two-couple situation. Five couples become unwieldy for precise work.

Such a four-couple marital group constitutes the most stimulating experience in the writer's whole psychiatric career. This is partly because the games between married couples have been going on for a long time. They are therefore played with strong feeling and confidence, quickly become evident, and are easily observed and understood by the other members of the group. And it is partly because true intimacy, which takes a long time to establish in a general group, if it can ever be established at all, is already present between married couples. Nothing is more edifying and touching to the onlooker than the expression of deep and real love between two human beings, especially when there are others present who are equally moved. Speaking rhetorically, whoever has been saddened by loss of confidence in the essential goodness of people should attend such a group. And sometimes it is the sickest people who give the most beautiful pictures of their souls. Among the members who share the therapist's feeling in this respect, two of them have described this group as "the greatest invention since the wheel."

There are ideally no criteria for election in a martital group. Experience so far demonstrates that the couples who present themselves fall into four significant classes.

1. People who misunderstand each other, but do not wish a divorce. This means people whose games are destructive, or are not being played satisfactorily, or are being grown out of, or are beginning to wear thin.

2. Those suffering from what might be called "an outbreak of script." A marriage may run along happily for years until one spouse makes an "impulsive" extramarital liaison. The significant consequence is not the domestic turbulence that follows, which is not necessarily a psychiatric problem, but the onset of psychopathology, usually something like obsessional jealousy, often with a homosexual tinge, which is shocking to both parties. As the incident is elaborated in fantasies and dreams into a whole drama of *mariage à trois,* it becomes evident that this is a script which has been

present but latent in the minds of both parties throughout the marriage.

3. Recently-divorced people who are willing to consider a reconciliation. Here the group fulfills exactly the function implicit in the laws of those states which provide a long waiting period between the interlocutory and final decrees.

Generally speaking, the prognosis in these three types of cases is not bad. Much poorer is the outlook for the fourth type.

4. Couples in which one or both spouses come to the group as part of a game of "See How Hard I've Tried," attempting to exploit the therapist by compliance with his game of "Psychiatry," so that they can then proceed to get a divorce with a "clear conscience."

This form of therapy is still in its infancy, at least as far as transactional analysis is concerned. Of the eight couples who entered the group, one was already divorced; in this and one other case the final outcome is not known. There have been no divorces among the other six (after a two-year follow-up).

2 THE STRUCTURE OF MARRIAGE

When the group was started, at least one spouse in each couple was familiar with structural and transactional analysis. All present understood that the project was in the nature of an experiment, and that neither the aims nor the procedure could be stated in advance. Things went so well, however, that by the third meeting the marital difficulties could be formulated in general transactional terms and the goals could be set. The nature of the marriage contract had been clarified in a way which was confirmed again and again as new couples entered the group.

The structure of marriage can be described from

three different aspects—that is, the American and Canadian marriage, the *mariage d'inclination*.

1. The *formal contract* takes place between the two Adults, and is contained in the marriage service, in the course of which the parties promise to adhere and be faithful to each other in various situations. The statistical evidence is that this contract is not always taken seriously. The Adult commitment is abrogated whenever there is a divorce or an extra-marital affair, since either of these events means the abdication of a position outwardly taken in solemn good faith.

2. The *relationship contract* is a psychological one which is not openly stated. During the courtship there is a tendency for one party to function as a Parent and the other as a Child. This may be in the nature of an implicit parasitic agreement, or it may be a sensible arrangement in which the parties switch attitudes as the occasion demands. If it is a parasitic agreement, it may be abrogated after the honeymoon is over when one of the parties may want to switch roles, whereupon the other party (quite justifiably under the circumstances) cries: "Foul!" If the woman has mothered the man during the courtship, he implicitly assumes, and she implicitly agrees, that this relationship will continue after the marriage, and it is essentially part of the secret marriage contract. If she now turns and demands that he take care of her instead of her taking care of him, trouble is likely to follow, and the situation may or may not be compromisable without outside help.

3. The essential basis of the marriage, however, is the secret contract between the two Children, the *contract of the script*. The selection of a mate from among all the possible candidates is based on this. Each prospective spouse is in the position of a casting director. The man is seeking a leading lady who will best play the role called for by his script, and the woman seeks a leading man to play the role adapted to her protocol.

During the try-out period, candidates are first sorted into those who give appropriate transactional responses, and those who do not. The field is then narrowed down among the former by game-testing. Provocative maneuvers are designed to reveal which of the transactionally eligible candidates will play the required games. Among the game-eligible candidates, the final choice falls on the one who seems most likely to go through with the whole script; that is, partners are drawn together by the intuitive assumption that their scripts are complementary.

Reik[2] quotes Freud as follows: "When making a decision of minor importance, I have always found it advantageous to consider all the pros and cons. In vital matters, however, such as the choice of a mate or a profession, the decision should come from the unconscious. . . . In important decisions of our personal life, we should be governed . . . by the deep inner needs of our nature." Experience in the marital group demonstrates that the "should" in this injunction can be changed to "will." In a free marriage, the choice is inevitably governed by the needs of the Child. The examples to be given shortly will illustrate some of the clinical and operational manifestations of the contract of the script. The ramifications of this contract are so complex that they cannot be systematically or exhaustively demonstrated in a limited space, but the illustrations will serve to clarify the underlying principles so that the terminology, at least, will become clearer. The reader will then be in a position to carry on his own observations and investigations in this matter, which will be far more convincing than any attempt to prove the point.

3 THERAPEUTIC GOALS

The therapeutic goals of transactional marriage therapy emerge naturally from the initial structure of the marriage contract. The object is to preserve the formal contract if possible while at the same time allowing each party to obtain as much satisfaction as possible under compromise of the relationship and script contracts. This goal is translated for the patients from the following clinical statement.

"The relationships and games in this marriage will have to be made optional instead of compulsive, so that destructive or unconstructive elements can be eliminated. After this is accomplished, the spouses may or may not be interested in each other. Time must be allowed for the emergence of more constructive relationships and games. Then each party can decide on rational grounds whether or not he wishes to perpetuate the marriage. This amounts to a psychological divorce within the framework of the formal contract. As each spouse emerges in a new form, an opportunity is offered for a psychological remarriage if they both desire it. If they do not, the therapy may result in a permanent abrogation of the formal contract."

In practice, the marriage is found to undergo progressive improvement as games and script elements are "peeled off" layer by layer, until the underlying sexual difficulty is laid bare in terms of the original protocols. At this point, the question arises: "What do we do now?" or "What do we do instead?" Then there is a strong temptation to relapse into the old patterns. If one partner steadfastly maintains the newly found position and will not relapse, then there is a tendency for the other spouse to seek an extra-marital partner who will either play the old games or else help carry the script rapidly to completion. If this temptation is warded off and the outcome is good, as it has uniformly been so far, a new relationship is formed within the marriage "on top of" the same old sexual conflicts, which remain unresolved, but are handled differently.

Presumably, if each partner went into psychoanalysis at the critical point where these conflicts are unmasked, their resolution would result in a more steadfast remarriage, either with the same partner or with another partner whose script complemented the new, less archaic needs. With transactional analysis alone there are so far three outcomes: at worst, a marriage with considerable but much better controlled turbulence; or compromise and resignation of many needs; or, at best, exhilaration at discovering hitherto dormant qualities and possibilities in each other. All three of these are beneficial to the actual children of the marriage, if any.

4 LOVE

The insufflation which is called love cannot be dealt with by transactional analysis any more than it can by any other psychotherapeutic system, and if this sentiment exists between the two parties, it is a bonus which is at present beyond the reach of psychiatric investigation. Love, however, would not be a necessary condition for the ideal marriage as expressed in structural and transactional terms. The latter would imply a free union with parental approval between two happy people (as previously defined) whose relationship and scripts were complementary and ultimately constructive. On this basis, two people who were devoted to their common standards and to each other might rate higher than Abélard and Héluise.

5   THE COURSE OF DISTURBED MARRIAGE

The typical American disturbed marriage sequence is more often seen in practice with women than with men. The first marriage, at sixteen, represents an extricative operation. The couple live together for ten days to ten months, and then there is an annulment or divorce. If there is a child, it is usually farmed out to one of the wife's relatives, otherwise the extricative function of the marriage is defeated. The girl has now established her civil independence, and is free to go ahead with her script, which is usually impractical and masochistic. The second marriage takes place about five years later and lasts about five years. It is broken off because of the husband's neglect or cruelty; he does what her script requires, but the script is no good. She then has to go to work to support the new children and they become a prime interest in her life. Her third marriage, at about thirty, takes care of the material needs, but the nostalgia of her script still persists to some degree and makes her dissatisfied, so that she beings to provoke her husband. Since he is actually a milder version of the second husband, with the same qualifications much less aggressively endowed, he responds to these provocations in the manner appropriate to her (and his) script. At this point the script has become Adult-ego dystonic to the woman; she feels that something has gone wrong, and seeks treatment either for the marriage or for herself. The husband, who is for the first time perhaps expressing his own needs by his misbehavior, may or may not be interested in the therapy.

The single marriage typically comes to treatment as follows. The union initially compares favorably in many respects to the ideal marriage. Self-determination is attained during the honeymoon or the premarital sexual affair, which has the qualities of a six-handed game with the parents of the young couple. During this period, sex is satisfactory to both parties because of the aggressive releasing elements involved in this complex game. After the first exhilaration wears off, underlying sexual difficulties begin to make themselves felt. The couple now becomes involved in a two-handed game which is a substitute for sex, and is designed to diminish the frequency of the feared sexual confrontation, while at the same time yielding covert gains to both parties. The wife may play "Frigid Woman"; she calls the man a beast, an uproar develops and often goes into a money game. In this way the threatening sexual intimacy is warded off without either party having to face the anxieties involved; meanwhile internal, secondary, and social gains are thriftily collected. The occasional intercourse, however, brings children. These are gratefully received for worthy reasons, but also serve as a welcome distraction. Both parties become heavily involved in the activities connected with child-rearing; this leaves little opportunity for sexual advances, and offers many legitimate reasons for postponing or interrupting love-making.

As the children grow older, however, the couple is more often left with leisure time. The old games are resumed. Difficulties arise because although they play complementary roles in the games, there are minor differences in the rules set up in the minds of each party. These differences, and slight differences in their scripts, become more and more important, so that the cry of "Foul!" is more and more frequently heard. As the couple approaches forty, the failure of their games and scripts bring some measure of despair. This leads them to seek professional help.

6 CLINICAL EXAMPLES

If someone in the group asked Mr. Quatry a question, he would answer readily. If someone asked Mrs. Quatry a question, he would answer that too. Mrs. Quatry protested against this. She said Mr. Quatry always acted like a father and treated her like a backward child. It was noted, however, that when she was offered an opportunity to speak for herself, she did not make use of it. Someone asked her why, and she characteristically replied that she was too stupid, she didn't understand the question. It was evident, therefore, that this relationship was maintained by mutual consent. Mr. Quatry was then instructed by the therapist to refrain from answering for his wife. Two phenomena could then be observed. First, Mrs. Quatry became angry when he didn't answer, saying that he didn't care about her any more. Secondly, whenever Mr. Quatry was off guard, he inadvertently returned to his old pattern. Then he would snap his fingers and say: "There I go again!" After a while, he began to find it amusing when he made such slips, and everyone in the group joined in the laughter except Mrs. Quatry. Nobody found it amusing, however, when they learned that during intercourse these roles were reversed. Instead of Mr. Quatry being the Parent and Mrs. Quatry the Child, he became the Child and she the Parent, so that intercourse was unsatisfactory for both of them. The therapeutic problem in regard to the relationship contract was to stabilize the Adult in each spouse, both in the group and during intercourse.

With the Pentys, the situation in the group was reversed. Mrs. Penty never allowed Mr. Penty to answer a question for himself. He bore this like a martyr, but sometimes protested. As the situation became clearer, however, it emerged that he suffered from severe erythrophobia, and was afraid that if he spoke up he might blush. Thus he was playing a game of "If It Weren't For You." He married the talkative, domineering Mrs. Penty as a protection against his erythrophobia, and then when she performed her function, he complained against her.

The Hechts came late in the life of the group, and were unable to understand the terminology. At their second session, the therapist said: "Hi!" as he sat down, principally to make Mr. Hecht comfortable. Mr. Hecht did not reply. Later in the session, Dr. Q mentioned this. Mr. Hecht said that such silly rituals were meaningless and he did not believe in them. Mrs. Hecht then remarked that Mr. Hecht was always surly like that and gave her short answers. He protested that if she asked him something or told him something, he said what was necessary and then shut up. He didn't see any use in a lot of unnecessary noise. Mrs. Hecht said that he always left her hanging with his abrupt replies. Mr. Hecht told a story about his office that illustrated his point. A secretary arrived at work one day and said "Good morning!" to the boss. The boss answered: "I didn't ask for a weather report, all I want is for you to get on the job." Mr. Hecht thought the boss showed a lot of sense. He said Mrs. Hecht had been brought up to believe in all that folderol. Mrs. Hecht said it made life pleasanter to be polite.

This gave Dr. Q an opportunity to introduce them to the idea of pastimes and games, which they had heard the rest of the group talking about. Mrs. Hecht wanted to play "Etiquette," and Mr. Hecht did not. That was one thing that was wrong with their marriage.

The Septims had a *mariage à quatre* with another couple. Mr. Septim became uneasy after about six months of this and "dragged" his wife to the group. Dr. Q took the position that this was a script they had in common, and that the marriage was unconsciously intended from the beginning to involve another couple.

They had each chosen a mate who would be interested in such an arrangement and had somehow known each other's potentialities in this direction before they were married. They both denied this vehemently and Mr. Septim said that it was preposterous. For his part, he was ready to break off with the other couple right now. The group's questioning, however, soon elicited not only pertinent fantasies on both sides, but even some tentative overt moves in the same direction before they were married. Mrs. Septim then declared that she wanted to live and experience things for the sake of her art, and that *mariage à quatre* was the way to do it. This couple did not return after the second meeting. Dr. Q had deliberately brought about a quick show-down because until the Septims decided which way they wanted to go, they hindered the progress of the rest of the group. This was a hard decision to make, but he had to decide where his responsibility lay, and that was what he came up with.

7 RESISTANCES

The favored form of resistance in a marital group, which is almost universally employed by unsophisticated members, is a game called "Court-room." The husband tells the group a long story about what the wife did, attempting to elicit support for himself as the plaintiff. The wife then states her defense, explaining to the group what her husband did to provoke her behavior. On the next round, the wife may be the plaintiff and the husband the defendant. In each case the group is expected to function as a jury and the therapist as a judge.

There are two ways to break this up. One is to expose the game by tentatively agreeing with the plaintiff and then asking him how that makes him feel. Then the therapist disagrees with the plaintiff and asks him how he feels in that case. This has already been illustrated in the case of Mrs. Quatry, who felt better when the therapist said she was right; when he said she was wrong, she replied: "I knew that all along." This device should be employed judiciously, however; in any case, it should not be used more than twice or thrice a year.

Another way is to interdict the game, and this can be done very elegantly by a simple maneuver. The group is told that they can speak either about themselves, in the first person, or to their spouses, in the second person, but that they must not use the third person.

This also helps with another kind of situation. There are certain couples who never talk to each other during the group meetings. They talk to other people, or about themselves or each other, but never to each other. The therapist states a moral axiom: "It is probably Good if spouses speak to each other occasionally." The statement of this precept, together with the interdiction of the third person, usually solves the situation. If the couple is hesitant, the group is usually in such a good humor by this time that everyone pitches in and helps.

NOTES

The game of marriage, as played among the upper classes in France in the first half of the nineteenth century, is amusingly described in detail by Balzac.[3] Compared with the modern bourgeois two-handed games of "Frigid Woman" and "If It Weren't For You," the three-handed Parisian game between the husband, the wife, and the elusive lover has an aristocratic finesse which leaves much more scope to the intellect and the imagination. In its time and place, it may have been no more unhealthy than the heavy-handed games of nowadays, and except for the bacteriological aspects covertly explored by Schnitzler in "La Ronde," it has a more esthetic quality. Balzac frankly uses the language of games, hence the light mood he induces. He speaks of "defenses," "mousetraps," "strategy," and "allies."

Some of the authors in Keyserling's symposium[4] likewise treat marriage as a game.

More seriously, nearly all the jokes about marriage, from the earliest "Quid est tibi ista mulier?" "Non est mulier, uxor est!" to yesterday's comic strip, recognize the antagonistic patterns involved. Curiously enough, this sad aspect is the comic one, while the deeper and more satisfying intimacies nearly always end, in literature at least, in tragedy. The real happiness of game-free devotion, the ideal goal of marriage therapy, remains largely unsung. Nobody is really thrilled by Philemon and Baucis, and the cotter's Saturday night seems as drab to most people as a poet writing in a country church-yard.

As of this writing, it appears that there is a constant quantity of pathology in every marriage, to be divided between the two partners and perhaps shared by the children. Thus when one party is healthy the other is not, and vice versa. Since low back pain is a common "psychosomatic" manifestation of this pathology, it may be used as a paradigm. One can speak then of "inflamed discs." Thus there are "four-disc marriages," "three-disc marriages," and "two-disc marriages." In a "four-disc marriage," one partner may be healthy and the other have "four discs"; or they may split the pathology, one partner having "three discs," and the other "one disc"; or they may each have "two discs," i.e., each may have a moderate degree of low back pain, instead of one being healthy and the other having severe pain.

If one partner is in therapy and the other is not, there is a tendency for the other spouse to become more disturbed or to have more symptoms as the patient gets better. In the language of game analysis, the spouse goes into a state of increasing despair (manifested, for example, by "more discs") as the patient deprives him of his gains by refusing to play the old game (the patient's improvement being manifested by "fewer discs"). The inference is that in most cases the only hope of reducing the total pathology is for both partners to go into therapy. The fable of the discs offers a convenient prognostic scale for rating marriages. On such a scale, a "four-disc" marriage may survive, although its course will be rocky; the future of a "five-disc" marriage is very dubious. A "one-" or "two-disc" marriage may be treatable by a non-psychiatric counselor, while a "three-disc" marriage should respond to psychiatric therapy.

REFERENCES

1. Jackson, J. & Grotjahn, M. "Concurrent Psychotherapy of a Latent Schizophrenic and His Wife." *Psychiatry* 22: 153–160, 1959.

2. Reik, T. *Listening with the Third Ear*. Farrar, Straus & Company, New York, 1949, p. vii.

3. Balzac, H. de *The Physiology of Marriage*. Privately printed, London, 1904.

4. Keyserling, H. *The Book of Marriage*. Blue Ribbon Books, New York, 1926.

CHAPTER NINETEEN

Regression Analysis

THE ultimate aim of transactional analysis is structural readjustment and reintegration. This requires first, restructuring, and secondly, reorganization. The "anatomical" phase of restructuring consists of clarification and definition of ego boundaries by such processes as diagnostic refinement and decontamination. The "physiological" phase is concerned with redistribution of cathexis through selective planned activation of specific ego states in specific ways with the goal of establishing the hegemony of the Adult through social control. Reorganization generally features reclamation of the Child, with emendation or replacement of the Parent. Following this dynamic phase of reorganization, there is a secondary analytic phase which is an attempt to deconfuse the Child.

The optimal situation for the readjustment and reintegration of the total personality requires an emotional statement from the Child in the presence of the Adult and Parent. The requirement that the Adult and Parent be fully commissioned during the whole experience detracts from the general value of psychological and pharmacological hypnotic procedures, since the essential function of most such artifacts is to liberate the Child by decommissioning other aspects of the personality. Psychoanalysis overcomes this difficulty through the device of free association. The drawback here is that the Child often expresses himself indirectly or in a spotty, macular fashion, so that a great deal depends upon the interpretive ability of the therapist and the receptivity of the patient to specialized interpretations.

The logical development of transactional analysis is a direct appeal to the Child in the waking state. Reasoning and experience lead to the belief that a Child expresses himself most freely to another child. Hence the closest approach to an ideal solution for the therapeutic problem of self-expression is the method of regression analysis. The evolution of this procedure is still in an embryonic state and requires some years of experiment and refinement in order to overcome some of the inherent difficulties and obtain the maximum therapeutic yield.

Regression analysis is a technique which is taught to the patient, and a prerequisite is a clear understanding of structural analysis. The indications are that the required relaxation of defenses or transfer of cathexis is least easily accomplished by patients such as the dogmatic Mr. Troy, who must maintain a Parental attitude, or like the intellectual Dr. Quint, who must maintain an Adult attitude. Others often attain a considerable degree of skill with surprising rapidity, and some who have a special aptitude (whose nature so far eludes understanding) may take to it immediately.

The rationale for attempting to revive the Child as an actually reexperienced ego state is an epistemological one. To review briefly, the Child is regarded functionally as the manifestation of a psychic organ or system, the archaeopsyche. *Phenomenologically,* the Child appears as a discrete, integrated ego state. It becomes known *behaviorally* through symptomatic physiological, psychological, and verbal signs, and *socially* through the quality of its transactions. The origin of these manifestations can be confirmed *historically* by establishing that they reproduce phenomena which were manifested during the actual childhood of the individual. But behavioral description and history are both Adult approaches. The patient and the therapist talk *about* the Child in an inferential way, which is what the epistemologists call "Knowledge by description." The therapeutic effect of this is usually appreciable and gratifying, but is of a different order from what happens if the archaic ego state itself is vividly revived in the mind of the patient rather than being inferred from external data. Such a revival is allied to the "abreaction" of Freud, the "gut-memories" of Kubie,[1] and the temporal lobe phenomenon of Penfield.[2] It is a non-inferential apprehension constituting "Knowledge by acquaintance" even in the strictest sense of the term.[1] Here it is not the Adult talking about the Child, but the Child itself talking.

In order to understand this clearly, it is necessary for the clinician to take it quite literally. The position is just the same as if there were two people in the room with the therapist: an observing adult and a pathological child, except that they are physically inseparable. The problem is how to separate them psychologically so that the child can speak for himself. (For the sake of simplicity the third party, the Parent, will be disregarded for the moment.) A separation by artificial means such as hypnosis is deleterious to the final outcome. It is one thing for a pediatrician to tell a waiting mother what her offspring said in the office, and another thing for the mother to hear it with her own ears.

When a previously buried archaic ego state is revived in its full vividness in the waking state, it is then permanently at the disposal of the patient and the therapist for detailed examination. Not only do "abreaction" and "working through" take place, but the ego state can be treated like an actual child. It can be nurtured carefully, even tenderly, until it unfolds like a flower, revealing all the complexities of its internal structure. It can be turned over and over in the hand, so to speak, until previously unobserved features come into full perception. Such an active ego state is not regarded in the manner of Kubie as a memory, but as an experience in its own right, more like Penfield's temporal phenomenon.

Iris had come to the group for several years, with occasional interruptions, and played an excellent game of "Psychiatry" in structural and transactional terms. By observation and inference she could diagnose her own and other people's ego states and analyze transactions. Eventually an opportunity arose for her to have intensive individual therapy, which both she and the therapist thought she was ready for. Her previous occasional interviews had been stereotyped and somewhat boring to herself and Dr. Q. They had both recognized that she was playing "Psychiatry," and that although this was of considerable help to her, it left something to be desired. (Specifically, she played three different varieties of this game: Mental Health, Psychoanalytic, and Transactional. She was weaned away from Mental Health, was allowed some leeway with her "wild analysis," and was actively encouraged in the Transactional variety because this seemed to be the most useful to her.) After she started regularly on the couch, she became a different person. The phenomenological Child began to emerge, and one day came out in full bloom. She could actually feel herself back in a certain servile situation, and recognized how influential these re-experienced feelings had been in determining her destiny. She now poignantly felt her dual identity as Adult and Child. The following day she reported: "You know, since yesterday I've felt clearer than I have for years. It's as though I were emerging from a fog. Recognizing the Child is one thing, but actually feeling it is another. It's frightening. Knowing that it's my Child doesn't make it any more comfortable for me, but it does relieve me: at least I know where those feelings are coming from."

Thus, regression analysis is a deliberate attempt to shift the study of the Child from an inferential basis to a phenomenological one. With a suitably prepared patient, one who has had plenty of experience with structural analysis, and has some understanding of transactional analysis and game analysis as well, the therapist makes the following statement:

"I am five years old and I have not yet been to school. You are whatever age you choose, but under eight. Now go ahead."

Here the therapist plays the role of a child who is not acquainted with polysyllables or circumlocutions. This is a special kind of role, since it is one he is well acquainted with: he has only to be what he was when he was five.

It is not easy to report the results of a session of regression analysis. The therapist's position is one of split cathexis. He must be half Child and half Adult observer of both his own and the patient's behavior. Whatever cathexis goes into his Child is subtracted from his usual therapeutic Adult, and the result is that it requires the utmost concentration on his (Adult) part to keep both ego states active simultaneously. The pertinent effect is an impairment of Adult memory. He can deal effectively at the time with what happens, but it is difficult to reconstruct the events afterward. The use of a tape recorder is contraindicated. The introduction of a tape recorder to two actual five- or six-year-old children will quickly demonstrate what a predominating artifact it is with such people. And since understanding of regression analysis is still so rudimentary, it would be at this time impossible to estimate the effect on the proceedings of having a recorder in the room.

An approximate reconstruction, however, will at least give the flavor of what happens. Mr. Wheat, whose father died when he was two years old, was talk-ing in an individual session about some of his Parental attitudes toward his own sexual peccadilloes.

Dr. Q: I am five years old and have not yet been to school. You are whatever age you choose, but under eight. Now go ahead.

Mr. W: My daddy is dead. Where's your daddy?

Dr. Q: He's out seeing sick people. He's a doctor.

Mr. W: I'm going to be a doctor when I grow up.

Dr. Q: What does dead mean?

Mr. W: It means you're dead, like when a fish is dead or a cat is dead or a bird is dead.

Dr. Q: It isn't the same, because when *people* are dead it's different. They have a funeral and everything.

Mr. W: How do you know?

Dr. Q: I just know. They have a funeral and they bury them in the cemetery. Is your daddy in the ceme-tery?

Mr. W: Yes, and he's up in heaven too.

Dr. Q: How can he be in the cemetery and in heaven too?

Mr. W: Well, he is.

Dr. Q: Where's heaven?

Mr. W: It's up in the sky.

Dr. Q: If he's in the sky he can't be in the ceme-tery.

Mr. W: Yes he can. Something comes out of him and it goes to heaven and the rest of him they put in the cemetery.

Dr. Q: Where does it come out of?

Mr. W: It comes out of his mouth.

Dr. Q: You're funny. I don't believe that. How do you know it comes out of his mouth? Can you see it?

Mr. W: No, but it does anyway.

Dr. Q: If you can't see it, how do you know?

Mr. W: Because my mommy told me. It's your real

daddy that goes to heaven and it's only his body they put in the cemetery.

Dr. Q: Well, I don't see how he can be in two places. What does he do up in the sky?

Mr. W: He sits beside Jesus and watches us. You know, you're funny looking. You have a skinny face.

Dr. Q: You're crazy to believe your daddy can be in two places.

Mr. W: I wish I had a real daddy. (Weeps.) Okay, I've had enough.

This brief experience made it clear to both the patient and the therapist how confused Mr. Wheat's Child was about the origin, function, and reality of his Parent. Previously, the whole problem of his father's influence, and his unconscious fantasies about his father insofar as they affected his behavior, had been matters of interpretation and speculation. Further regression analysis revealed how profuse those fantasies were, and how impossible it was for his Child to reconcile the contradictions about death: his anatomical father shivering under the frozen ground in the snow-covered cemetery, and some other kind of father who came out of the mouth sitting blissfully beside mild-mannered Jesus, his serenity periodically shattered by the deeds of his offspring, who would be held in sad accounting when his own time came and he went to his eternal judgment before God the Father and the spirit (fully clothed in custom-tailored pre-World War I elegance) of his own father.

In normal social intercourse, the Child "programs" the Adult, in the cybernetic sense; here the situation is reversed, and the Adult of the therapist must "program" his Child. Some of the technical difficulties become apparent even in the brief extract given. Would a five-year-old boy like the therapist be so persistent in pursuing one subject? Is it ever permissible to use the word "crazy" with a patient, even if this is the natural word for a five-year-old boy? Can the patient really ever stop regarding the therapist as a parent, and talk to him as though he were another child? It is evident that regression analysis is still in a highly experimental stage, and can only be employed with the utmost care in the selection of cases.

The use of this technique in group therapy yields equally interesting results.

Dr. Q: I am five years old and I have not yet had any schooling. Each of you is whatever age you choose, but under eight. Now go ahead.

Heather: My granddaddy does bad things to me.

Magnolia: I can't remember any of my male relatives doing anything improper.

Dr. Q: Magnolia goes to school and she uses big words that I don't understand. What's "improper"?

Camellia: I know, because my mommy told me. "Improper" means you do something you're not supposed to.

Daisy: You must have had a close relationship with your mother, Camellia.

Dr. Q: That lady, Daisy, is listening to us, and she uses big words too.

Iris: Sometimes I'm afraid to play here because I know that lady, Daisy, is watching us.

Dr. Q: Why did you all come to my house to play?

Rosita: I like to go to a boy's house and play. You can have all kinds of fun and you can do bad things like my mommy does with some men that come to see her.

And so on, for about twenty minutes. Afterward, each of the members said that this episode had had an unusual effect on her. Camellia had a severe pain in the chest, reminiscent of early stomach-aches; Rosita felt as though she were floating; Heather's hands were shaking; Poppy was weeping; Daisy had a bad headache, and said she hadn't had a headache since she was seven or eight years old; Magnolia's heart was pounding; Iris was aghast at the new memories which came to her in profusion; and Hyacinth had had difficulty throughout in not bursting into giggles.

So impressed were these women with the power of this instrument that when Heather proposed that they repeat the procedure at the next session, they all voted against it, and it was several weeks before they were ready to go ahead again. In the meantime, those who were in concurrent individual therapy had many new things to talk about.

Eight years is chosen as the critical age for the patient's regression because there are very few people who claim amnesia beyond that: therefore all the patients are likely to have some basis for proceeding, and "complete amnesia" is not readily available as a resistance. Five years is chosen as the age for the therapist because it implies some development of reality sense, but only a limited pre-school vocabulary. The vocabulary limitation makes it easy to confront people who are not participating, and who reveal this by verbal sophistication. It offers a cogent way of illustrating to them what is required; if they cannot take such a broad hint, then it is probable that they are resistive rather than merely unclear.

Regression analysis is a kind of psychodrama, but it seems to be more precise in its theoretical background and its technique.[5] It is more limited in scope, and also less artificial, since without exception all the participants, including the therapist, have played their roles before in blood and sweat and tears. It is perhaps more closely allied to the "direct analysis" of Rosen,[6] particularly in the use made of the material.

Since this is at present the farthest frontier of transactional analysis, everything known about it so far is tentative, and any further statements would be ill-advised. Perhaps further light on the subject will come from the work of Chandler and Hartman[7] with LSD–25, which has much in common with regression analysis, and seems to be free of some of the drawbacks of other pharmacological regressions.

REFERENCES

1. Kubie, L. *Loc. cit.*
2. Penfield, W. *Loc. cit.*
3. Runes, Dagobert D. *Dictionary of Philosophy.* Philosophical Library, New York, n.d. "Acquaintance, Knowledge by"; "Description, Knowledge by"; "Epistemology," Section f.
4. James, W. *Psychology.* Henry Holt & Company, New York, 1910. p. 14.
5. Moreno, J. L. *Psychodrama,* Vol. 1. Beacon House, New York, 1946.
6. Rosen, J. *Loc. cit.*
7. Chandler, A. L. & Hartman, M. A. *Loc. cit.*

CHAPTER TWENTY

Theoretical and Technical Considerations

1 THEORY

A SYSTEM cannot be generalized from within. The minutest examination of the Earth will not reveal its place in the universe until the investigator finds courage to look upward at the skies. A generalization is made by asking: "What is this an example of?" An elegant illustration can be found in modern number theory. The properties and relationships of prime numbers have been the subject of intensive and persistent examination by some of the best intellects of the past twenty-two centuries. Yet the field remained relatively sterile and full of approximations ever since the original researches of Eratosthenes. Recently, however, a way was found of answering the question: "What is the series of prime numbers an example of?" The answer is that there are many possible varieties and infinite instances of such "mathematical sieves."[1] Even to a layman it is evident that this generalization of Eratosthenes's advice has interesting possibilities of further theoretical development and practical application. Mathematicians generally welcome such broadening insights, which have the advantage of bringing together under one comprehensive concept areas which were previously difficult to correlate.

There are indications that structural and transactional analysis might possibly serve a similar function.

For example, experiments in translating into structural language textbooks, monographs, and papers on the socio-clinical sciences have already revealed two advantages. First, the increase in clarity and conciseness can reduce the bulk of such works by a considerable amount; and secondly, it helps the "interdisciplinary" problem by supplying a common relevant terminology for hitherto disparate disciplines.

By way of acknowledgment, it should be said that structural analysis is only the apple of which psychodynamics is the core. Conscientious students will find that the core slips neatly into the apple; hasty attempts to force the apple into the core can only result in a deplorable mutilation of the fruits of clinical experience.

2   ROLE-PLAYING

Ego states must be differentiated from "roles," unless the concept of role-playing is reduced to an absurdity by including everything. The position of structural analysis should be defined in this respect.

When an accountant speaks at a Rotary Club dinner, he may act the way he thinks an accountant is expected to act. This is role-playing. But when he is concentrating on a column of figures in his office, he is not playing the role of an accountant, he *is* an accountant. He maintains a certain ego state, the ego state which is necessary for adding a column of figures.

If a therapist plays the role of a therapist, he will not get very far with perceptive patients. He has to *be* a therapist. If he decides that a certain patient needs Parental reassurance, he does not play the role of a parent; rather he liberates his Parental ego state. A good test of this is for him to attempt to "show off" his Parentalism in the presence of a colleague, with a patient toward whom he does not *feel* parental. In this case he is playing a role, and a forthright patient will soon make

clear to him the difference between *being* a reassuring
Parent and playing the role of a reassuring parent. One
of the functions of psychotherapeutic training establish-
ments is to separate trainees who want to play the role
of therapists from those who want to *be* therapists.

A patient may play a role in the script or game of
another patient; but as an individual, he is not playing
a role when he is Parent, Adult, or Child; he exists in
the ego state of one of these three. A patient in the ego
state of a Child may decide to play a role; but whatever role he plays, or however he switches from role to
role, his ego state remains that of a Child. He may
even play the role of a certain kind of child, but that is
only one possible choice of his Child ego state. In the
same way, actual children playing "House" may take
the respective roles of Mother, Doctor, and Baby, but
they all remain children of a certain age while they are
playing these roles.

3   TRAINING

Training in structural analysis is not as arduous as
training in psychoanalysis, but it is arduous enough,
and requires the same critical attitude toward previous
conditioning, including previous psychoanalytic training. At least a year of weekly seminars, with daily
practice, is necessary in order to get the proper clinical
feeling. The writer was once asked to give a twenty-
minute paper on transactional analysis, and a discus-
sant was assigned who had no experience with this approach. This was like giving a twenty-minute paper on
the theory and practice of transistor circuit design before an aggressive association of vacuum tube manufac-
turers, none of whom had ever seen a transistor. As
Freud once remarked, it is one thing to flirt with an
idea, and another thing to be married to it. This epigram may be paraphrased: "You never know a woman

until you have lived with her," and an occasional stroll in the park with transactional analysis will hardly reveal all its possibilities. The relatively short training period for the transactional analyst is not because transactional analysis is necessarily simpler or less important, but because the material emerges more spontaneously and more intrusively than the material of other psychotherapeutic systems.

4   THERAPEUTIC HINTS

1. The beginner is advised to concentrate on learning to differentiate the Adult from the Child. The Parent can be left alone until its recognition is forced on him by the material. Similarly with a new patient.

2. The system should be introduced well behind the clinical material. For example, it is wise to have at least three diagnostic illustrations from the patient's productions. If the patient does not understand the first example, the second can be offered. If this is also refused, resistance or bad timing rather than lack of understanding should be suspected. The third example is then kept in reserve until it can be used later to confirm some other approach.

3. Later, diagnosis of the Parent or the Child must be confirmed from actual historical material. One of the patient's functional parents, or the patient himself in childhood, must have behaved in the manner indicated. If such confirmation is not forthcoming, the diagnosis must be suspended.

4. The trichotomy must be taken quite literally. It is just as if each patient were three different people. Until the therapist can perceive it this way, he is not ready to use this system effectively. For example, the patient seeks treatment for three different reasons: one is the reason his mother (or father) would have brought him there; another is the rational explanation; and the third

is the reason he might have come as a pre-school child, perhaps to get candy or its substitute. Again, one of his aspects may have resisted coming, and the other two have dragged him there.

When there is any difficulty in understanding what is going on at an individual interview, it can often be cleared up by analyzing it as though there were actually six different people in the room: for example, the therapist, his father, and himself as a little boy; and on the patient's side, a little girl, an objective neutral governess, nursemaid, or pediatrician, and the patient's mother.

5. Once more, the words "mature" and "immature" have no place here. Every patient is assumed to have a structurally complete Adult. The question is how to get it cathected. There is always a radio, the problem is how to get it plugged in.

6. The word "childish," since it has taken on a derogatory sense, must likewise be excluded. The Child may be confused or loaded with unconstructive feelings, but child-like qualities are potentially the most valuable aspects of the personality.

7. For the most part, the examples given have concerned the behavioral and social aspects of the Child because those are the objective observations. Discussion of these offers only intellectual insight. For the best results, it is necessary for the patient to experience the ego state itself, the phenomenological Child, to be once again the muddy little boy, the girl in the tattered dress, and to see her childhood intimates around her with almost eidetic imagery.

8. It should be remembered that the concept of games is a very precise one. A game is not just a habit, an attitude, or a reaction, but a specific sequence of operations, to each of which a specific response is expected: first move, response; second move, response; third move, response; checkmate!

9. It may take some time to see that games and pastimes are not occasional occurrences, but take up the large bulk of time and effort spent in society.

10. When it is noted that a patient plays a certain game, it will eventually be seen by both patient and therapist that this does not mean an occasional sally, but that it is played almost incessantly, hour by hour, day by day, with varying degrees of intensity.

11. The ideal intervention is the "bull's-eye," one which is meaningful and acceptable to all three aspects of the patient's personality, since all three overhear everything that is said.

During a tense moment in the group, Mr. Hecht took a candy bar from his pocket and gave half of it to his wife. Both these young people then curled up in their chairs and munched like two high-school children. Dr. Q remarked: "Now I see why you got married. You're like two waifs in the wood fleeing from the domineering parents you told us about." Mr. Hecht added: "And we have chocolate together." Dr. Q elaborated: "Yes you make sweet chocolate together." Everyone laughed, and Mrs. Hecht put in: "Honi soit qui mal y pense!"

Dr. Q's joke was close to a bull's-eye. It pleased the Hechts' saccharine Parents because of the word "sweet." It pleased their Adults because it was pertinent and amusing. And it reached at least Mrs. Hecht's Child, since she caught the intentional anal flavor of the remark, which was meant to hint at the nature of their script contract.

12. After the beginner gathers momentum, there will be a period of enthusiasm. This may be followed by a phase of revulsion, particularly against using the terminology. This recoil should not arouse anxiety or cause a resignation, since it is a normal part of the learning process. Indeed, if such a reaction does not occur, it is questionable whether any deep conviction can be at-

tained. It is precisely when a new professional discipline is about to become an integrated part of the personality and a permanent commitment is impending, that deeper resistance may be temporarily aroused. This seems to be part of any professional training, and is probably a natural structural phenomenon.

5   RESULTS

The reader has now become familiar with some of the things that transactional analysis can do. In the writer's practice during the past four years, about 100 people gave it a fair trial (at least seven consecutive weeks, sometimes as long as two or three years). Twenty of these were pre-psychotic, psychotic, or post-psychotic. In the majority of cases the treatment ended with the patients, their families, and the therapist all feeling better. The experiences of other therapists using this form of treatment are similar in many instances. Patients who had previously been treated by one or more other psychiatrists using orthodox psychoanalysis, psychoanalytic therapy, and various other approaches were particularly gratifying to work with because they were so well prepared. These usually left in good spirits with a very favorable attitude toward transactional analysis.

Some of the patients, particularly those who did not use transactional analysis in a meaningful way, showed little change in attitude or behavior. Three cases were outright failures, patients whose treatment terminated in (voluntary) hospitalization; these were all people who had had previous psychiatric hospitalizations.

The least distressing and most instructive of the three failures was Mrs. B, the first alcoholic with whom game analysis was attempted. She appeared to gain some insight and one day, after two individual interviews and ten weekly group sessions, she appeared in the group and asked them to tell her what they thought of her. Everyone was impressed because this was the first time she had actively participated. The therapist recognized that she now felt comfortable enough to begin to play her game. The group members responded in an objective, justifiably complimentary way. Mrs. B protested, saying that she wanted "the truth," obviously meaning some disagreeable comments. The group did not comply. In the language of games, they refused to play persecutors in her game of alcoholic. She went home and told her husband that if she ever took another drink he must either divorce her or send her to a hospital. He agreed. She quickly became intoxicated and he took her to a hospital. After her discharge they were divorced.

δ THE PSYCHIC APPARATUS

An example was discovered recently in which there appeared to be a split in a single uncontaminated ego state, a condition which could not be accounted for on the basis of the theory so far formulated. In attempting to explain this anomaly, it was discovered that certain new elements had to be inferred which immediately proved their usefulness in clarifying some obscurities.

The clinical paradigm for introducing these new elements concerns Mr. Decatur, a successful traveling salesman in his thirties who returned home in a high state of sexual tension following one of his long trips. After a satisfactory single intercourse with his wife, he resumed work the next morning in his home town. The one intercourse had merely taken the edge off his healthy sexual appetite, and he was looking forward to more when he got back home that night. It was not surprising, therefore, that in talking to and listening to his women clients during the day, he found himself at times having sexual fantasies about them. He made the observation that at such periods, his Adult was divided into two parts, a sexual part and a business part. The writer was inclined to agree with this diagnosis. The sexual fantasies seemed to be free of pregenital elements. They were intrusive, considerate, and well adapted to the reality possibilities to each situation; in principle they met the criteria for realistic genital sexual "object interest," if not love, and they were based on healthy biological instinctual pressures. Since there were neither inhibitions nor archaic elements, they could not be regarded as anything but Adult, free of exteropsychic and archaeopsychic influences, and controlled by reality-testing.

While these fantasies were proceeding, he continued to talk and listen in his usual effective business-like way, and this represented also an Adult activity. Hence it had to be admitted that his Adult was for all clinical purposes split into two different states of mind which functioned simultaneously. He did mention, however, that while the fantasies were interesting and his business activities successful, there was something missing in the intensity of each of them. From these remarks it could be inferred that there was some splitting of cathexis between the two aspects, so that neither of them was as energetic as each was ordinarily when they functioned separately. He also stated that what helped him keep part of his mind on his business, so that he did not relapse completely into fantasy while he was listening to a long dissertation from one of his clients, was a feeling of duty or "oughtness."

The ensuing discussion can be read most profitably by those who have a sound clinical foundation in transactional analysis. Otherwise the inferred elements, which are practical clinical necessities, may appear to be merely another gratuitous set of concepts such as are only too common in academic psychologies.

We shall now speak of three *instances;* determinants, organizers, and phenomena. The *phenomena* are already familiar as ego states: Child, Adult, and Parent. The *organizers* are also familiar as psychic "organs": archaeopsyche, neopsyche, and exteropsyche. *Determinants* are factors which determine the quality of the organization and the phenomena, that is, they establish their programing. *Internal* programing arises from indigenous biological forces. These may influence any of the organizers, and hence the resultant phenomena. *Probability* programing arises from autonomous data-processing based on past experience. *External* programing arises from incorporated external canons.

In the case of the traveling salesman, the phenomenon was an Adult ego state, a manifestation of the neopsyche. But there was on the one hand a strong internal biological determinant, and on the other a strong external (moral) determinant. His solution was a split Adult ego state, one segment of which was instinctually determined, and the other maintained by a sense of duty. The executive power, however, at all times remained with the neopsyche, so that his behavior was correct and well-tested against the reality potentials.

The next step is to postulate that each organizer has two functions, and the essential point is that these two functions are independent. One function is to organize determinants into effective *influences*, and the other function is to organize phenomena. (The independence of these two functions may be easily accounted for on the basis of cathectic balances. The most actively cathected organizer will take over the executive, the less actively cathected will merely act as influences.) Since instincts are phylogenetically archaic, it may be logically postulated that the archaeopsyche organizes internal programing. Because the neopsyche is concerned with data-processing, it may be regarded as the organizer for probability programing. And since the exteropsyche is the organ concerned with borrowed ego states, it may be alloted the task of organizing external programing.

We are now in a position to review some of the ambiguities encountered in structural analysis. An ego state is the phenomenological and behavioral manifestation of the activity of a certain psychic organ, or organizer. These same organs have the independent task of effectively organizing whichever determinants are most active at a given moment. This results in two parallel series, with nine simple cases: Child, with internal, probability, or external programing; Adult, with the same possibilities; and Parent, with the same possibilities. Not all these cases will be attempted, but a few of them may profitably be discussed.

The characteristic of the archaeopsyche is what Freud calls primary process; that of the neopsyche, secondary process; and that of the exteropsyche, something akin to identification. Hence the tendency of the Child will be toward primary process; but probability programing will tend to interfere with this. Then tendency of the Adult will be secondary process, but internal (instinctual) programing will tend to impair this function. The tendency of the Parent is to function according to borrowed parameters, but this may be affected by internal or probability programing.

These situations sound similar to some of those which have been discussed previously under the name of contamination, and their relationship to that phenomenon remains to be clarified. Contamination has been described in spatial terms, while the present discussion is from the functional point of view.

The Parent has been described as having two attitudes: nurturing and prohibitive. These attitudes can now be accounted for functionally, where previously their clarification rested on historical data. Their functional explanation depends on whether the concept of a death instinct is admissible or not. If it is, then both attitudes may be regarded as internally programed exteropsychic ego states: the nurturing attitude determined by libido, the prohibitive attitude determined by mortido (or "destrudo," as some prefer to call the energy of the death instinct). If the death instinct is not admissible, then the nurturing Parent is still internally (e.g., endocrinologically) programed, and the prohibitive Parent may be regarded as externally programed.

The Parent has also been described on the one hand as an influence ("as mother would have liked"), and on the other as an active ego state ("like mother"). It is now clear that the first refers to external programing (as when the Adult of the traveling salesman carried on his business from a sense of duty), while the second still refers to an active ego state which may be programed in any one of three ways or in any combination of the three ("like mother when she was nursing me through an illness" (internal); "like mother when she was arguing about the grocery bill" (probability); "like mother when she was spanking me" (external, or internal mortidinal)). It is evident that this also has a bearing on the second-order structure of the Parent, described from the functional rather than the phenomenological point of view.

The distinction between the adapted Child and the natural Child is now also simpler to state. The adapted Child is an archaeopsychic ego state externally programed, while the natural Child is an archaeopsychic ego state internally programed. The precocious Child may be added for the sake of completeness as the probability programed Child, although in practice of course the determinants have, as in all cases, a more complex relationship. The examples given are intended only as schematic illustrations or abstractions of what may be seen in the living tissue.

The inference or concept of programing is particularly necessary in attempting to clarify the difficulties encountered in many instances concerning Adult ego states. One example of its usefulness here is in distinguishing between "rational" authorities and "authoritarian" authorities. A rational authority may be anyone from a dictator or monarch like King Solomon to a certain kind of traffic policeman. A common example in modern times is the overseas British of Australian colonial administrator. Their *approach* to native populations is typically that of a statistical data-processor, but their *attitude* is paternalistic and their solutions to problems are usually oriented toward the childlike aspects of their changes.[2] This may be characterized as a Parent-programed Adult, represented in Figure 20A. The authoritarian authority is the dictator, big or small, as he is popularly pictured: one whose approach is primarily to inflict his will on his subjects, but who maintains an attitude of rational justification, so that his propaganda presents statistical data calculated to justify his tyranny. Since his "real Self" is Parent, "he himself" may believe what he is saying. This is the Adult-programed Parent represented in Figure 20B. (For the sake of completeness, the unpredictable autocratic authority may be added, the Child-programed Roman emperors who tried to realize their archaic fantasies in unrestrained cruelty and abandon.)

On a more universal level, referring to Figure 17D, the ethical Adult, "Ethos," may be regarded functionally as the Parent-programed Adult, the denotation being that good mothers behave ethically toward their infants. The feeling Adult, "Pathos," may be understood as a Child-programed Adult, referring to the fact that at a certain age little brother cries when bigger brother is in pain.

What are here called determinants, generalized from

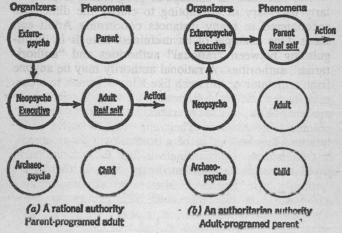

(a) A rational authority
Parent-programed adult

(b) An authoritarian authority
Adult-programed parent

FIGURE 20

the clinical material of transactional analysis, resemble another set of concepts derived much earlier from similar material. This correspondence is gratifying, since it tends to support the validity of both systems by independent sets of observations. The concepts of id, ego, and superego have become somewhat jargonized in the hands of Freud's followers, and it is preferable in a formal discussion to stick to Freud's original formulations.[8]

The id. "It contains everything that is inherited, that is present at birth, that is fixed in the constitution—above all, therefore, the instincts, which originate in the somatic organization and which find their first mental expression in the id in forms unknown to us. . . . This oldest portion of the mental apparatus remains the most important throughout life." This description is quite competent to take care not only of the popular conception of "id activity," but also of genital sexual factors and maternal nurturing behavior, and in this sense id activity resembles "internal programing."

The ego. "It has the task of self-preservation ... it performs that task by becoming aware of the stimuli from without, by storing up the experiences of them (in the memory), by avoiding excessive stimuli (through flight), by dealing with moderate stimuli (through adaptation), and, finally, by learning to bring about appropriate modifications in the external world to its own advantage (through activity) ... in relation to the id, it performs that task by gaining control over the demands of the instincts, by deciding whether they shall be allowed to obtain satisfaction, by postponing that satisfaction to times and circumstances favorable in the external world or by suppressing their excitations completely." Such an agency resembles the self-programing probability computer with special characteristics which is the model for neopsychic programing.

The superego. "The long period of childhood, during which the growing human being lives in dependence upon his parents, leaves behind it a precipitate, which forms within his ego a special agency in which this parental influence is prolonged. . . . The parents' influence naturally includes not merely the personalities of the parents themselves but also the racial, national, and family traditions handed on through them ... an individual's superego in the course of his development takes over contributions from later successors and substitutes of his parents." In effect, the superego is a reservoir for exteropsychic influences.

And in summary: ". . . the id and superego have one thing in common: they both represent the influences of the past (the id the influence of heredity, the superego essentially the influence of what is taken over from other people), whereas the ego is principally determined by the individual's own experience."

Freud does not raise any question of systematic

phenomenology, and it is here that structural analysis can usefully fill a gap in psychological theory, just as transactional analysis fills a gap in social theory by setting up elementary units (transactions) and larger units (games and scripts) of social action.

NOTES

Structural analysis first began to be used with some regularity by the writer in the fall of 1954, after a few years of preliminary evolution. By 1956, the need for and the principles of transactional and game analysis had emerged with sufficient clarity to indicate a more systematic, ongoing therapeutic program. The results obtained during the initial phases from September 1954 to September 1956 have been given elsewhere,[4] and are summarized, as given, in the table below. The criteria used were similar to those mentioned in the present text. "F" denotes failures, patients whose treatment terminated in (voluntary) hospitalization. "O" denotes those who showed little change in attitude or behavior. "I" denotes those who improved steadily according to whatever consensus of opinion was available in each case. Line "P" includes all pre-psychotics, psychotics, and post-psychotics, and line "N" includes all other patients.

	Number			Percentages		
Total	F	O	I	F	O	I
P 23	2	3	18	10	12	78
N 42	0	14	28	0	33	67

The value of such figures is at best open to question, and at worst they may be misleading to the patients, the professional and lay public, and the therapist who compiles them. The question of drawing up similar tables for the patients mentioned in the text was discussed with some colleagues and with some of the patients themselves, and the responses were almost unanimously dubious or adverse. The patients, who are the people chiefly concerned, were quite willing to co-operate in any evaluative procedures that the therapist might suggest, but by and large they seemed to regard statistical scales as having little serious relation to the realities of psychotherapeutic progress. One woman gave as an example: "This morning I happened to look at my washing machine and it looked *real*. That made me very happy. Things didn't look that way before I came here." The question was: "How do you know how much that means to me, and how are you going to prove it to anybody?" Outright failures are easy to categorize, but successes, at least in private office practice, are difficult to quantify conscientiously.

Seven weeks are chosen as the minimum acceptable exposure to treatment because of what appears to be a natural biological period. It usually takes from 39 to 45 days for ego boundaries to make a metastable shift into a new position. This is the "crystallization" period,[5] for example, in "getting used" to a new house (for people who are interested in their living quarters). Hence it is pragmatically indicated in making surveys to take seriously only those patients who keep their appointments regularly for at least seven weeks in succession, regardless of how frequent those appointments are, providing they are at least once a week. If they are less frequent than once a week, another period has to be considered which would make each appointment a "new experience" and thus break the continuity. Evidently, the continuity is also broken if a week is missed during the initial period.

A surprising number of psychoanalysts have noted structural phenomena, that is, shifts in ego state, or have been told by patients about what are here called the Adult and the Child. The surprise lies in the fact that none of them, except Federn and his pupils, have given any serious thought to the matter. H. Wiesenfeld has drawn my attention to a paper by Ekstein and Wallerstein[6] in which they emphasize these very observations, but in the end abandon the naturalistic approach to become involved in a technical discussion of defense mechanisms. Interesting though their conclusions are, they seem banal in contrast to the promising and exciting initial observations. This paper demonstrates in a fascinating way the shifts between archaeopsychic, neopsychic, and exteropsychic ego states in borderline and psychotic children.

REFERENCES

1. Hawkins, D. "Mathematical Sieves." *Scientific American.* 199: 105–112, December, 1958.

2. *Pacific Islands Monthly.* Pacific Publications Pty., Sydney. Passim.

3. Freud, S. *An Outline of Psychoanalysis. Loc. cit.,* pp. 14–18.

4. Berne, E. "Ego States in Psychotherapy." *Loc. cit.*

5. Stendhal. *On Love.* Peter Pauper Press, Mount Vernon, N. Y., n.d.

6. Ekstein, R. & Wallerstein, J. "Observations on the Psychology of Borderline and Psychotic Children." *Psychoanal. Study of the Child,* IX, 344–369, 1954.

Appendix

A TERMINATED CASE WITH FOLLOW-UP

THE following case illustrates the procedure and outcome in a completed course of structural and transactional analysis. Because the systematic use of this approach from beginning to termination has only recently become possible with the full flowering of its theoretical development, the follow-up is relatively short. Nevertheless, this is not an isolated instance, and whether by good luck or because the therapy accomplishes its purpose, there now exists a small group of cases whose ultimate outcome will be observed with special interest through the years. This consists of patients who made unexpectedly rapid (by former standards) symptomatic and social improvement under controlled therapeutic conditions.

Before taking up in more detail the case of Mrs. Enatosky, the case of Mrs. Hendrix, a 30-year-old housewife, is worth considering briefly. Mrs. Hendrix was first seen ten years ago, when she was suffering from an agitated depression. She was treated by conventional supportive methods ("offering oral supplies," as it is colloquially called) for one year, in the course of which she recovered.

When she returned a decade later, she was, if anything, worse than she had been during her previous episode, with more active suicidal fantasies. This time she was treated by structural and transactional analysis, and within six weeks she improved more than she had during the whole year of therapy in her former episode; this in the opinion not only of herself and the therapist, but also of her family and intimates; and this improvement was brought about by a procedure decidedly different from "supportive" offering of

275

"supplies." After another six weeks, she was coping better than she had ever done in her life, having relinquished some of her long-standing autistic ambitions in favor of living in the world. She had also given up an unhealthy tendency to postulate her position or her unfortunate childhood; instead of playing "Wooden Leg" and "If It Weren't For Them," she was beginning to find her identity within the framework of new possibilities which unfolded in her family life. This case is mentioned because it offers about as well-controlled a situation as it is possible to hope for in clinical practice: the same patient with two similar well-defined episodes separated by a distinct interval, treated by the same therapist with two distinct approaches.

To return now to Mrs. Enatosky. As recounted at the beginning of Chapter 14, this woman complained initially of "depressions" of sudden onset. It may be recalled that she had had three previous forms of treatment: Alcoholics Anonymous, hypnosis, and psychotherapy combined with Zen and Yoga. She showed a special aptitude for structural and transactional analysis, and soon began to exert social control over the games which went on between herself and her husband, and herself and her son. The formal diagnosis is best stated as schizo-hysteria. The case will now be reviewed session by session with significant extracts.

1. APRIL 1

The patient arrived on time for her initial interview. She stated she had been going to other therapists but had become dissatisfied and had called a municipal clinic, and after some discussion with a social worker had been referred to Dr. Q. She was encouraged to proceed and at relevant points appropriate questions were asked in order to elicit the psychiatric history. She stated that she had been an alcoholic for ten years and had been cured by Alcoholics Anonymous. She dated the onset of her drinking from her mother's psychosis when she was 19. She said that her depressions began at the same time. The nature of her previous psychiatric treatment was discussed. The preliminary demographic information was obtained so that she could be placed as a native-born 34-year-old once-married Protestant housewife, a high school graduate, whose husband was a mechanic. Her father's occupation, the length of her marriage, her sibling position in years and months, and the ages of her children were noted. A preliminary search for traumatic events elicited that her father drank heavily and that her parents separated when she was seven years old.

The medical history revealed headaches, and numbness of one arm and leg, but no convulsions, allergies, skin afflictions, or other physical disorders with common psychiatric implications. Her age at the time of all operations, injuries, and serious illnesses was noted. Her childhood was explored for gross psychopathology such as sleep-walking, nail-biting, night terrors, stammering, stuttering, bed wetting, thumb sucking and other pre-school problems. Her school history was reviewed briefly. Chemical influences such as medications and exposure to noxious substances were also noted. A cautious exploration of her mental status was undertaken, and finally she was asked to relate any dream that she could remember. Recently she dreamed: "They were rescuing my husband from the water. His head was hurt and I started to scream." She mentioned that she often heard inner voices exhorting her to health, and once, two years ago, an "outer" voice. This satisfied the requirements for preliminary history-taking, and the patient was then allowed to wander as she pleased.

Discussion: The history-taking was carefully planned so that at all times the patient seemed to have the initiative and the therapist at most was curious rather than formal or openly systematic in gathering information. This means that the patient was allowed to structure the interview in her own way as far as possible and was not required to play a game of psychiatric history-taking. Because of her complaint of numbness she was referred to a neurologist for examination.

2. APRIL 8

The neurologist suspected cervical arthritis, but did not recommend any specific treatment. The patient conducted this interview as a kind of psychological survey. She spontaneously mentioned wanting approval and rebelling "like a little girl," as some "grown-up part" of her judged it. She said the "little girl" seemed "childish." It was suggested that she let the "little girl" out, rather than try to clamp down on her. She replied that that seemed brazen. "I like children, though. I know I can't live up to my father's expectations, and I get tired of trying to." This also includes her husband's "expectations." Such expectations were generalized for her as "parental expectations," since she had practically said as much herself. She sees the two most important "parents" in her life as her husband and her father. She is seductive toward her husband and recognizes that she was the same with her father. When her father and mother separated she thought (age 7): "I could have kept him." Thus she has not only a conflict about compliance, but also an attitude of seductiveness, toward parental figures.

Discussion: The patient's special aptitude for structural analysis is already evident. She herself makes the separation between "the little girl" and "a grown-up part" and recognizes the compliance of "the little girl" toward certain people whom she relates to her parents. It was only necessary, therefore, to reinforce this trichotomy in a nondirective way. With many other patients this might not have been undertaken until the third or fourth session, perhaps even later.

3. APRIL 15

She resents people who tell her what to do, especially women. This is another reaction to "parents." She mentions a feeling of "walking high." It is pointed out that this is the way a very small girl must feel, that this is again the Child. She replied: "Oh, for heaven's sake, that's true! As you said that I could see a little child . . . it's hard to believe, but that makes sense to me. As you say that, I feel I didn't want to walk: a little girl in rompers. . . . I feel funny now. They pull you up by your right shoulder and you're outraged . . . yet I do the same to my own son. I disapprove while I'm thinking 'I don't disapprove, I know just how he feels.' It's really my mother disapproving. Is *that* the Parent part you mentioned? I'm frightened a little by all this."

It was at this point that it was emphasized that there was no mysterious or metaphysical aspect to these diagnostic judgments.

Discussion: The patient has now experienced some of the phenomenological reality of the Child and has added to the behavioral, social, and historical reality she established in the previous interviews. The indications, therefore, are favorable for treatment with transactional analysis.

4. APRIL 22

"This week I've been happy for the first time in fifteen years. I don't have to look far to find the Child, I can see it in my husband and in others too. I have trouble with my son." The game with her son was clarified in an inexact but timely and illustrative way in terms of Parent (her disapproval and determination), Child (her seductiveness and her sulkiness at his recalcitrance), and Adult (her gratification when he finally did his work). It was hinted that an Adult approach (good reason) rather than a Parental approach (sweet reason) might be worth a try.

Discussion: The patient is now involved in transactional analysis proper and the idea of social control has been suggested.

5. APRIL 28

She reports that things work better with her son. Regression analysis is attempted to find out more about the

Child. She relates: "The cat soils the rug and they accuse me and make me wipe it up. I deny that I did it and stammer." In the ensuing discussion she remarks that both Alcoholics` Anonymous and the Anglican Church require confession to "messes." For this reason she gave them both up. As the session ends she asks: "Is it all right to be aggressive?" Answer: "You want *me* to tell you?" She understands the implication that she should decide such things on Adult grounds rather than asking Parental permission, and replies: "No, I don't."

Discussion: During this session some of the elements of her script are elicited. It can be anticipated that she will try to repeat with the therapist in some well-adapted form the cat situation. Her question "Is it all right to be aggressive?" is perhaps the first move in this adaptation. This gives the therapist an opportunity to decline to play and to reinforce her Adult. The patient has made such good progress in understanding structural and transactional analysis that she is already considered adequately prepared for fairly advanced group therapy. The group she is to enter consists largely of women.

6. MAY 4

A dream. "I look at myself and say: 'That's not so bad.' " She liked the group but it made her uncomfortable during the rest of the week. She relates some memories, including homosexual play during childhood. "Oh! That's why I didn't like AA. There were two homosexual women there and one of them called me sexy." She complains of vaginal itching. "My mother and I slept together and she bothered me."

Discussion: The manifest content of her dream is taken to be Adult and indicates the possibility of a good prognosis. The experience in the group has activated sexual conflicts, and this is the first indication of their nature.

7. MAY 11

She felt highly excited on leaving the group meeting.

"Things are moving quickly. Why did they make me laugh and blush? Things are better at home. I can kiss my son now and my daughter for the first time came and sat on my lap. I can't be a good lover when things are monotonous."

Discussion: The analysis of her family games, part of which has been outlined in Chapter 14, has resulted in the establishment of some Adult social control. It is evident that this improved control has been perceived by her children and for the first time in a long while they have the feeling that she can maintain her position and they react accordingly. Her excitement in the group and her statement that she can't be a good lover when things are monotonous indicate that she is involved in a sexual game with her husband.

An experience in the group later this week rather clearly showed her need for parental figures in some of her games. There was a new patient in the group, a male social worker, and she was very much impressed by his occupation. She asked him what they were supposed to do there. It was pointed out that she knew more than he did, since it was his first meeting and her third. She says she resents it when people tell her what to do, yet peasant-like, in spite of her superior experience, she asks a novice for instructions because she appears to be impressed by his education: evidently an attempt to set up a game. This interpretation strikes home. She recognizes how she "cons" a likely candidate into being parental and then complains about it.

8. MAY 18

She was upset by regression analysis in the group. It made her think of her fear of insanity, and of her mother in the state hospital. Her own production was of some elegant gates leading into a beautiful garden. This is a derivative of a Garden of Eden fantasy from before the age of five. The material indicates that the garden has become adapted to the gates of the state hospital where she visited her mother many years ago. This experience in the group offered a timely opportunity to mention to her that she might want to be hospitalized and so relieved of responsibility.

She has visited her mother only once in the past five or six years and it was suggested that it might be advisable for her to do that again. This suggestion was very carefully worded so as to be Adult rather than Parental. Any implication that she was a bad girl for not visiting her mother had to be avoided. She was able to understand the value of such a visit as an exercise for her Adult and as a means of preventing future difficulties between her Parent and her Child if her mother should die. The good reception of this suggestion was manifested by her bringing up new information. Her husband never washes his hair and always has a good excuse, which she accepts. He has not washed it for many months. She says it doesn't bother her too much. The therapist said she must have known that when she married him. She denied it.

9. MAY 25

She said she has always been more afraid of sick animals than of sick people. This week her cat was sick, and for the first time she was not afraid of him. Once when she was little her father hit her and her dog jumped on him, whereupon he gave the dog away. She told her children that her mother was dead. Whenever she would think of her mother she would start to drink. One time she was told that when her mother was eight months pregnant, her father tried to poison her. They saved the patient and thought her mother was a goner, but then she was revived. The aunt who told her this story says: "Your life has been a mess since birth."

Discussion: The import of this is not clear. It is evident, however, that she is working through some rather complex conflicts concerning her mother. Her maintenance of social control with the sick cat is evidence that a visit to her mother may be possible in the near future.

10. JUNE 1

"Frankly, the reason I'm afraid to visit my mother is that I might want to stay there myself." She wonders: "Why do I exist? Sometimes I doubted my existence." Her parents' marriage was a shotgun wedding and she has always felt that she was unwanted. The therapist suggested that she get a copy of her birth certificate.

Discussion: The patient is now involved with existential problems. Her Adult has evidently always been shaky because her Child has implanted doubts about her existence, her right to exist, and the form in which she exists. Her birth certificate will be written evidence that she does exist, and should be particularly impressive to her Child. As social control is established and she learns that it is possible for her to exist in a form which she herself chooses, her desire to retreat to the state hospital should diminish.

11. JUNE 8

She describes her husband's alcoholic game. At AA she was told that she should bless him and comfort him, and that made her sick. She tried something different. "One day I said I would call the ambulance for the hospital, since he didn't appear to be able to take care of himself, so he got up and didn't drink again." He said he was only trying to help her stay sober by drinking himself. This comes up because he was drinking heavily last week and she had pain in her shoulders and wanted to hit him, but told him off instead.

It appears from this that their secret marriage contract is based partly on the assumption that he will drink and she will function as a rescuer. This game was reinforced by AA to her benefit. When she refused to continue as a rescuer and became a persecutor instead, the game was thrown off and he stopped drinking. (Evidently it was reinstituted due to her insecurity of the past week.)

This outline was presented to her. She first said: "It couldn't have been part of our marriage contract, because neither of us drank when we met." A little later in the interview she suddenly said: "You know, now I remember I did know when we were married that he didn't wash his hair, but I didn't know that he drank." The therapist said that the unkempt hair was also part of the secret marriage contract. She looked skeptical. Then she thought a minute and said: "By golly, yes, I did know he drank. When we were in high school we used to drink together all the time."

It now appears that in the early years of their marriage, they played a switchable game of alcoholic. If she drank, her husband didn't; and if he drank, she stayed sober. Their relationship was originally based on this game, which they later interrupted, and must have exerted considerable effort to forget about.

Discussion: This session helped to clarify for the patient the structure of her marriage, and also emphasized the amount of time and effort which is required to keep marital games going, and equally, the amount of energy involved in their repression without conscious control.

12. JULY 6

There has been an interval of a month for summer vacation. The patient returns with a sore shoulder. She has been to the state hospital, and her mother sent her away. This made her feel hopeless. She has some olfactory illusions. She thinks she smells gas in the office, but decides it is clean soap. This leads into a discussion of her mental activity. During her recent Yoga training, she developed imagery which was almost eidetic. She would see gardens and wingless angels with sparkling clarity of color and detail. She recalled that she had had the same kind of imagery as a child. She also had images of Christ and her son. Their complexions were clear and lively. She sees animals and flowers. As a matter of fact, when she walks through parks she likes to talk secretly but aloud to trees and flowers. The longings expressed in these activities are discussed with her. The artistic and poetic aspects are pointed out, and she is encouraged therefore to write and

to try finger painting. She has seen her birth certificate
and her existential doubts are less disturbing.

Discussion: These phenomena and the auditory manifestations she had previously mentioned, are not necessarily
alarming. They point to childhood restitutive tendencies
related to a deeply disturbed relationship between her and
her parents. The conventional approach would be to give
her "supportive" treatment and help her repress this psychopathology and live on top of it. Structural analysis
offers another possibility which requires some boldness: to
allow this disturbed Child to express herself and profit
from the resulting constructive experiences.

13. JULY 13

She went to her internist and he gave her Rauwolfia
because her blood pressure was high. She told her husband
she was going to fingerpaint and he got angry and said:
"Use pastels!" When she refused, he started to drink. She
recognizes what happened here as a game of "Uproar" and
feels some despair at having been drawn into this. She
says, however, that if she does not play "Uproar" with
him then *he* will feel despair, and it is a hard choice to
make. She also mentions that the gate on the beautiful
garden is very similar to the gate on the day nursery where
her mother used to send her when she was very small. A
new problem now arises: how to distinguish the effect of
psychotherapy from the effect of Rauwolfia. She is eager
to help with this.

14. JULY 20

She is losing interest and feels tired. She agrees it is
possible that this is an effect of the medication. She reveals
some family scandals she has never mentioned to anyone
before, and states now that her drinking did not begin after
her mother became psychotic, but after these scandals.

At this session a decisive move was made. During her
therapeutic sessions, the patient habitually sits with her
legs in an ungainly exposed position. Now she complains

again about the homosexual women at AA. She complains that the men also made passes at her. She doesn't understand why, since she did nothing to bring this on. She was informed of her exposed position and expressed considerable surprise. It was then pointed out to her that she must have been sitting in a similar provocative way for many years, and what she attributes to the aggressiveness of others is probably the result of her own rather crudely seductive posture. At the subsequent group meeting she was silent most of the time, and when questioned she mentioned what the doctor had said and how this had upset her.

Discussion: This is a crucial session. At the price of sacrificing the possibilities of a normal family life, the patient has obtained a multitude of gains, primary and secondary, by playing games with her husband and other men and women. The primary external gain is the avoidance of pleasurable sexual intercourse. If she can relinquish these gains, she may be ready to undertake a normal marital relationship whose satisfactions should more than repay her for her abdication. The schizoid elements in her Child are clear from her symptomatology. The hysterical elements are most clearly manifested in her socially acceptable game of "Rapo." Hence the diagnosis of schizo-hysteria.

In her case, the naming of the game is avoided since she is still too soft-boiled to tolerate such bluntness. It is simply described to her without giving it a name. In very sophisticated groups, however, it is known technically as "First-degree Rapo." It is the classical game of hysterics: crude, "inadvertent," seductive exhibitionism, followed by protestations of surprise and injured innocence when a response is forthcoming. (As previously noted, "Third-degree Rapo," the most vicious form, ends in the courtroom or the morgue.) The therapeutic problem at the moment is whether her preparation has been adequate and the relationship between her Child and the therapist sufficiently well understood to make this confrontation effective. In a sense, her life and those of her children hinge on the therapist's judgment in these matters. If she should decide to become angry and withdraw from treatment, psychiatry might be lost to her for a long time afterward, perhaps, permanently. If she accepts it, the effect could be decisive, since this particular game is her chief barrier to marital happiness. The therapist, naturally, has not ventured to bring the matter up without considerable confidence of success.

15. AUGUST 10

The therapist returns after a two-week vacation. The confrontation has been successful. The patient now describes an assault by her father in early puberty while her stepmother pretended to be asleep. He also molested other children, but her stepmother used to defend him. She relates this "assault" to her own seductiveness. This situation she discusses at some length, eliciting her feeling that sex is dirty or vulgar. She says she has always been very careful sexually with her husband because of this feeling and has tried to avoid sex with him for this reason. She understands that the games she plays with him are an attempt to avoid sex, as she feels she cannot let go enough to enjoy it and it is merely a burden to her.

Discussion: The patient is evidently shocked at the therapist's directness, but is gratified because it lays bare still further the structure of her marriage and indicates what could be done about it.

16. AUGUST 17
(Terminal Interview)

The patient announces that this is her last session. She no longer fears that her husband will think she is dirty or vulgar if she acts lusty. She never asked him if he thought so but just assumed that he did. During the week, she approached him differently and he responded with gratified surprise. For the last few days he has come home whistling for the first time in years.

She also realizes something else. She has always felt sorry for herself and tried to elicit sympathy and admiration because she is a recovered alcoholic. She recognizes this now as a game of "Wooden Leg." She feels ready at this point to try it on her own. She also feels different about her father. Maybe she contributed even more than she thought to the seduction. The remark about her skirts being too short shocked her but helped her. "I would never admit I wanted sex. I always thought I wanted 'attention.' Now I can admit I want sex." During the week she visited her father who was ill in another city in a hospital. She was able to observe her visit with considerable objectivity. Now she feels that she has divorced him and doesn't want him any more. That is why she was able to proceed sexually with her husband. She feels the transfer was accomplished through the intermediary of the therapist, who took her father's place for a while at first; but now she doesn't need him any more. She can talk freely to her husband about sexual repression causing her symptoms, and about her sexual feelings for him. He said he agreed with her and reciprocated her feelings. After she thought all this out, following the last visit, she had a dream that night in which there was a beautiful, feminine, peaceful woman, and it made her feel really good inside. The children are different too; they are happy, relaxed, and helpful.

Her blood pressure is down and her itching is gone. The therapist thought the improvement might be due to the medicine. She replied: "No, I don't think so, I would know the difference, I've taken it before. The medicine makes me feel tired and nervous when it's taking hold, but this is an entirely new feeling."

She reports that she is drawing instead of finger-painting, doing what she wants; she feels this isn't wrong, it's like learning to live. "I don't feel sorry for people any more, I feel they ought to be able to do this too if they went about it right. I no longer feel I'm below everyone although that feeling isn't completely gone. I don't want to come to the group any more, I'd rather spend the time with my husband. It's like we're starting to go with each other again when he comes home whistling, it's wonderful. I'll try it for three months and if I feel bad I'll call you. I don't feel so 'neurotic,' either: I mean having psycho-somatic symptoms and guilt feelings and my fear of talking about sex, and like that. It's a miracle, is all I can say. I can't explain my feeling of being happy, but I feel we [you and I] worked together on it. There's more closeness and harmony with my husband and he's even taking over the children like he's becoming the man of the house. I even feel a little guilty about AA because I used them in my game of 'Wooden Leg.' "

She was asked directly whether structural analysis helped and whether game analysis helped, and in each case replied: "Oh, yes!" She added: "Also the script. For example, I said my husband had no sense of humor and you said 'Wait a minute, you don't know him and he doesn't know you because you've been playing games and acting out your scripts, you don't know what either of you is really like.' You were right because now I've dis-covered that he really has a sense of humor and that not having it was part of the game. I'm interested in my home and I'm grateful for that. I can write poetry again and express my love for my husband. I used to keep it in." At this point the hour was drawing to a close. The therapist asked: "Would you like a cup of coffee?" She replied: "No thanks, I've just had some. I've told you now how I feel, that's it, that's all, it's been a great pleasure to come here and I enjoyed it."

General Discussion: There is no need to regard this gratifying improvement with either skepticism, alarm, or pursed lips, in spite of the apparent raggedness of the above extracts. The patient herself has already answered many of the questions which might occur to an experienced reader.

For example, she herself perceived the substitution of the therapist for her father and the subsequent substitution of her husband for the therapist, so that this cannot be labeled a classical blind cure. The most impressive items are the changed attitudes of her children and, particularly, of her husband. Such indirect criteria are usually more convincing than the opinions of either the therapist or the patient. There is evidence that the original therapeutic aim has been systematically accomplished. She has given up playing many of her games and has replaced them with more satisfying direct relationships and intimacies. Her dress and behavior are more modest, and at the same time she looks more sexually attractive and sexually satisfied. A concise interpretation of what happened at the archaic level can be offered. She came to the therapist with a provisional fantasy of being dominated and hypnotized, as had happened with her other male therapists. She had slowly to give up this fantasy as she was confronted with her games, and the remark about her seductive posture made it clear to her that he was not going to be seduced. With her strengthened Adult she was then able to make the decision to relinquish her child-like ambitions and go about her grown-up business.

Although in some current thinking the course of this case may not indicate that the improvement is stable, it requires only one assumption to take a more optimistic view, and that assumption is borne out by experience; namely, that playing games and playing through one's script are optional, and that a strong Adult can renounce these in favor of gratifying reality experiences. This is the actionistic aspect of transactional analysis.

A few days short of the three-month trial period she had suggested, the patient wrote the therapist as follows: "I feel fine. I don't have to take any pills and have been off those blood pressure pills for a month now. Last week we celebrated my thirty-fifth birthday. My husband and myself went away without the children. The water was beautiful, and the trees. Gosh, if only I could paint them. We saw a huge porpoise, the first time I have ever seen one, and it was beautiful to watch, so graceful in movements. . . . My husband and I are getting along so nicely. Night and day such a difference. We have become closer, more attentive, and I can be me. That's what seemed to stump me most of the time. I always had to be polite, etc. He still comes whistling up the stairs. That does more good for me than anything. I am so glad you suggested drawing. You have no idea what that alone has done for me. I am getting better and I might try paints soon. The children think they are very good and have suggested that I exhibit some of them. Next month I am going to take swimming lessons, no fooling, something I would never have been able to do. As the time gets closer I am a little afraid but I have made up my mind I am going to learn. If I can learn to put my head under water, that alone will be a great thrill for me. My garden looks so nice. That's another thing you helped me with. By golly, I go out there at least twice a week now for several hours and no one objects. You know I think they like me better this way.

"I didn't intend to ramble on this way but it seemed I had so much to tell you. I'll write and let you know how my swimming progresses. Love from all of us in Salinas."

This letter reassured the therapist of two things:

1. That the patient's improvement persisted even after the medication for her blood pressure was discontinued.

2. That the improvement in the patient's husband and children persisted even after psychotherapy was discontinued.

It should be added that the husband now washes his hair. The most pessimistic thing which can be said about this case so far is that it represents a flight into a healthy family life. The only clinical demand that can legitimately be placed on transactional analysis is that it should produce results which are as good as or better than those produced by any other psychotherapeutic approach, for a given investment of time and effort. In the case of Mrs. Enatosky, there were 16 individual interviews and 12 group sessions.*

* The improvement was still maintained on a one-year follow-up.

In this connection, and for purposes of comparison, the words of a thoughtful psychoanalyst of wide experience[1] should be borne in mind: "What we conquer are only parts of psychogenesis: expressions of conflict, developmental failures. We do not eliminate the original source of neurosis; we only help to achieve better ability to change neurotic frustrations into valid compensations. The dependence of psychic harmony on certain conditions make immunity unattainable. Freud's 'Analysis Terminable and Interminable' brought for those of us who nourished unlimited therapeutic ambitions both disappointment and relief."

REFERENCES

1. Deutsch, H. "Psychoanalytic Therapy in The Light of Follow-up." *J. Amer. Psychoanal. Assoc.* VII: 445–458, 1959.

Patient Index

Author Index

294

Subject Index

abreaction, 248
actionism, 151
active cathexis; *see* cathexis, three
  states of
adaptability, 66
adaptation, 118
Adult, 12-17, 19, 27, 48-56, 66-
  69, 82, 86, 97, 143-159, 246-248,
  258, 266-268; defined, 3-4; *see
  also* individual case histories in
  Patient Index
Adult ego state; *see* ego state
"Alcoholic," 107-110
antagonism, 137
antipathy, 137
"Anti-Schlemiel," 107
archaeopsyche, 3, 12, 17, 54, 77,
  265
archaeopsychic elements, 212
archaeopsychic relics, 17
archaic fears, 12
assimilation, 37
autistic thinking, 12

behavioral diagnosis, 67, 162
biological fluidity, 66
biological gain, 101, 115*n*
bound cathexis; *see* cathexis, three
  states of
boundary symptoms, 51

case history with follow-up, 275-
  292
cathectic dominance, 144
cathexis, 13, 26*n*, 29, 30, 144, 247;
  flow of, 20-21; lability of, 34;
  three states of, 23-24
character neurosis, 41-42
Child, 12-17, 19-22, 27-28, 47-56,
  66-69, 82, 86, 97, 143-148, 246-

248, 258, 265-267; defined, 3-4;
  see also individual case histories
  in Patient Index
Child ego state; *see* ego state
Child structure analysis, 223-227
complementary relationship, 90,
  133
complementary transactions, 90,
  101, 152
conjunctive vector, 133, 134, 135
contamination, 31-34
conversion hysteria, 54
"Court-room," 242-243
crasis, 81
crossed transactions, 90-91, 101
cultural "psychopathies," 219-220

decontamination process, 149-150,
  158, 246
delusions, 50-51
demeanor, 62
depersonalization, 52-54
despair, 107
determinants, 265, 268-269
diagnosis, 58-69; *see also* behavioral diagnosis; historical diagnosis; operational diagnosis; social diagnosis
diagnostic criteria, 61-66
"direct analysis," 254

ego, 270, 277
ego boundaries, 21-22, 35, 50-52,
  246
ego dystonic, 22-23
ego image, 70*n*
ego model, 70*n*
ego state(s), 3, 10-11, 12, 13, 14,
  24-25, 31, 33-34, 48-49, 58, 60-
  61, 66-69, 145, 208, 215*n*, 246,

296